What People Are S

Kids' Adventures Around San Francisco Bay

"This is definitely a great resource! *Kids' Adventures Around San Francisco Bay* will certainly be an indispensable guide for our family."
— **Kristi Yamaguchi**
Olympic Gold Medalist—Figure Skating

"Following and Leading Kids!
Children's minds are sponges that soak up what they experience... Importantly, kids, being kids, absorb and retain material better when it is presented in a fun way. Look on it as planting seeds that have the potential to grow and develop a brain to its best capacity. You too may find these many and diverse gems of interest. By educating our kids we educate ourselves. ...Whether you are local resident or a tourist, you will find this work stimulating and fun, just as it is for your kids."
— **Dr. Glenn Austin, M.D., F.A.A.P.**
Past President, the American Academy of Pediatrics

"Feel like you and your kids have done everything there is to do in Northern California? Think again. Elina Wong's *Kids' Adventures Around San Francisco Bay* is likely to become any parent's new favorite resource, offering countless suggestions for fun and educational activities for children of every age."
— **Diablo Magazine**

"Los Gatos Author Cultivates a Love of Art and Science
...This lively new book can help parents and educators introduce children to new things and support their learning through the area's vast array of exhibits, events, performances, outings and classes.
— **Bay Area Parent**

"**Get out:** Pick pluots in Brentwood, rent rowboats at Lafayette Reservoir, cruise Oakland Harbor in FDR's yacht, tour Fairfield's Jelly Bellies factory: Elina Wong's Kids' Adventures Around San Francisco Bay ... is more fun for the postpubescent set than its title suggests."
— **East Bay Express**

Greater San Francisco Bay Area City Locator Map

Greater San Francisco Bay Area City Locator Map

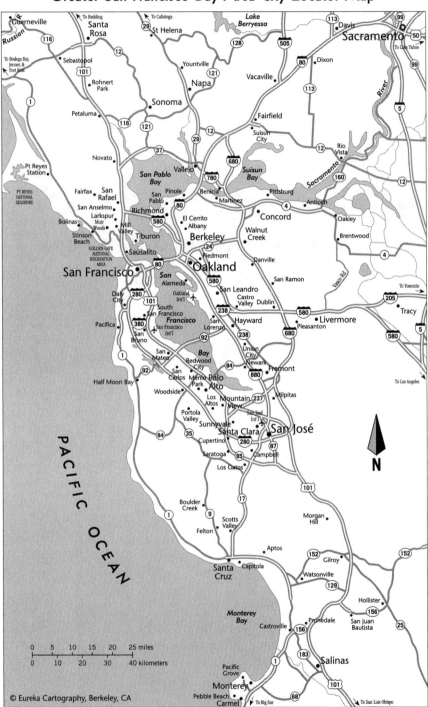

Kids' Adventures
Around San Francisco Bay

Educational Places to Go, Things to Do, & Classes to Take
in the North Bay, Peninsula, East Bay, Silicon Valley & Santa Cruz

Elina Wong
Copyright ©2004

Kids' Adventures Around San Francisco Bay:
Educational Places to Go, Things to Do, and Classes to Take in the North Bay, Peninsula, East Bay, Silicon Valley, & Santa Cruz

Attention corporations and non-profit organizations: Quantity discounts available for fundraisers, premiums, and gifts. Please contact us.

Published by:
Kids EdVentures
Post Office Box 1090
Los Gatos, CA 95031-1090, USA
Tel: (408) 356-2450; Fax: (408) 356-2714
www.KidsEdVentures.com

Printed in the United States of America
Cover Design: Robert Howard Graphic Design
Editors: Diane Feldman, Despina Gulides; Book Interior Design: Folio Bookworks
Back Cover Writing: Susan Kendrick Writing

Publisher's Cataloging-in-Publication
(Provided by Quality Books, Inc.)

Wong, Elina
  Kids' adventures around San Francisco Bay : educational places to go, things to do, and classes to take in the North Bay, Peninsula, East Bay, Silicon Valley, and Santa Cruz / Elina Wong.
  p. cm.
  Includes index.
  Contents: Animal Kingdom — Plant Kingdom — Bees, Butterflies, & Bugs — Science Museums — Planetariums & Observatories — Transportation Favorites — How Things Work — Art & Performing Arts — Historical Outings — Seasonal Events — Local Resources — Science and Arts Education — Physical Activities
  LCCN 2003095650
  ISBN 0-9743617-1-2

  1. San Francisco Bay Area (Calif.)—Guidebooks.
  2. Children—Travel—California—San Francisco Bay Area— Guidebooks.
  I. Title.

F868.S156W6395 2004   917.94'60454
                          QBI03-200659

Distributed to the trade by Independent Publishers Group.
10 9 8 7 6 5 4

Contents

Section I
Places to Go & Things to Do

Section I
Places to Go & Things to Do (Cont'd)

Section II
Classes to Take

Section II
Classes to Take (Cont'd)

Appendices

Acknowledgments

The companies, product brands, organizations, and services mentioned in *Kids' Adventures Around San Francisco Bay: Educational Places to Go, Things to Do, and Classes to Take in the North Bay, Peninsula, East Bay, Silicon Valley, and Santa Cruz* retain all rights, trademarks, and service marks that belong to them.

Neither the author nor the publisher has any ownership nor received any compensation from any of the companies, products, organizations, or services included in this book.

Carolyn Holm, author of *Everyday Art*, graciously granted her permission to quote her definitions of "open art" and "closed art." Thank you.

A big thank you to the people who helped make this book a reality. Ruby Wong: Thanks for reviewing the book and your moral support and input. Ellen Gee: Thanks for reading the manuscript, providing suggestions, and catching the details I missed. Alison Ahmed: Thanks for our many memorable outings that helped form the foundation and inspiration for this book. Thanks for sharing your knowledge of art education and the art world and for reviewing the art sections. Maria Mancini: Thanks for listening and your encouragement. Marcie Cayton: Thanks for evaluating the Web site on how airplanes fly and your feedback and moral support. Anna Rozovsky: Thanks for reviewing the music sections and your encouragement. Deanna Graham: Thanks for helping me realize that the Bay Area means different things to different people and fine tuning the book's title. Stanford and Margaret Gee: Thanks for your friendship and support without which this book would not have been introduced to the marketplace. My husband, for taking over the nighttime chores, for giving me the time to write the book, and for providing computer and moral support.

Finally, I'd like to thank my team: my editors, cover designer, distributor, printers, publicists, Web site developers, back cover writer, and Publishers Marketing Association for making this such a wonderful journey. Thank you all!

11

Disclaimer

This book is designed to provide information on the educational and community resources available in the greater San Francisco Bay Area. It is sold with the understanding that the publisher and author are not providing any professional services. If expert professional assistance is required, the services of a competent professional should be sought.

Efforts have been made to make this guide as complete and as accurate as possible. However, there may be mistakes, both typographical and in content. Information can change. This text should be used as a general reference guide. To avoid disappointment, check the information with the organization prior to embarking on your trip.

Inclusion in this book should not be considered to be a recommendation, endorsement, or referral, nor a guarantee of the quality of the products, organizations, and services presented. Each individual must use his best judgment before purchasing products or engaging in any activities.

The author and Kids EdVentures are not liable nor responsible to any person, organization, or entity with respect to any loss or damage caused, or alleged to have been caused, directly or indirectly, whether or not negligent, by the information contained in this book.

By purchasing this book, the reader agrees to exempt the author and the publisher from any responsibility.

Introduction

I hear, I forget.
I see, I remember.
I do, I understand.
—Chinese Proverb

Children learn through play. From play, they explore their world, test their theories about how things work, and learn through *all* of their five senses. Experiences that allow all their senses to be engaged help them to remember and understand. That's why it's so valuable to provide fun adventures to engage our children. When they play and experience, they are studying and learning about their world.

In 1997, milestone articles came out from the scientific community regarding the brain development of children. They answered the age-old question of nature versus nurture. Both play a role and interact with each throughout our lives. There are windows of opportunity when exposure to certain types of learning is the most optimal. The infant brain is born with billions of neurons and connections, but when the child's brain is not exposed to the necessary stimuli, the corresponding neurons are shut down since the brain deems them unnecessary. Besides being lots of fun, engaging experiences stimulate a child's natural curiosity about the world and help to develop his brain.

Earlier research has shown that the first few years of a child's life are critical. Most of the child's brain development happens prior to his entering kindergarten. The infant, toddler, and preschool years are critical to the child's overall development.

While parents must decide which activities should be undertaken, and when, it is important to remember that children need time to just day-dream or play, so that they are *not* overscheduled and overburdened. It is important to keep a balance between downtime and all the fun and educational adventures just outside our doorsteps.

Outings and field trips allow children to experience and learn from all of their senses. Being out in nature helps children understand how things are related. Exposure to the fine arts helps encourage and develop their creativity and imagination. Sports and physical play are important to their physical development and well-being. In today's world, where schools provide just the basics, it's more important than ever for parents to find resources in the community to provide the enrichment in science, art, music, drama, and sports that our schools are hard-pressed to offer due to the lack of funds. The saving grace is that our community is rich in resources and we can get much of this enrichment without tremendous expense from our local parks, parks and recreation departments, and community groups that provide theater and concerts at affordable rates, and sometimes for free.

Finally, because motor skills are one of the first skills babies develop and continue to do so during their toddler, preschool, and elementary school years, I've included physical activities and parks that your child might enjoy.

I've lived in the Bay Area for over twenty-five years, and I'm still finding new experiences and resources, especially now that I have become a parent. Some of these I learned from other moms I've met who provided insider's tips to the abundant resources in our community. I've also seen travelers' guides to the Bay Area with an overwhelming list of things to see and do and Web sites with an equally overwhelming number of destinations. But I was frustrated trying to find the appropriate outings for an educational goal I had in mind. As a result, I've organized this book with an educational focus to help you find resources, outings, and classes based on an educational goal.

The outings and classes in this book cover a wide range of topics to help your child learn about the ocean, land, air, and space as well as art, music, dance, drama, and history.

This book is divided into two major parts. The first part focuses on places to go and things to do. The second part is dedicated to classes for kids.

"Places to Go and Things to Do" includes both destinations and outings:

- Destinations are museums, zoos, aquariums, nature centers, gardens, farms, planetariums and observatories, parks, etc.
- Outings include boating, air shows, factory tours, whale-watching, tide pooling, fruit picking, living history demonstrations, shows and concerts, and annual seasonal events such as the Chinese New Year's Parade, Cinco de Mayo, July 4th celebrations, the Renaissance Faire, Holiday Tea Parties, etc.

"Classes to Take" provides information on the resources available for kids' classes covering a wide range of topics from art, music, drama, and science to dance, swimming, gymnastics, ice skating, and bowling. Many of these can be done also as one-time outings.

I've provided:

- a calendar to help you plan outings year-round.
- a free activities index to help you find fun things to do without ove-stretching your budget (and these are plentiful!).
- an alphabetical index to make your search for things to do easier.

I hope this book is helpful and useful. Let me know what you think as you go out to explore and enjoy!

Elina Wong

How to Use This Book

This book should be used as a general reference and for information purposes only. While I've researched the information and collated it to make your search easier, and I've tried to be as accurate as possible, please double check and confirm dates, hours, times, locations, etc. prior to your outing to avoid any disappointments.

Age appropriateness: When the entry is listed with a minimum age requirement, the age requirement is established by the facility. Some facilities are just not designed for younger children, so please pay attention to the minimum age requirement. Some facilities have an age recommendation. These are shown as "Recommended Age." When the entry says (Ages #+), it is my suggestion as a general guideline and not a requirement nor a recommendation of the facility. Use your best judgment based on the interest, attention span, maturity, physical development, etc. of your child to guide you to determine if it is an appropriate activity for your child. The recommendation is just a general guideline, and each child has his own interests and characteristics.

Most facilities will host birthday parties. It is a rare facility that does not host birthday parties these days. Nature Centers or Visitor Centers at Nature Preserves often provide a less expensive alternative for birthday parties, and the kids love them!

The classes section is an additional outing resource because many facilities will allow one-time visits such as ice skating, bowling, etc. Gymnastics, ice skating, bowling, art, and music are great activities for birthday parties, too.

Some facilities will not provide tours to individuals or small groups but will provide programs and tours for larger groups such as the Scouts or school groups. If you have some friends who are also interested in a specific activity or you belong to a parent's group, consider setting up a group to do these outings so you can take advantage of the programs that are offered only to groups. Note that facilities that have programs for school groups or Scout groups may require advanced reservations up to a year in advance.

Remember that many museums have specific days when admission is free to the public. But you have to plan ahead to take advantage of those days.

Tips for a Great Trip

1) Print out the visitor maps provided by the local Convention and Visitor Bureaus. Here are their Web sites:
- San Francisco has Bay Area wide, San Francisco citywide, and detailed area maps: < www.sfvisitor.org/maps/index.html >
- Oakland has East Bay and Oakland downtown maps: <www.oaklandcvb.com/maps.html>
- San Jose has Bay Area wide, San Jose downtown, uptown, and central San Jose area maps: <www.sanjose.org/global/gethere/maps.html>
- Santa Cruz has the Santa Cruz County map: <www.santacruz.org/places/county.html>
- Monterey has a Monterey County map: <http://montereyinfo.org/?p=4382>
- Carmel has city map: < www.carmelcalifornia.org/images/Carmel_Map.pdf>
- San Francisco Bay City Guide's Web site has great maps on transportation including BART, Bay Area ferries, and MUNI (with cable car routes) as well as Bay Area wide, downtown San Francisco, Fisherman's Wharf, and Golden Gate Park maps: <www.baycityguide.com/maps.html>. The site also has a huge collection of on-line coupons to attractions, shops, restaurants, tours, etc.

2) Before you start your trip, call to confirm dates, times, and costs

and to get specific directions. Look up their Web sites for maps and directions. Sometimes the maps from the Internet mapping software are wrong. Confirm directions to avoid getting lost. While every effort has been made to provide accurate information, things change frequently and without notice.

3) Prepare your younger child by explaining a bit about your destination and/or reading about the topic prior to your outing, to ensure an enriching experience. I've suggested some materials where appropriate to help you prepare your child.

4) Bring some cash, in various denominations from quarters and dollar bills to larger bills. This will come in handy for parking (both metered and parking lots), food, and other necessities. Most facilities require cash for food, even if they will accept credit cards at the entrance for admissions.

5) Have extra changes of clothing and shoes in the car (at least for the kids, but it's a good idea for the adults, too) for unexpected messes.

6) Bring lots of bottled water or drinks because fun can be a thirsty business. It's always a great idea to have some fruit, yogurt, cheese sticks, or other snacks handy for the trip home.

7) It's a good idea to have binoculars, camera, jackets, sunscreen, sunglasses, and umbrellas stocked in your car so they'll be handy at a moment's notice.

8) As a general rule of thumb, many museums are closed on Mondays and are open during some federal holidays like Memorial Day, July 4th, Labor Day, etc.

I have excluded directions to the facilities because directions are so easily available from the Web sites of the facilities, from mapping software on the Internet, or by calling the sites for specific directions.

Book's Web Site
www.KidsEducationalAdventures.com

- Links to the Web sites that appear in this book are provided to readers for one-stop convenience of locating up-to-date information.

- Provide information on current family educational events in the Greater San Francisco Bay Area.

- Community forum for readers to share their experiences and to seek others' reviews of the facilities and services that appear in this book. When sending in a review or when reading a review, please keep in mind that different people have different standards and expectations.

- Be a vehicle for readers to give feedback. Your feedback is greatly appreciated and much sought after! While I may not be able to respond to your feedback individually, please know that readers' feedback will be addressed as a whole wherever possible and appropriate.

Section I

Places to Go & Thing to Do

Chapter 1
Animal Kingdom

The animal kingdom is extremely diverse. From the smallest shrew to the giant blue whale, size is only one feature among many that differentiate us. We can expose our children to barnyard animals in local farms; to more exotic and colorful animals at zoos and aquariums; but, best of all, we can expose them to animals in their natural habitats. This section covers farms, zoos and wildlife museums, aquariums, nature preserves, beaches for tide pool animals, and whale-watching cruises for marine life.

Farms

Help your child learn that eggs come from chickens, milk from cows, and sweaters from sheep's wool. You can take farm tours to gather the eggs that the hen has laid, feed the sheep, and learn about wool shearing. Recreational farms such as Ardenwood and Hidden Villa are wonderful places to learn that eggs, milk, and butter come from chickens and cows and not from the shelves of the local grocery store. I recommend visiting Ardenwood first, because the animal feedings are scheduled during convenient times and there are a variety of fun experiences.

Ardenwood Historic Farm (Ages 2 +)

(510) 796-0663; 34600 Ardenwood Boulevard, Fremont, CA 94555
<www.ebparks.org/parks/arden.htm> or City of Fremont's site for Ardenwood:
<www.fremont.gov/recreation/ardenwoodpark/default.htm>

Description: This farm has an historic house, the Patterson House; gardens; farm animals; a horse-drawn train; and a blacksmith shop. Plan your trip to coincide with the animal feeding and blacksmith demonstrations. Best days to visit are Thursday–Sunday for the animal feeding. Learn from the staff which part of the hay the animals love to eat. Follow the staff around to harvest the eggs the chickens have laid, feed the animals, and get them settled for the evening. Better yet, time your visit with the many special events that are offered.

Hours: *Tues–Sun:* 10am–4pm. Closed Monday.
Animal Feeding: Thur–Sun 3pm.
Summer Season (April to mid-November):
• Patterson House tours: Thur, Fri, Sat, & Sun
• Horse-drawn train: Thur, Fri, & Sun 10:15am–3:30pm
• Blacksmith demonstrations: Thur, Fri, & Sun
• Farmyard Café is open
• Family programs and naturalist programs are held on Sat & Sun.
Winter Season (mid-November–March 31):
The horse-drawn train and the blacksmith shop are closed during the winter season.

Cost: Tues, Wed, Sat: $1/adult or senior, 50 cents/child, free/child under 4 years old. Thur, Fri, & Sun: $5/adult, $4/senior, $3.50/child, and free/child under 4 years old. Special event fees are higher.

Bathrooms: Yes.

Facilities: Dirt trails. Strollers are OK.

Food: Café open Thur, Fri & Sun only. Picnic tables available.

What to Bring: Sunscreen, sunglasses, hat, picnic lunch and drinks, or cash for food.

Follow-Up Activities: For the calendar of special events, check the Web site: <www.fremont.gov/Recreation/ArdenwoodPark/Events.htm> or <www.ebparks.org/events/byloc/arden.htm#D29012>. Special events include: spring activities at the farm such as baby animals, butterflies, farm chores for kids, puppets of the world, old-fashioned games, corn planting, learning to knit, gardening and farming, candle making and bees, sheep and wool, rope making, and more. There are many historic events, including Johnny Appleseed Day, Highland Scottish Games, a Civil War Reenactment on Memorial Day, an Old-Fashioned Independence Day Celebration on July 4th, Historic Rail Fair over Labor Day weekend, Cajun-Zydeco Festival in late September, Harvest Festival in mid-October, Halloween trains on weekend evenings during the second half of October, and "Christmas at Ardenwood" in early to mid-December.

Casa de Fruta (All Ages)

(800) 548-3813, (800) 543-1702 Mail Order, (831) 637-0051 Office
6680 Pacheco Pass Highway, Hollister, CA 95023
<www.casadefruta.com>

Description: Besides being a roadside stand and café, Casa de Fruta has a zoo, miniature train, children's playground, and rock shop. The zoo has buffalo, llamas, birds, cows, and white deer originally from Hearst Castle's menagerie in San Simeon. The rock shop and mining sluice have panning for gemstones and gold.

Hours: Closed January & February. From March–December, hours are generally 7am–9pm. Call ahead to confirm the zoo hours and the train schedule.

Cost: *Fun Pass:* $4.99/person includes 1 ride on the train, 1 admission to the zoo and a bag of popcorn. *Two-Day Fun Pass:* $9.99/person with unlimited rides on the train and unlimited admission to the zoo. *Annual Pass*: $14.99/person with unlimited admission to the train and zoo, 10% discount at the motel, and birthday party packages.

Bathrooms: Yes.

Facilities: Stroller friendly.

Food: Casa de Coffee restaurant (open 24 hours), a deli, and a fruit stand for snacks. Casa de Sweets has ice cream, coffee, and pie. Picnic grounds.

What to Bring: Sunscreen, sunglasses, camera, picnic lunch, and cash.

Follow-Up Activities: For a more detailed list of special annual events, visit the Web site: <www.casadefruta.com/events.htm>. 1) Easter Egg Hunt (free) in April. 2) At the end of May there is a Native American Pow-Wow featuring over 34 Indian tribes, sharing their dance, food, arts and crafts. 3) Civil War Reenactment in mid-June, with sutler encampments, medical facilities, cannons, military headquarters, etc. 4) Renaissance Pleasure Faire from mid-September to mid-October. 5) Pumpkin patch in October.

Deer Hollow Farm (Ages 2+)

(650) 903-6430, (650) 965-FARM for Farm Tour Reservations
Rancho San Antonio County Park, Cristo Rey Drive, Cupertino, CA 95014
<www.openspace.org/preserves/deer_hollow_farm/deer_hollow_farm.html>

Description: Deer Hollow Farm is located inside the Rancho San Antonio Preserve. It is a very small farm with chickens, goats, pigs, and sheep. It requires about a mile walk from the parking lot to the farm.

Hours: *Tues–Sun:* 8am–4pm. See the chicks and ducklings in the spring by taking the farm tours on the third Saturday of the month, from April through July. Tours are at 10am & 11:30am and last 45 minutes. Call for reservations. For additional information, visit the Friends of Deer Hollow Farm Web site: **<www.svpal.org/~fodhf/>**

Cost: Free.

Bathrooms: At the main entrance to the park.

Facilities: Stroller accessible, but during a farm tour, consider putting younger ones in a baby carrier.

Food: Food kiosk serving hot dogs, icees, etc. during the summer only.

What to Bring: Sunscreen, hat, sunglasses, and water bottles.

Emma Prusch Farm Park (Ages 2+)

(408) 926-5555; 647 South King Road, San Jose, CA 95116
<www.ci.san-jose.ca.us/cae/parks/pfp>

Description: This farm has a small birds area that includes free range chickens, some rather territorial (and aggressive) geese, a peacock, and some rabbits. The barn houses a few cows and two sheep. Unfortunately, this farm doesn't have tours for families on a regular basis. Visit this farm for the community gardens and orchards, but visit Hidden Villa or Ardenwood Farm for animals and animal feedings. This farm has two demonstration orchards: a rare fruit orchard and a deciduous fruit orchard featuring some of the fruit grown here in Santa Clara Valley, previously known as "Valley of Heart's Delight." School groups can reserve farm tours. These tours include animal visits, butter making by the students and butter tasting, and a brief presentation of the history of the farm.

Hours: Daily from 8:30 am to sunset. Visitor Center open from 8:30am–4pm. Closed Thanksgiving, Christmas, & New Year's Days.

Cost: Free admission and parking.

Bathrooms: Indoor bathrooms available at the Meeting Hall building.

Portable toilets available in the park and community gardens.

Facilities: Stroller friendly.

Food: No food sales. Picnic tables available, some with barbecues, and one vending machine that sells drinks located on the side of the Meeting Hall building.

What to Bring: During the summer remember to bring sunscreen, sunglasses, and picnic lunch and drinks if you're thinking of staying for a picnic.

Follow-Up Activities: Happy Hollow Park and Zoo and the Children's Discovery Museum are close by.

Hidden Villa (All Ages)

(650) 949-8653; 26870 Moody Road, Los Altos Hills, CA 94022
<www.hiddenvilla.org>

Description: This is one of my favorites; it is truly an oasis. Nestled in the Los Altos Foothills, just beyond Foothill College, Hidden Villa is the former estate of the Duvenecks. There's an organic garden, a small farm, a hostel, an environmental education center, and hiking trails. Don't miss the farm tour and the beautiful organic garden, which has a grapevine cave and a gourd vine tunnel that kids love. Learn about different plants and composting. Past the garden, there is a big barn where the cows and sheep are housed. Continue walking up the dirt road and you'll come to a T-intersection. Make a left at the T-intersection, just past the little bridge, and you'll see a small white barn on your left. Some of the horses and goats are housed here. On your right, across the way from the small white barn, there's a white house. Walk behind the white house into the yard to see the chicken coop. If you're lucky, you may be able to see the freshly laid eggs inside the henhouse. The roosters and the hens are left to roam in the yard on alternate days. There's a very small barn in the back of the yard that houses the pigs. The placards on the outside wire fence identify the names of the pigs.

Hours: Tues–Sun during daylight hours. Closed to the public in the summer for summer camps except for certain weekends. Check the schedule on the Web site for summer weekend hours. Visitor Center: Tues–Sun: 10am–4pm. Guided farm and garden tours on most weekends at 11am and 1pm, rain or shine.

Cost: $5 parking fee per car—"honor box." Guided farm tours are $5/person, free/child under 2. Reservations are required. Other costs vary by program.

Bathrooms: Yes, at the Visitor Center, the Education Building, and the Office in the Duveneck House. Pick up a trail map at the Visitor Center (the first building next to the first parking lot once you pass the farm stand at the entrance).

Facilities: Dirt and gravel paths. Strollers are fine here.

Food: No food available. Picnic tables available if you want to bring your own lunch/snack. No trash cans; plan on bringing your trash home.

What to Bring: Bag lunch and drinks. Don't forget the sunscreen, sunglasses, and camera.

Follow-Up Activities: 1) Nature programs such as nature walks, wildflower hikes, bird walks, and Saturdays on the Farm for Kids (ages 6–10) series 10am–12pm. 2) Birthday parties. 3) Summer camps. 4) Cultural programs and concerts throughout the year. Past programs have included "African Cultural Celebrations." 5) Celebrate Earth Day Fun-on-the-Farm in late April from 10am–3pm with Maypole dancing, butter churning, sheep shearing, wool spinning, storytelling, face painting, animal visits, blacksmith demonstrations, garden fun, a tour of the new sustainable buildings, and tours of the Duveneck House. Earth Day admissions: $15/adult, $10/child 12 & under, free/child 2 & under, or $45/family of four.

Lemos Farm (All Ages)

(650) 726-2342; 12320 San Mateo Road (Hwy 92), Half Moon Bay, CA 94019

Description: Petting zoo, pony rides, train, hayride, and jumper. Haunted house, pumpkin patch, and hayrides during Halloween. November and December, Christmas trees available. Traffic can be challenging during special events such as the Pumpkin Festival Weekend.

Hours: Sat & Sun: 9am–5pm.

Cost: Free admission, but rides cost extra. *Rides:* $4/pony ride, $2.50/train ride, $4/child, $2.50/hay ride, and $4/child on the jumper. **Day pass:** $13/person for unlimited rides.

Bathrooms: Yes.

Facilities: Stroller friendly.

Food: Yes.

Follow-Up Activities: If you can brave the traffic, consider visiting the Annual Half Moon Bay Art and Pumpkin Festival, which is held on the

Saturday and Sunday following Columbus Day 10am–5pm. Events include costume contests, Great Pumpkin Parade, pumpkin carving contest, music and family entertainment on three stages. It is held on Main Street, in Half Moon Bay. Admission is free. For more information: <www.miramarevents.com/pumpkinfest/family_fun.html> For tips and directions: <www.miramarevents.com/pumpkinfest/ tips.html>.

McClellan Ranch Park (Ages 2+)

(408) 777-3149, (408) 739-5482 4H membership (Jan Bressington) or 4H Email: 4Hkristylr@pacbelll.net
22221 McClellan Road, Cupertino, CA 95014
<www.netsurge.com/trillian/4h>
<www.friendsofblackberryfarm.org/fobbf_McClellan.html>

Description: This hidden park will surprise you. It is used frequently by professional photographers for portraits because of the beautiful diffused lighting afforded by the trees. This preserve is home to a Junior Nature Museum; Community Gardens; and the Headquarters of the Audubon Society, Santa Clara County chapter; and the Rolling Hills 4-H Club. The Junior Nature Museum features some snakes, insects, silkworms, etc. depending on the seasons. It is also the site for afterschool and nature classes sponsored through the Cupertino Parks and Recreation Department. Community organic garden plots are available for city residents of Cupertino. School groups can sign up for tours of the farm buildings and the Junior Museum. This preserve is also a good place for bird watching. The Rolling Hills 4-H Club 5-18 raises rabbits, chickens, sheep, pigs, and cattle. The 4-H Club has many child-led projects such as web design, raising rabbits, or any other project in which the child is interested.

Hours: Tues–Sat: 10am–2pm, or later depending on activity. Call ahead to confirm hours and for the latest events. Tues–Fri: avail for group tours.

Cost: Free.

Bathrooms: Yes.

Facilities: Strollers OK, but not on the trails.

Food: No.

What to Bring: Sunscreen and sunglasses.

Follow-Up Activities: 1) Wildlife Education Day in early October from 10am–2pm. Call the Audubon Society at (408) 252-3747 for details.

It has talks on bats, crafts for kids, insects set up, and insect collection displays. 2) To find out events happening at the Junior Nature Museum, e-mail Barbarab@cupertino.org to subscribe to her electronic newsletter. 3) Check with Cupertino Parks and Rec. for after school classes. See Cupertino Parks and Rec. entry in the Local Parks and Recreation Departments section.

San Francisco Zoo (All Ages)
Family Farm at the Children's Zoo
(415) 753-7072, (415) 753-7080; One Zoo Road, San Francisco, CA 94132
<www.sanfranciscozoo.org>

Description: At the Family Farm, get involved with animal care by feeding the animals their breakfast (10:45 am, weekends year-round, and every day during the summer), grooming them, and taking care of their hooves. Learn about the history of domestic farm animals at 1pm on weekends throughout the year, and every day during the summer. At the hatchery, help collect eggs, feed, and water chicks (11am–noon, weekends and during the summer). You can also help feed the ducks in the pond. There are goats, sheep, miniature horses, ponies, a pig, ducks, and chickens.
Hours: Daily: 10am–5pm 365 days a year, including Christmas Day and Thanksgiving Day. Children's Zoo: 11am–4pm. During the summer (Memorial Day–Labor Day), Children's Zoo 10:30 am–4:30pm.
Cost: $10/adult, $7/youth (12–17) or senior (65+), $3/child (3–11), free/child 2 & under.
Bathrooms: Yes, throughout the park. No baby changing facilities. Get a zoo map at the entrance.
Facilities: Stroller friendly.
Food: Cafés throughout the park. Menus available on the Web site under "Visit the Zoo" icon, then the "Guest Services" icon.
What to Bring: Jacket, even in the summer, because San Francisco can be foggy and cold. Don't forget the sunscreen, hat, sunglasses, and camera.
Follow-Up Activities: See entry in the following Zoos & Wildlife Museums section.

Slide Ranch (All Ages)
(415) 381-6155; 2025 Shoreline Highway, Muir Beach, CA 94965

Description: This ranch is located off Hwy 1, with beautiful views of the Pacific Ocean. The ranch has an animal area, an organic garden, an observation beehive, and access to trails and tide pools. Time your visit with the Family Farm Days or other special event days such as "Farm Days," the "Spring Fling," and the Harvest Festival. There are special hands-on activities to allow interaction with the farm animals during these special events when the ranch is fully open. The farm animals are not available for hands-on interaction except during these special event days. Pre-registration is required. Plan your outing in advance to avoid disappointment since tickets do sell out. The "Spring Fling" event in early April features newborn baby animals including chicks, lambs, and kids (baby goats). There are demonstrations on sheep shearing and wool spinning, local organic cuisine, face painting, arts and crafts, and egg dyeing activities. This event includes live performances in a country fair environment. The Farm Days revolve around themes such as "Sheep to Shawl" and "Ocean Exploration," which includes a tide pool visit. The "Mother's Day Celebration" provides an opportunity to visit animal moms and their newborns. Special workshops on composting and bee keeping are available for adults and older children.

Hours: 10am–4pm.

Cost: Free. Event days cost extra. See the "Programs & Events" section on the Web site for details. For example, Spring Fling Event: $12/person in advance, $15/person at the gate, $55/families 5 or more, free/child 2 & under.

Bathrooms: Portables only.

Facilities: Stroller friendly on the ranch, but not on the trails.

Food: No, except during the "Spring Fling" special event.

What to Bring: Picnic lunch and drinks. If you plan on visiting the bee keeping workshop, dress in heavy clothes, gloves, and boots.

Follow-Up Activities: 1) Special programs and events throughout the year. Once on the Web site, click on "Programs & Events" then the "Family Program" button for more details on events. 2) Summer camps. 3) School programs.

Tilden Nature Study Area & Little Farm (Ages 2+)
Tilden Regional Park

(510) 843-2137 Swimming at Lake Anza; (510) 524-6773 Merry-Go-Round;
(510) 527-0421 Pony Ride
600 Canon Drive, Kensington, CA 94708
Wildcat Canyon Road & Grizzly Peak Boulevard, Berkeley, CA
<www.ebparks.org/parks/tilden.htm>

Description: The Nature Study Area is next to the Little Farm with animals. There's also a pony ride, a carousel, a train, and a botanical garden. The Botanic Garden offers tours and lectures year-round.

Hours: 8am–10pm unless posted otherwise. *Trains:* 11am–6pm weekends and holidays. *Merry-Go-Round:* 11am–5pm weekdays, holidays, and on weekends during spring and summer breaks. After Labor Day, the Merry-Go-Round is open on weekends only 11am–5pm. *Pony rides:* 11am–5pm on weekends and 11am–4pm daily during the summer (June 14–Labor Day). *Lake Anza:* 11am–6pm. The lake is open for fishing year-round.

Cost: Free parking. *Lake Anza Swim Area:* $2.50/person ages 16–61, $1.50/youth under 16. *Merry-Go-Round:* $1/ride or $10/13-ride ticket book. *Steam Train:* $1.75/ride or $7/5 ride family ticket. *Pony ride:* $3/ride or $25.50 for 10 rides.

Bathrooms: Yes, at steam train, Lake Anza, and the Botanic Garden Visitor Center. Lake Anza has changing rooms and a snack bar.

Facilities: Stroller friendly.

Food: Snack stands at Lake Anza and merry-go-round.

What to Bring: Picnic lunch, sunscreen, sunglasses, and drinks.

Follow-Up Activities: Naturalist programs through the visitor center and the botanical garden. Visit the Web site for program and event information: <www.ebparks.org/events/byloc/tilden.htm>. See Chapter 2: Plant Kingdom—Gardens & Arboretums section for details on the Regional Parks Botanic Garden.

Zoos & Wildlife Museums

Learning about animals helps us appreciate the circle of life, so beautifully illustrated in Disney's *Lion King*. Animals help us learn to respect animal habitats and the beautiful world we've inherited. They help us appreciate that we each have a special place on earth.

If you have a little one who loves the zoo and animals, consider purchasing a membership from one of the zoos since one membership provides free admission to many zoos across the country. For example, Happy Hollow Zoo, Oakland Zoo, Coyote Point Museum and Zoo, and the San Francisco Zoo all have reciprocal memberships. This means membership in one zoo allows free or reduced admission to all the other zoos on the list. Membership costs are different depending on the zoo. The best "value" was Happy Hollow Zoo when I had a membership, but check the zoos for the most current membership fees. Keep reciprocal memberships in mind for museums and other facilities, too. Research the "Reciprocal" list and the prices to determine which membership provides the best value for you. The zoo you choose will be the one that will provide the detailed mailings and class/event information.

The Bay Area Science Alliance has a Web site that provides a calendar of events for all the science-related family events and exhibits in the Bay Area. It's a consolidated calendar with information from the many Bay Area science-related organizations to help you plan your monthly outings. The Web site is <www.basa.info/cs/basa/cal/20>.

California Academy of Sciences (Ages 3+)
Golden Gate Park
(415) 750-7145; 55 Concourse Drive, San Francisco, CA 94118 (Reopening in 2008); *Temporary Location:* 875 Howard Street, San Francisco, CA 94103 <www.calacademy.org>

Description: The California Academy of Sciences consists of the Natural History Museum, Steinhart Aquarium, and Morrison Planetarium where your child can learn about the earth, the oceans, and the universe. It also has a dinosaur skeleton (T-Rex) and an Insect Room with an exhibit of butterflies and moths, to show how camouflage and mimicry can be used to fool one's enemies. See the respective entries under Steinhart Aquarium and Morrison Planetarium for more detailed information for each and the full entry in Chapter 4: Science Museums.

Coyote Point Museum (Ages 2+)

(650) 342-7755; 1651 Coyote Point Drive, San Mateo, CA 94401
<www.coyoteptmuseum.org>

Description: The museum has exhibits on the water cycle, the weather, and recycling and trash. Outside of the main museum building, there are animal exhibits of river otters, foxes, coyotes, snakes, etc. Don't miss the animal feedings and talks.

Hours: Closed Mondays. Tues–Sat: 10am–5pm. Sun: noon–5pm.
Fox feeding: daily at 11:30am. *River Otter feeding:* daily at 12:15pm.
Animal Talks: weekends at 2pm at the Wildlife Amphitheater.

Cost: $4 parking, $6/adult, $4/senior or child (13–17), $2/child (3–12). Free admission on the first Wednesday of each month, excludes groups of 10 or more.

Bathrooms: Yes.

Facilities: Stroller friendly.

Food: No. Picnic tables outside the museum.

What to Bring: Cash for parking and picnic lunch.

Follow-Up Activities: 1) Birthday parties. 2) Family programs covering topics such as volcanoes, earthquakes, hurricanes, geography, and gardening. The museum even has storytime and toddler programs. See "Calendar" icon on the Web site. 3) Classes for preschoolers through middle school students. Topics include insects, gardens, bats, oceans, rainforests, and more. Check the Web site for more detailed information: <www.coyoteptmuseum.org/education/facilities.htm>. 4) Tide pool visits at Fitzgerald Marine Reserve registration through the museum. See Tide Pool section for more information.

Happy Hollow Park & Zoo (Ages 2+)

(408) 277-3000; 1300 Senter Road, San Jose, CA 95112
<www.happyhollowparkandzoo.org>

Description: The park has a small zoo, including a petting zoo with interesting and rare animals, a rides area perfect for preschoolers, a puppet show, and play areas. The rides and puppet show are included with the price of admission. When my daughter was three and four years old, we came at least every other week spring–fall.

Hours: Daily: 10am–5pm. *Summer* (July 6–August 25): 10am–6pm. *Puppet Show:* Mon–Fri: noon & 2pm, Sat & Sun: noon, 2pm & 4pm. *Train* open during spring and summer, depending on staffing. Summertime can be quite crowded with summer camps that have field trips here. *Winter:* Rides and park are closed, but the zoo is open.

Cost: *Parking:* $5/car when kiosk is attended (summer). There is a 50% discount on parking for military personnel/veterans (with ID), seniors, the disabled, and members with 10-visit or annual parking passes. *Admission:* $5/person (2–64), $4.50/senior (65–74) & disabled, free/person under 2 or over 74. *Train rides:* $1.75 per person. Every so often, there is $1 admission to the park. Check the event calendar on the Web site for specific dates.

Bathrooms: Yes, but no changing stations.

Facilities: Stroller friendly. Stroller rentals are available by the main entrance.

Food: Café. You may also bring your own food to the park. There are picnic tables by the rides and food concession areas.

What to Bring: Cash for parking, sunglasses, sunscreen, and plenty to drink during hot weather. The kids can work up quite a thirst running around. Consider bringing a picnic lunch and picnic gear. Don't forget to bring a few quarters for the petting zoo, to buy food for the animals.

Follow-Up Activities: 1) Classes for tots to older kids are available, but advanced registration and additional fees are required. Check the Web site for additional class information: <www.happyhollowparkandzoo.org/education/classes>. 2) Also at Kelly Park are the Japanese Friendship Garden and History Park, San Jose with a wonderful Trolley Barn filled with antique trolleys and cars. The trolley runs on weekends. See respective entries for more detailed information in Chapter 2: Plant Kingdom—Gardens & Arboretums and in Chapter 9: Historical Outings.

Lindsay Wildlife Museum (Ages 2+)
(925) 935-1978; 1931 First Avenue, Walnut Creek, CA 94596
<www.wildlife-museum.org>

Description: This small museum focuses on native California wildlife and natural history. It has exhibits on birds of prey: hawks, owls, eagles, falcons, etc. It also features foxes, bobcats, raccoons, reptiles, amphibians, and more. There is an eagle or bobcat feeding or a stage presentation of a wild animal on a daily basis. Call for details before your trip. There is a discovery room for young children. The museum is surrounded by four demonstration gardens: a wildlife garden, a drought tolerant garden, a woodland garden, and a garden with deer-resistant plants.

Hours: Closed Mondays. Tues–Fri: noon–5pm, Sat & Sun: 10am–5pm. *Summer* (mid-June–end of August): extended hours Tues–Fri: 10am–5pm.

Cost: $6/adult, $5/senior, and $4/child (3–17)

Bathrooms: Yes.

Facilities: Stroller friendly.

Food: No. Picnic area in adjacent park.

What to Bring: Picnic lunch, sunscreen, sunglasses, and drinks.

Follow-Up Activities: 1) Preschool classes for children ages 2½ and 3½. In addition, there are classes for various age ranges through age 12. 2) There is a summer camp for children ages 4–9. Check the "Just for Kids" page on the Web site for current information. 3) Adult classes, trips, and tours are also available in the "Classes, Trips, and Tours" section of the Web site. Some of the classes have included an introduction to bird watching, wetland animals, a tarantula hike, and a Brooks Island outing. 4) Birthday parties.

Oakland Zoo (All Ages)

(510) 632-9523; 9777 Golf Links Road, Oakland, CA 94605
<www.oaklandzoo.org>

Description: Oakland zoo features animals from various environments, including the African savanna, tropical rain forest, and Australian out-back. There's a children's zoo and a playground. The children's zoo is being renovated, with the new children's zoo slated for reopening spring 2005. The lower park has a separate entrance, to the right of the main entrance, and features rides and a mini-roller coaster for little ones. However, these rides are not included with park admission and require additional ticket purchase. Don't miss the aerial tram for a beautiful view of the Bay Area and a bird's eye view of the zoo.

Hours: Daily 10am–4pm. Closed Thanksgiving, Christmas, and during inclement weather. Wildlife Theater, an educational animal show for kids, is usually on the weekends. Check the Animal Feeding schedule at the main entrance.

Cost: Parking fee: $3, zoo admission: $7.50/person ages 15–55, $4.50/child (2–14) and seniors (55+). Parking is free on the first Monday of each month, excluding holidays. Rides cost $1–$2 each.

Bathrooms: Yes.

Facilities: Stroller friendly.

Food: Café. You may also bring a picnic lunch.

What to Bring: Sunscreen, hat, sunglasses, camera, and plenty to drink. You will also need some extra cash to pay for parking and the rides at the lower park.

Follow-Up Activities: 1) Family events and classes for children throughout the year. Check the calendar on the Web site for the most current information: <www.oaklandzoo.org/services/calendar.html>. 2) Birthday parties. 3) Summer camps for pre-K to grade 12. Registration begins in March.

Old Borges Ranch (Ages 4+)

(925) 934-5860; 1035 Castle Rock Road, Walnut Creek, CA 94598
<www.ci.walnut-creek.ca.us/openspace/osborges.htm>

Description: This was a former ranch that is now home to a ranger station and animals including goats, sheep, pigs, and chickens. It has a child's fishing pond, a play area, and an amphitheater on the grounds. This ranch gives us a glimpse of how folks lived in the old West, with historical displays of turn of the 20th century artifacts.

Hours: *Ranch Area:* Daily sunrise to dusk. *Ranch House:* Weekends: 1–4pm.

Cost: Free.

Bathrooms: Yes

Facilities: Dirt paths, baby carrier recommended.

Food: No. Picnic tables available.

What to Bring: Picnic lunch, sunscreen, sunglasses, and hat. If you're attending Heritage Day, don't forget to bring $5/family cash for shuttling from Northgate High School at 435 Castle Rock to the ranch.

Follow-Up Activities: 1) *Heritage Day* on the 2nd Saturday in June from 10am–5pm has music, cowboys, horse rides, Indians, crafts, and food. *Holiday Hoe Down* is on the 1st Saturday in December. 2) Living history programs are available to groups to learn about the ranching experience.

These are available Tuesdays–Thursdays. Call for reservations. 3) For ranger-led tours, visit this Web site for dates and times: <www.ci.walnut-creek.ca.us/openspace/default.htm>.

Palo Alto Junior Museum & Zoo (Ages 3+)

(650) 329-2111; 1451 Middlefield Road, Palo Alto, CA 94301
<www.cityofpaloalto.org/ross/museum>

Description: This is a small museum and zoo. The zoo is small, but with a nice collection of animals, including owls, bats, and interesting birds. The museum has changing exhibits.

Hours: *Museum*: Tues–Sat: 10am–5pm. *Zoo*: Tues–Sat: 10am–4:30pm, Sun: 1–4pm. Closed Monday.

Cost: Free. Donations appreciated.

Bathrooms: Yes.

Facilities: Stroller friendly.

Food: No.

What to Bring: Picnic lunch.

Follow-Up Activities: A wide range of science classes is offered through the Palo Alto Parks and Recreation department. Check the Palo Alto *Enjoy!* Catalog at <www.paenjoy.org> for details.

Randall Museum (Ages 2+)

(415) 554-9600; 199 Museum Way, San Francisco, CA 94114
<www.randallmuseum.org>

Description: This small museum has exhibits on science, nature, and art. It has animals native to California; an insect exhibit; a small petting zoo with lizards, birds, snakes, and mice; as well as a see-through beehive.

Hours: Tues–Sat: 10am–5pm. Saturdays (1–3:30pm): special one-time workshops for art and science projects.

Cost: Free. Workshops require a small fee.

Bathrooms: Yes.

Facilities: Stroller friendly.

Food: No.

What to Bring: Picnic lunch.

Follow-Up Activities: 1) Classes and workshops for ages 3+. 2) Birthday parties organized by the Buddy Club. For additional info on Birthday parties, call: (510) 236-7469.

Ringling Brothers and Barnum & Bailey Circus (Ages 3+)

(415) 421-TIXS San Francisco, (510) 762-2277, (650) 478-2277
<www.ringling.com> or <www.ticketmaster.com>
Usually performs at Oakland Arena, Cow Palace, San Jose Arena, and other venues in the Bay Area.

Description: Circuses are great fun. It's one of the ways to actually see these animals in action, albeit artificially since they have been extensively trained. But it's a treat to see tigers, horses, elephants, and acrobats performing gravity defying stunts. Arrive 90 minutes before the show to meet the animals up close in the center circle, included with the price of admission. *Note:* Clowns can be scary for little ones. You may want to gauge your child's reaction to a clown before taking him to the circle.

Hours: Comes around to local Bay Area arenas once a year, usually in August. Tickets go on sale in July. Check Web site for current schedule and ticket information.

Cost: Varies, usually between $11–$50 per seat, depending on seating and date. Check Web site for most current information.

Bathrooms: Yes.

Facilities: Not generally stroller friendly, but depends on the facility.

Food: Hot dogs, candy, sodas, etc.

What to Bring: Camera—if you go early, you can visit with the clowns and other performers before the show begins. There, you have a great opportunity to take pictures with the performers and the animals. Bring cash for food, souvenirs, and parking.

San Francisco Zoo (All Ages)

(415) 753-7080; 1 Zoo Road, San Francisco, CA 94132
<www.sanfranciscozoo.org>

Description: The San Francisco Zoo is probably my favorite Bay Area zoo because it has such a variety of activities appropriate for little ones. These include the Family Farm at the Children's Zoo, the Insect Zoo, the colorful lorikeets, not to mention the Little Puffer Train and Carousel. Don't miss the lorikeets at Lorikeet Landing, the Wildlife Theater, and the bird area within the Children's Zoo to learn about eagles, falcons, and other birds of prey. You can feed the beautiful, rainbow-colored lorikeets right out of your hand. Purchase a tiny paper cupful of nectar at the entrance to the exhibit for one dollar. You can also purchase a picture of you or your child feeding the lorikeets at the exit of the exhibit. Animal feeding is also great fun. See what lions, tigers, elephants, and penguins eat every day. The Insect Zoo is a great place to watch a beehive and learn about bugs. Try to time your arrival at the Insect Zoo with the "Incredible Insects in Action" event to get the best experience.

Hours: Daily:10am–5pm. 365 days a year, including Christmas Day and Thanksgiving Day. Children's Zoo: 11am–4pm. During the summer (Memorial Day–Labor Day), the Children's Zoo has slightly extended hours 10:30am–4:30pm. Here is the feeding schedule. Confirm on the Web site: <www.sfzoo.org/kids/activities.htm#4>

Daily schedule:
- Asian Elephant exhibit: 1:30pm daily.
- Big Cats in the Lion House: 2pm daily (except Mondays).
- Penguins at Penguin Island: Fri–Wed: 3pm; Thur: 2:30pm.
- Lorikeet Landing: check at the gate.

On weekends and daily during the summer:
- Meerkats and Prairie Dogs: 2pm.
- Incredible Insects in Action: 2:30pm.
- Native American Animals: 3:15 and 3:45pm

Cost: $4 fee in the parking lot. Street parking is free.

Zoo admission: Free admission on the first Wednesday of each month. $10/adult, $7/youth (12–17) or senior (65+), $4/child (3–11), free for children 2 and under. Little Puffer Train and carousel rides cost $2/person. See Trains section for more details on train and carousel. San Francisco residents have discounted admission rates: $8/adult, $3.50/youth (12–17) or senior (65+), $1.50/child (3–11), free/child 2 and under.

Bathrooms: Yes, throughout the park. Get a zoo map at the entrance.

Facilities: Stroller friendly.

Food: Cafés throughout the park. Menus on the Web site under "Visit the Zoo" then "Guest Services."

What to Bring: Jacket, even in the summer, because San Francisco can be foggy and cold. Don't forget the sunscreen, hat, sunglasses, camera, and binoculars. Bring some dollar bills to feed the lorikeets, and other small bills to purchase tickets for the train, carousel, and rides. Consider bringing some sand equipment for playground use.

Follow-Up Activities: 1) Weekend workshops for children ages 3 and up. Look up the Web site: <www.sfzoo.org/education/classes.htm> for additional class information. 2) Spring and summer camps. 3) Birthday parties.

Nature Preserves

Nature preserves allow us the opportunity to view wildlife in their natural habitat. Bird watching, tide pooling, visiting the northern elephant seal, and whale-watching are some of the many activities available to view wildlife in their natural habitat here in the Bay Area.

California is on the migratory path of many birds. Bird watching can be a bit tricky to the novice. Since I am a novice, I looked for resources that will help in the identification of birds. Here are some resources that I found very useful.

1) *Local Birds of the San Francisco Bay Area: "Quick Guide"* to commonly seen local birds instantly identifies backyard-trail and shore-water birds. This is a quick reference laminated foldout card that's easy to carry along on a bird watching trip. It is only 5.5" x 6.5" and very thin. It has color illustrations and a brief description of each bird, with separate sections for shore birds, backyard birds, and trail birds commonly found in the Bay Area.

2) *Birding at the Bottom of the Bay: A Birder's site guide from Santa Clara Valley Audubon Society, Third Edition.* This book provides information on where and when to go for bird watching trips in the local area. You can purchase this book directly by mail from the Santa Clara Valley Audubon Society: SCVAS, 22221 McClellan Road, Cupertino, CA 95014 or by credit card by calling (408) 252-3747.

3) You can also purchase the laminated card and the book from the Wild Bird Center, (408) 358-4673, 792 Blossom Hill Road, Los Gatos, CA 95032. The Web site is: <www.lovethembirds.com>

4) Santa Clara Valley Audubon Society has bird watching trips that are open to members. Membership costs $15/year. Check the Web site: <www.scvas.org> in the "calendar" section for trips and events. The society is located at the McClellan Ranch site in Cupertino: 22221 McClellan Road, Cupertino, CA 95014. (408) 252-3747.

5) Many naturalist programs at the Nature Preserves and Parks with Visitor Centers also provide docent- or naturalist-led bird watching walks. These include Baylands, Elkhorn Slough, Arastradero, Sunol, Lindsey Wildlife Museum, Point Reyes National Seashore, California Academy of Sciences, and Crissy Field.

For bird watching trips, don't forget to bring your binoculars and your bird identification card!

Elkhorn Slough Reserve in Moss Landing, Baylands Nature Preserve in Palo Alto, and Point Reyes National Seashore in Marin provide wonderful bird watching opportunities. Arastradero Preserve in Palo Alto provides a habitat for in-land birds.

Elkhorn Slough and Baylands are both wetlands and salt marsh environments. This environment provides a transition zone between the freshwater and saltwater of the bay and ocean. The wetlands serve as a diverse habitat for wildlife, from migrating birds to sharks, crabs and shrimp, marine worms, and microscopic algae known as diatoms. The ecology lab inside the Lucy Evans Interpretive Center located at the Baylands and the Visitor Center at Elkhorn Slough have microscopes to view the microscopic life that inhabits these environments.

Año Nuevo State Reserve and Point Reyes are breeding grounds for the northern elephant seal. Point Reyes National Seashore also provides opportunities to view birds, elk, whales, and other wildlife.

Año Nuevo State Reserve (Ages 5+)

(650) 879-0227, New Years Creek Road, Pescadero, CA 94060
(650) 879-2025 Reserve office: 8:30am– 3:30pm
(800) 444-4445 Guided Walk Reservations (Required between December 15 and March 31. Reservations open in late October for individuals.)
<www.parks.ca.gov/central/bayarea/ansr228.htm>

Description: Located between Santa Cruz and Half Moon Bay, Año Nuevo is the largest breeding colony in the world for northern elephant seals. Come see their mating ritual and the seal pups from December to March. Tours require visitors to hike for about 3 miles.
Hours: During the breeding season (December–March), access to the

Reserve is open only for guided walks. The walks last 2 hours and the hike is about 3 miles. They depart every 15 minutes 9:15 am–2:30 pm.
Cost: $5/person.
Bathrooms: Yes, at the Visitor Center.
Facilities: Not stroller friendly.
Food: You can picnic at the picnic tables next to the Visitor Center.
What to Bring: Drinks/water bottles, warm jacket, picnic lunch, binoculars, and very comfortable walking shoes for the hike.

Arastradero Preserve (Ages 4+)
(650) 329-2423
Arastradero Road, Palo Alto, CA (½ mile west of Page Mill Road)
<www.arastradero.org>
<www.city.palo-alto.ca.us/ross/naturepreserve/arastradero.html>

Description: Located in the Palo Alto foothills, Arastradero Preserve is an open space preserve with rolling grasslands and a lake where wildlife abounds, including many varieties of birds such as bluebirds, wrens, chickadees, flycatchers, and even barn owls.
Hours: Open daily from 8am to sunset.
Cost: Free parking.
Bathrooms: Yes, next to the parking lot.
Facilities: Stroller friendly.
Food: No.
What to Bring: Sunglasses, sunscreen, picnic lunch, drinks, binoculars, and bird identification card.
Follow-Up Activities: Nature programs through the Palo Alto Parks and Recreation department. Check the Palo Alto *Enjoy!* Catalog under the "For Everyone" section or call (650) 329-2423. Past classes have included "Nesting Birds at Arastradero Preserve" and "Ethnobotany Walk," a program that explains how the Ohlone people used plants for food, shelter, basketry, and medicine.

Baylands Nature Preserve (For Ages 4+)
(650) 329-2506; 2775 Embarcadero Road, Palo Alto, CA
<www.paloaltoonline.com/paw/paonline/things_do/baylands.shtml>
<www.abag.ca.gov/bayarea/baytrail/vtour/map3/access/Btpalto/Btpalto.htm>

Description: The Baylands Nature Preserve and Shoreline Park are prime bird watching areas, with 150 species of wild birds, including some endangered species. There is a duck pond on your way to the Interpretive Center with different species of ducks and other birds. Learn about wetlands/salt marshes as habitats for diverse wildlife at the Lucy Evans Baylands Nature Preserve Interpretive Center. Plan on visiting the Preserve on the weekend so you can take advantage of the slide show, educational video, and nature walks with expert naturalists who can enrich and add depth to your experience. While on a docent-led walk on a November Saturday afternoon, I saw black-necked stilts, dowitchers, and sandpipers, along with the ubiquitous seagulls.

Hours: *Winter Hours:* Closed Mondays. Tues & Wed: 10am–5pm, Thur–Fri: 2–5pm. Don't miss the ecology lab: open in the afternoons. Weekends: 1–5pm. On weekends, educational videos: 1 and 4pm, slide show on salt marsh life: 2pm, and nature walks with naturalists: 3pm. *Summer Hours:* Tues–Fri: 2–5pm, Weekends: 1–5pm. On weekends, educational videos at 1 and 4pm, slide show on salt marsh life at 2pm, nature walks with naturalists at 3pm. *Note: The naturalist may be the only staff at the Visitor Center; when the naturalist is conducting the nature walk at 3pm, the Visitor Center is temporarily closed.*

Cost: Free.

What to Bring: Binoculars, sunscreen, sunglasses, water bottles, and bag lunch if you're planning to eat here. Dress in layers, as it can be windy. Wear good walking shoes that you don't mind getting muddy.

Bathrooms: Yes, inside the Interpretive Center. Portable bathrooms are located at the very end of the road.

Facilities: Stroller friendly. However, if you're planning to go on the nature walks with the naturalist, consider using a baby carrier or backpack instead.

Food: No, but picnic tables available.

Follow-Up Activities: 1) Plan ahead and register for one of the weekend programs such as "Fall and Winter Birding at the Baylands" and "Mysteries of the Mud Workshop" through the Palo Alto Parks and Recreation department. These programs are free. For program details, visit the Web site <www.paenjoy.org> to find the Palo Alto *Enjoy!* Catalog in the "Open Space" or "Everyone" section. 2) 2-week session summer camps in the summer. 3) *Environmental Volunteers*, a group of wonderful docents who provide science and environmental education to school groups at the Baylands, can be reached at: (650) 961-0545 or by mail at

3921 E. Bayshore Road, Palo Alto, CA 94303-4326. 4) Consider visiting the Shoreline Park in Mountain View, just a few miles off Highway 101, before your visit to Baylands Nature Preserve. You can have a wonderful day trip by first visiting Shoreline Park. Take a quick look inside the Rengstorff House, go on a paddleboat ride, and have lunch at the Lakeside Café in the morning. After lunch, visit the Baylands Natural Preserve and learn about the diverse animals and marine life that call the salt marshes home.

Bolinas Lagoon Preserve – Audubon Canyon Ranch
(415) 868-9244; 4900 Highway One, Stinson Beach, CA 94970
<www.egret.org>

Description: Best known for its heron and egret nesting grounds, the preserve is open to the public only during the heron and egret season. While there are no guided walks, guides are stationed at various points of the preserve to answer visitor questions.

Hours: Open only during the heron and egret nesting season (from the 2nd weekend in March through the 2nd weekend in July) on weekends and holidays: 10am–4pm.

Cost: Free.

Bathrooms: Yes.

Facilities: Stroller friendly.

Food: No.

What to Bring: Sunscreen, sunglasses, binoculars, and picnic lunch. Don't forget to wear comfortable walking shoes.

Follow-Up Activities: School programs for 4th and 5th graders are available to elementary schools for free. Call for reservations.

Don Edwards San Francisco Bay National Wildlife Refuge
Visitor Center: (510) 792-0222; One Marshlands Road, Newark, CA 94560
Environmental Education Center: (408) 262-5513; 1751 Grand Boulevard, Alviso
<http://desfbay.fws.gov>

Description: The Don Edwards San Francisco Bay National Wildlife Refuge is dedicated to preserving the wetlands and wildlife around the San Francisco Bay. The refuge is on the Pacific Flyway for migratory birds and is home to some endangered species such as the California Clapper

45

Rail bird. The refuge has two sites for visitors. The Visitor Center in Newark has wildlife exhibits as well as an auditorium and an observation tower. The Environmental Education Center is located in Alviso. Both the Visitor Center and the Environmental Education Center have interpretive programs and guided walks. Visit the Web site for the event schedule. Bay Area Science Alliance's site, <www.basa.info>, has events as well.

Hours: *Visitor Center:* Tues–Sun: 10am–5pm. Closed all national holidays. *Environmental Education Center:* Weekends: 10am–5pm. Open Mon–Fri to school groups by reservation only. Closed all national holidays.

Cost: Free.

Bathrooms: Yes.

Facilities: Stroller friendly.

Food: No.

What to Bring: Sunscreen, sunglasses, binoculars, and picnic lunch.

Follow-Up Activities: Environmental education programs offered to schools and other groups.

Elkhorn Slough Reserve (Ages 3+)

(831) 728-2822; 1700 Elkhorn Road, Watsonville, CA 95076
<www.elkhornslough.org>

Description: Elkhorn Slough, the largest remaining coastal wetlands in the state, is considered one of the premier bird watching sites that attract many visitors from all over the country. It is a haven for almost 300 varieties of birds including owls, woodpeckers, hawks, falcons, pelicans, jays, warblers, grebes, and more. Elkhorn Slough Rookery in the north marsh is a nesting site for great blue herons and great egrets, which nest in the treetops of Monterey Pines here in the spring (late January–early March). The Visitor Center has educational exhibits and microscopes to view the microscopic life that lives in the slough and the mud flats. For close-up pictures of microscopic life, such as the diatom (microscopic plants that live in the water and form the base of the food chain), check out the Web site's "Under the Scope" section <www.elkhornslough.org/micro2.htm>.

Hours: The reserve and visitor center are open Wed–Sun: 9am–5pm. Docent tours and nature walks on weekends at 10am and 1pm. Early bird walk on first Sat of the month at 8:30am.

Cost: Visitor Center is free. Entrance fee for the reserve: $2.50/adult 16 and older.

Bathroom: Yes.

Facilities: Stroller friendly.
Food: No.
What to Bring: Binoculars. Dress warmly and wear walking shoes.
Follow-Up Activities: *Elkhorn Slough Safari Nature Tours* offers naturalist guided tours on a pontoon boat of the slough. It provides the opportunity to view sea otters, seals, migratory birds, and shorebirds up close. $26/adult, $19/child 14 & under, and $24/senior 65+. Visit <www.elkhornslough.com> for schedules and reservations or call: (831) 633-5555. Departures from Harbor District lot off Sandholt Road in Moss Landing.

Midpeninsula Open Space Preserve (Ages 4+)
(650) 691-1200; 330 Distel Circle, Los Altos, CA94022
<www.openspace.org>

Description: This organization acquires and maintains open space and provides information on 26 preserves with almost 50,000 acres of land along the peninsula, from San Carlos to Los Gatos. Click on the "Preserves" button on the Web site to locate the 26 preserves. There are many nature programs for families throughout the preserves.
Hours: Open all year from sunrise to ½ hour after sunset. Visit the Web site and look under "Hikes & Activities" button on the top bar, then "Calendar of Activities" on the left column for most current events, times, and dates.
Cost: Free.
Bathroom: Yes.
Facilities: Strollers friendliness varies based on the preserve.
Food: No.
What to Bring: Sunscreen, picnic lunch, binoculars, and camera.

Point Lobos State Reserve (All Ages)
(831) 624-4909; 3 miles south of Carmel, Highway 1, Carmel, CA
Mailing Address: 1 Box 62, Carmel, CA 93923
<http://pt-lobos.parks.state.ca.us>
Trail Map: <http://pt-lobos.parks.state.ca.us/map/TrailMap.html>

Description: This breathtakingly beautiful park is rich not only in scenic beauty, but also in the diversity of wildlife and cultural history. Wildlife includes birds, land mammals, marine life such as seals and otters, and monarch butterflies. The reserve has been home to American Indians, Chinese, Japanese, and Portuguese whalers. Learn more about this rich heritage from tours and the wonderful Web site.

Hours: 9am–5pm. Last admission ½ hour prior to closing. Extended hours until 7pm during Daylight Savings time. Museum tours (Whalers Cabin & Whaling Station Museums) are open as staffing permits, usually 11am–3pm. Ranger- or docent-led nature walks, cabin tours, and slide programs require advanced reservation by groups or school groups.

Cost: $5 parking fee/car.

Bathroom: Yes.

Facilities: Stroller friendly only along paths.

Food: No.

What to Bring: Sunscreen, sunglasses, picnic lunch, binoculars, and camera. Dress warmly and wear walking shoes.

Follow-Up Activities: The Web site is worth perusing, as it has a wealth of information on the natural and cultural history of this beautiful reserve.

Point Reyes National Seashore (All Ages)
<www.nps.gov/pore/home.htm>

Description: Point Reyes National Seashore provides a treasure trove of experiences. These include learning about the Miwok Indians at Kule Loklo, a replica coast Indian village[1]; watching birds, marine life, elephant seals, whales, and tule elk in their natural habitat; and learning about maritime history, environment, and marine fossils at the Kenneth C. Patrick Visitor Center and the Lighthouse Visitor Center. This park has multiple facilities with their own hours, exhibits, and special programs.

For wildlife viewing, try to visit the park when the rangers are conducting their naturalist programs. However, if you are unable to attend during these workshops, you can take self-guided tours. Don't forget your binoculars!

Here's a list on where to go: *Abbots Lagoon*: Best bird watching site during fall and winter for shorebirds, waterfowl, sparrows, hawks, and osprey. *Drakes Estero:* Largest harbor seal breeding colony in Point Reyes.

[1] See "Native American Indians" section under Chapter 9: Historical Outings for the entry on Kule Loklo.

Elephant Seal Overlook: Breeding colony of elephant seals can be observed from December through March. During this season, docents provide information, binoculars, and spotting scopes from 11am–4pm on weekends and holidays. *Five Brooks Pond:* Watch green-backed herons, grebes, hooded mergansers, and ring-necked ducks. See bats in the early evening feeding on insects. Salmon working their way up Olema Creek can be viewed from the bridge from December through February. *Lighthouse:* View turkey vultures, ravens, hawks, and even peregrine falcons. The colony of murres can be seen on the rocks north of the lighthouse during their spring and summer nesting season. This is also a good place to watch the gray whale migration from January through early May. Visit the Web site for more specific information about these locations, directions, and maps: <www.nps.gov/pore/activ_view.htm>. Here's a list of the Point Reyes visitor centers.

Bear Valley Visitor Center
(415) 464-5100; Bear Valley Road in Olema, CA

Hours: Mon–Fri: 9am–5pm, Sat/Sun & Holidays: 8am–5pm. Closed Christmas Day.

Description: Exhibits on the ecosystems and cultural heritage of the park. It has a weather station, seismograph, and touch table. Kule Loklo, the replica Miwok village, is a short ½ mile walk from the Bear Valley Visitor Center. See the "Native American Indian" section in Chapter 9: Historical Outings for more information on Kule Loklo.

Bathrooms: Yes.

Facilities: Stroller friendly.

Food: No.

Kenneth C. Patrick Visitor Center
(415) 669-1250; Drakes Beach off Sir Frances Drake Blvd.
30 minutes from Bear Valley Visitor Center

Hours: *All Year:* Weekends & Holidays: 10am–5pm. Closed Mon–Fri & Christmas Day. *Summer (Memorial Day to Labor Day only):* Fri–Tues, 10am–5pm.

Description: Exhibits on 16th century maritime exploration, marine fossils, and marine environments. A 250-gallon saltwater aquarium highlights life from Drakes Bay. A minke whale skeleton hangs from the ceiling.

Bathrooms: Yes, and showers, too.

Food: Picnic tables and barbecues. Drakes Beach Café is located next door.

Follow-Up Activities: Labor Day Sunday Sand Sculpture Contest each year from 9am–3:30pm. Registration held at the Visitor Center starting at 9am. Judging begins at 1pm. Awards at 3:30pm. Call (415) 464-5100 to verify and for more information.

Lighthouse Visitor Center
(415) 669-1534; Point Reyes Headlands, end of Sir Frances Drake Blvd. 45 min. from Bear Valley Visitor Center. There is a ½ mile walk (mostly uphill) from the parking lot to the Lighthouse Visitor Center.

Hours: Thur–Mon: 10am–4:30pm. Closed Tues, Wed, & Christmas Day.
Description: Exhibits on whales, wildflowers, birds, and maritime history.
Bathrooms: Yes.
Facilities: Not stroller friendly—has stairs.
Food: No.

Point Reyes Historic Lighthouse
(415) 669-1534; ½ mile from the parking area down some 300 steps

Description: The equipment building shows how the fog signal was used at Point Reyes. The historic lighthouse has exhibits on the history of the light and the keepers. The lens room includes the original clockworks and a 130-year-old first order Fresnel lens in working condition.

Hours: Thur–Mon: 10am–4:30pm, weather permitting. Closed Tues & Wed. Closed when wind speeds exceed 40 miles per hour. Lighthouse history programs on the first and third Saturday each month April–December. Reservations required. Call (415) 669-1534 between 10am–4:30pm.
Cost: Free .

Follow-Up Activities:
Naturalist Programs on the Weekends with the Park Rangers:
Wonderful programs on the weekends cover a variety of topics. They include: Kule Loklo Walk and Work Days, whale-watching from the Observation Deck and learning about whales and their migration, elephant seal watching and learning about their life cycle at the Elephant Seal Overlook, whales and wildflowers, Habitat Restoration

Workdays, lighthouse history, and more. These programs are based in different facilities. Visit the Web site for more detailed information: <www.nps.gov/pore/activ_classes_guided.htm>. Alternatively, from the home page of Point Reyes, select the "Activities & Recreation" tab on the top bar, then "Programs & Classes" tab on the lower bar.

Educational Programs at Point Reyes:

Junior Ranger Program: There are 2 programs. One provides a study of the lighthouse. The other explores the Coast Miwok Indians' history and culture. For more information on the program, visit either the Bear Valley Visitor Center or the Lighthouse Visitor Center.

Summer Nature Science Camps for kids ages 7–16. Different sessions and age groupings with 4-day sessions for kids 7–9, 5-day camps for kids 9–11 and 10–12, and a 6-day camp for teens 13–16. Camp activities: canoeing, tide pooling, backpacking, bird and mammal observation, night hikes, storytelling, arts and crafts, etc. For detailed information of the camps, visit the Web site: <www.ptreyes.org/camp>.

Safari West (Ages 3+)

(707) 579-2551; (800) 616-2695; 3115 Porter Creek Road, Santa Rosa, CA 95404
<www.safariwest.com>

Description: This is a nature preserve for endangered animals. Naturalist guided tours are 2½ hours long. The tour has two parts. The first part takes place in a safari vehicle; the second half is a walk to meet the birds and animals firsthand.

Schedule: Spring and fall tour times: 9am, 1pm, 3pm. Winter tour times: 10am & 2pm. Call for tour reservations.

Cost: $58/adult, $28/child. Free for children under 3.

Bathrooms: Yes.

Facilities: Not stroller friendly.

Food: Restaurant on site. Lunch: $15/adult, $12/child. Dinner: $25/adult, $15/child. You must make reservations.

What to Bring: Sunscreen, hat, sunglasses, comfortable clothes and shoes, camera, and binoculars.

Follow-Up Activities: Take a virtual tour on the Web site to see the types of animals you will learn about.

Nature & Visitor Centers

Shorebird Nature Center (Ages 4+)
Berkeley Marina
(510) 644-8623; 160 University Avenue, Berkeley, CA 94710
<www.ci.berkeley.ca.us/marina/marinaexp/naturecenter.html>

Description: The nature center has a 100-gallon saltwater aquarium with marine life from the San Francisco Bay. There's a touch table, animal models, and other wildlife exhibits. Time your visit with the Berkeley Bay Festival for the most enriching experience. During the school year, it is geared to school groups. Summer camps offered to students ages 5–13.

Hours: Tues–Sat: 8:30am–5pm. Mornings are devoted to classroom programs. Open to the public: 1–5pm.

Cost: Free.

Bathrooms: Yes.

Facilities: Stroller friendly.

Food: Nearby restaurants at the Berkeley Marina.

What to Bring: Cash for food, jacket, sunscreen, and sunglasses.

Follow-Up Activities: 1) Saturday programs for families include a tour of the Nature Center and the marina. 2) Birthday parties at the Adventure Playground where kids can build, paint, and play on recycled materials. The Adventure Playground is open Sat & Sun from 11am–5pm. 3) Marine biology summer camps on the rocky shore and marina environment for ages 5–13. Registration starts early May. Other summer programs available on boating and related topics. 4) *Berkeley Bay Festival* in late April (around Earth Day) starts at 12noon and ends at 5pm. This festival features free sailboat rides, mini-tours by Hornblower Yachts, dockside tours of many boats, food, music, hands-on activities, a freshwater aquarium, a traveling *Insect Discovery Lab* with insects from around the world, and a portable planetarium to see the stars. The Insect Discovery Lab is an outreach program offered to schools and other groups by the Center for Ecosystem Survival: <www.savenature.org> or (415) 648-3392. It is located at 699 Mississippi, Suite 106, San Francisco, CA 94107. 5) High-tide and low-tide programs available for both school and other groups to learn about the marine environment.

Crab Cove Visitor Center (Ages 3+)

(510) 521-6887; 1252 McKay Avenue, Alameda, CA 94501
<www.ebparks.org/parks/crab.htm>

Description: There is a small exhibit area with a few small animals and some pelicans. Visit during a naturalist program on the weekend to have an enriching experience. During low tides, the mudflats are exposed. The mudflat is a very rich environment for inter-tidal animals, including small crabs and shrimp, marine worms, and microscopic life.

Hours: Wed–Sun: 10am–4pm *March through November only*. Naturalist programs schedule on the weekends: <www.ebparks.org/events.htm>.

Cost: $5 parking fee, seasonal. Most programs are free or require a small fee. Some require pre-registration.

Bathrooms: Yes.

Facilities: Stroller friendly.

Food: No.

What to Bring: Binoculars, cash for parking, and picnic lunch.

Follow-Up Activities: 1) Whale-watching lecture and cruises in March. 2) Shorebird watching, low tide and minus tide explorations, marine life and land mammal nature programs conducted on weekends. 3) They have special classes for 3– to 5-year-olds and for 6– to 8-year-olds. Program offering changes with the season. Regular attendance throughout the year will provide quite a wonderful series of science classes. 4) Birthday parties.

Crissy Field Center, Presidio (Ages 4+)

(415) 561-7690; 603 Mason Street, Presidio, San Francisco, CA 94129
Hotline: (415) 4-Crissy; Cafe: (415) 561-7756; Warming Hut Cafe: (415) 561-3042; Bookstore: (415) 561-7761; Warming Hut Bookstore: (415) 561-3040
<www.crissyfield.org>
<www.crissyfield.org/html/cfc-prog/index.html>

Description: This open space and Visitor Center is now a part of the Golden Gate Recreation Area. The Visitor Center has a media lab, library, arts workshop, urban ecology lab, and many programs for children and adults.

Hours: Wed–Sun: 9am–5pm. *Center Café:* open only when the center is open. *Warming Hut Café:* (415) 561-3042, open daily 9am–5pm.

Cost: Varies from free to small fee, depending on the program.

Bathrooms: Yes.

Facilities: Stroller friendly.

Food: Two cafés, see hours above.

Follow-Up Activities: 1) Summer camps for children age 6–14. 2) School programs. 3) The *Kids and Families* programs include art projects, ecology of the wetlands, bird watching, and damselflies. There is also a media/ computer lab to model the weather and explore whales, birds, and the Australian Great Barrier Reef and its inhabitants. There are even simulated submarine rides and field trips such as whale-watching and guided tours of the Bay Model Museum, etc. These weekend programs are usually for children ages 5+.

Hayward Shoreline Interpretive Center (Ages 3+)

(510) 670-7270; (510) 881-6700 Reservations;
4901 Breakwater Avenue, Hayward, CA 94545
<http://hard.dst.ca.us/index.html>

Description: Hayward Shoreline Interpretive Center provides an introduction to the San Francisco Estuary's ecology. The Interpretive Center has exhibits, programs, and activities showcasing the natural and human history of this area. Join the naturalist on a weekend program to help enrich your family's experience.

Hours: Sat & Sun: 10am–5pm. School groups can visit Wed–Fri, with advanced reservations. Office closed Mon & Tues.

Cost: Free for the Interpretive Center, but fee varies with the naturalist program selected.

Bathroom: Yes.

Facilities: Stroller friendly.

Food: No.

What to Bring: Picnic lunch, cash for programs, and jacket.

Follow-Up Activities: 1) Naturalist programs on the weekends. Once at the Web site, click on "Signature Facilities," then "Hayward Shoreline Interpretive Center" for naturalist program schedule. 2) Summer camp for preK–6th grades. 3) May Day celebration of spring and the May Pole Dance in May. For the above activities, see the "Quarterly Brochure" on the Web site listed under the "Program & Classes" icon. These programs are offered as part of the Greater Hayward Area Recreation and Park Foundation. The parks and recreation catalog, "Quarterly Brochure," lists the classes, programs, summer camps, etc. that are available at the Sulphur Creek and Hayward Shoreline Interpretive Centers.

Rancho Del Oso Nature & History Center (All Ages)

Big Basin Redwoods State Park

(831) 427-2288; 3600 Highway #1, Davenport, CA 95017
<www.santacruzstateparks.org/parks/rancho/>;
<www.parks.ca.gov/default.asp?page_id=863>

Description: This nature center has naturalist programs. For more details, call and plan to visit during a naturalist program.
Hours: Sat & Sun: 12–4pm. *Guided nature walks*: every 2nd Sat. of the month: 1–3:30pm. *Cultural history tours*: every 2nd Sun of the month: 1–2pm.
Cost: Free.
Bathrooms: Yes.
Facilities: Stroller friendly only at the Visitor Center. Some trails are fine with a buggy.
Food: No.
What to Bring: Picnic lunch, binoculars, comfortable walking shoes, sunscreen, sunglasses, and lots of bottled water to drink.
Follow-Up Activities: 1) Annual bird count walk in late December/ early January time frame from 8am–noon and again at 1–4pm. 2) Programs on mushrooms and fungus with a mycologist (fungus expert) during the rainy season.

Redwood Grove Nature Preserve (Ages 3+)

(650) 917-0342; reservations after school programs, and birthday parties: (650) 941-0950; 482 University Avenue, Los Altos, CA 94022
<www.ci.los-altos.ca.us/recreation/fall/nature-preserve.pdf>

Description: This small preserve is located in a residential area of Los Altos. It has a small creek, a grove of redwoods, and a small Nature Center. The Nature Center has some small animals, including a bird and an iguana. There's a play table with some fossils, sand, and a brush, for children to play being at an excavation site. Naturalist Keith Gutierrez provides age appropriate and mesmerizing talks that kids love.
Hours: Open Houses in September, January, and May, on the third Sunday of these months from noon–3pm.
Cost: Free.
Bathroom: Yes.

Facilities: Stroller friendly.
Food: No. Picnic tables.
What to Bring: Binoculars for bird watching and picnic lunch.
Follow-Up Activities: 1) Sponsors birthday parties for ages 4–11 with music, games, animal visit, and nature walk. Program lasts approx. 1 hour and can be conducted indoors in case of rainy weather. 2) School and scouting groups have special programs available: Learning about Nature (preschooler–2nd grade), Ohlone Native Americans (2nd grade), Gold Rush program (3rd grade), and an overnight program for scouts. 3) After school classes and summer camps: sign up with the Los Altos Parks and Recreation Dept.

Sulphur Creek Nature Center (Ages 3+)
(510) 881-6747; 1801 D Street, Hayward, CA 94541
<http://hard.dst.ca.us/index.html>

Description: This Nature Center has exhibits of coyotes, foxes, opossums, hawks, owls, and a variety of reptiles and amphibians in their natural habitats. It also has a changing hands-on display featuring selected animal groups. Best of all, there's a pet lending library that rents hamsters, guinea pigs, rats, and mice for a week for young children to experience the responsibility of caring for a pet. There is a Discovery Room dedicated to the watersheds and creeks as a habitat for plants and animals.
Hours: Tues–Sun: 10am–4:30pm. Closed Mondays.
Cost: Free.
Bathrooms: Yes.
Facilities: Gravel pathways. Baby carrier or backpack recommended.
Food: No.
What to Bring: Sunglasses, sunscreen, and picnic lunch.
Follow-Up Activities: 1) School and scout groups have access to wildlife education programs. 2) Naturalist programs and classes for children 3–12. See the Greater Hayward Area Recreation and Park Foundation in the Parks and Recreation Section for contact information. The parks and recreation catalog, "Quarterly Brochure," lists the classes, programs, summer camps, etc. that is available at the Sulphur Creek and Hayward Shoreline Interpretive Centers. 3) Annual Wildlife Fair in early June (10am–4pm) for $5/person, free/child 3 & under. Activities based on a water theme include aquatic discoveries, crafts, music, face painting, storytelling, and games. 4) Birthday parties.

Sunol Regional Wilderness (Ages 3+)
Sunol Visitor Center
(925) 862-2601; Southeast end of Geary Road, Sunol, CA
<www.ebparks.org/parks/sunol.htm>

Description: This preserve is home to eagles, bobcats, mountain lions, and tule elk. The Little Yosemite area is a scenic two-mile hike from the Visitor Center; there's a sandstone outcrop with fossils embedded, the remnants of an ancient sea floor.

Hours: *Park:* 7am–dusk. *Visitor Center:* Sat & Sun: 10am–4:30pm.

Cost: $4 parking fee seasonal, weekends & holidays.

Bathrooms: Yes.

Facilities: Stroller friendly on some trails.

Food: No.

What to Bring: binoculars, sunscreen, sunglasses, picnic lunch, water, and comfortable walking shoes.

Follow-Up Activities: 1) Naturalist programs on the weekends. These include wildflower hikes, geology walks, science for little tykes, Ohlone and the old ways workshops, etc. Check the Web site: <**www.ebparks.org/events/byloc/sunol.htm**> for program details. Call for reservations. 2) Niles Depot Train Station is close by.

Fossil Sites

We can learn about geological history from the fossils that have been found. Mount Diablo State Park, Sunol Regional Wilderness, and Seacliff State Beach have sea life fossils and conduct guided walks to explain the formation and history of these fossils. Fossil collecting is not allowed. If your child loves to dig for treasure and wants to play at being a paleontologist, Bamboola has a pretend dinosaur dig.

Bamboola (Ages 2–6)
(408) 448-4FUN (4386); 5401 Camden Avenue, San Jose, CA 95124
<www.bamboola.com>

Description: Kids can play at being a paleontologist at Bamboola's sand area, outside of the arcade area. This area has dinosaur tracks and cement dinosaur bones that kids can pretend to dig up. Bamboola has mostly indoor play zones for young preschoolers. It has a crafts area, face painting, dress-up area, a water play area, a pretend house and grocery store with carts, a rock climbing area, a maze, an arcade, and a ball bouncer and tunnels.

Hours: Closed Monday. Tues: 10am–5pm, Wed–Sat: 10am–9pm, Sun: 10am–6pm. Free after 5pm on Wed–Sat only. The outdoor section is closed in the winter.

Cost: $9.95/ Child 3–12, $4.95/Child 1–2 years old, Free/ Adult. Ask about summer and yearly passes, which offer substantial discounts from the single entry price.

Bathrooms: Yes, wonderful bathroom for little ones. The toilets are just their size!

Facilities: Stroller friendly.

Food: Café available with pizza, sandwiches, salads, coffee, juice, milk, and soda.

What to Bring: Extra cash for food and arcade games, and an extra change of clothes for little ones who love to play in the water play area. Socks are required on the adventure playground, and rubber soled shoes are required for climbing rocks.

Follow-Up Activities: Birthday parties offered.

Mount Diablo State Park (All Ages)
(925) 837-2525; 96 Mitchell Canyon Road, Clayton CA 94517
(925) 943-1945, (925) 256-9250 Summit Center
<www.mdia.org>
<www.cal-parks.ca.gov/default.asp?page_id=517>

Description: Fossils embedded in the rocks at Fossil Ridge. You cannot collect fossils here. Summit Visitor Center displays the natural and cultural history of Mount Diablo. The walls of the Visitor Center are made of fossil-embedded sandstone. The Mitchell Canyon Interpretive Center has exhibits on the wildlife, geology, and plants of the park. For more information on park geology, visit the site: <www.mdia.org/geology.htm>.

Hours: *Summer:* 11am–5pm. *Winter:* 10am–4pm. *Summit Visitor Center* is open Wed–Sun. *The Mitchell Canyon Interpretive Center* is open on weekends and some holidays only from 9am–3pm in the winter and 8am–4pm in the summer.

Cost: $4 park entry fee.
Bathrooms: Yes.
Facilities: Stroller friendly.
Food: No.
What to Bring: Picnic lunch, water, binoculars, sunscreen, sunglasses, camera, and comfortable walking shoes.
Follow-Up Activities: 1) Many ranger-guided walks such as wildflower hikes, fossil walks, etc. For event schedule, visit this Web site: <www.mdia.org/events.htm>. 2) Star gazing parties on select Saturday evenings. Call (925) 837-2525, then press "4" and "#" for recorded information on most current star gazing parties. The Mt. Diablo Astronomical Society's Web site: <www.mdas.net>.

Seacliff State Beach (Ages 2+)
(831) 685-6442; 201 State Park Drive off Highway 1, Aptos, CA 95003
<www.parks.ca.gov/default.asp?page_id=543>
<www.santacruzstateparks.org/parks/seacliff/index.php>

Description: Fossils are embedded in the cliffs along the edge of the beach. This is also a good beach to hunt for seashells. Check with the Visitor Center for exact times and dates for naturalist programs.
Hours: 8am–sunset. Fossil walk scheduled on select Sundays at 12:15 pm. Visitor Center has programs on the weekends geared toward families.
Cost: $5 parking fee.
Bathrooms: Yes, with showers throughout the beachfront.
Facilities: Stroller friendly off the beach.
Food: Snack bar.
What to Bring: Beach gear, sunscreen, sunglasses, picnic lunch, and cash for parking.
Follow-Up Activities: Naturalist programs for families on weekends.

Sunol Regional Preserve (Ages 3+)
(925) 862-2601; Southeast end of Geary Road, Sunol, CA
<www.ebparks.org/parks/sunol.htm>

Description: Sandstone outcrop with embedded fossils. Geology walks are sometimes scheduled on the weekend. Check the Web site for current times and dates: <www.ebparks.org/events/byloc/sunol.htm#D29756>.

See full entry for details in Chapter 1: Animal Kingdom – Nature & Visitor Centers section. Call for advanced reservations.

Museum of Paleontology (Ages 5+)
University of California, Berkeley
(510) 642-1821; 1101 Valley Life Sciences Bldg., Berkeley, CA 94720
<www.ucmp.berkeley.edu/museum/publicexhibits.html>

Description: This research museum is the official state repository for all fossils found in California. Unfortunately, due to space and budget constraints, very little of the collection is available for public viewing. On display at the lobby of the ground floor are *Tyrannosaurus rex* and *pteranodon* mounts, and a few displays of California fossils and dinosaur material. On the second floor, there are additional displays, mostly of the evolution of the dinosaurs into birds. Plan your visit for Cal Day in April when the university opens its doors to visitors offering hands-on, kid friendly activities and tours that cover a huge range of topics (music, art, anthropology, engineering, chemistry, paleontology, and more).

Hours: *During the semester the building is open:* Mon–Thur: 8am–10pm, Fri: 8am–5pm, Sat: 10am–5pm, Sun: 1–5pm. *Holiday and Summer* Hours: visit the Web site and look under the "Biosciences & Natural Resources Library:" <www.lib.berkeley.edu/AboutLibrary/hours.html#Branches>. Cal Days are usually on a weekend day, in early April every year. For most current Cal Day information: <www.berkeley.edu/calday>.

Cost: Free.

Bathrooms: Yes, in the building.

Facilities: Stroller friendly.

Food: No. Cafeterias and restaurants available on and off campus, but may be a bit of a walk.

What to Bring: Cash for parking and food. Don't forget the camera or video camera with film and batteries.

Follow-Up Activities: 1) This museum's hidden treasures are its extensive on-line exhibits. The virtual exhibits in the "History of Life" section include information about phylogeny (the "tree of life"), geology, and evolution: <www.ucmp.berkeley.edu/historyoflife/histoflife.html>. 2) Dinosaurs, dinosaurs, dinosaurs, … and birds? Visit the dinosaur on-line exhibit: <www.ucmp.berkeley.edu/education/dinolink.html>. 3) Docent-led tours are available to schools and groups with a maximum of 25 people per group. Call the Education Department at (510) 642-4877 to schedule. For more information on the tours: <www.ucmp.berkeley.edu/education/docent.html>.

Directions: Map and directions to reach UC Berkeley: <www.ucmp.berkeley.edu/museum/bayarea.html>. Map of the Valley Life Sciences Building at UC Berkeley: <http://ib.berkeley.edu/vlsb/VLSBmap.html>.

Marine Life

There are many kinds of marine life besides fish. These include mammals that live in the sea such as sea lions, otters, whales, and dolphins. We can visit aquariums, tide pools, and nature preserves and take whale–watching cruises. For an answer to "Can fish hear?" visit this Web site: <www.worldkids.net/critters/pets/fish/fishears.htm>.

Aquariums & Marine Life Centers

Aquarium of the Bay (All Ages)
1-888-SEA-DIVE (732-3483);
Pier 39, Beach Street & The Embarcadero, San Francisco, CA 94133
<www.aquariumofthebay.com>

Description: This walk-through aquarium features the marine life of San Francisco Bay. Behind-the-scenes tours present information on what the divers wear to keep warm, how the aquarium keeps the water clean, where the water comes from, what happens when the fish get sick, and how they prepare food for the fish.

Hours: Mon–Fri: 10am–6pm, Sat & Sun: 10am–7pm. Closed Christmas Day. *Summer extended hours:* 9am–8pm. *Behind the Scenes Tours* (~40 min.): Fri, Sat, Sun, & Mon starting at noon, 2pm & 5pm. For reservations (which are recommended): (415) 623-5376. *Feeding Schedule:* Bat Ray Feeding: Tues, Thur, & Sun: 11:30 am; Grab A Bite (narrated): Tues, Thur & Sun: 3pm; Seven Gill Shark feeding: Thur & Sun: 1:30pm. Call

(415) 623-5333 for bay cruise schedules.

Cost: $12.95/adult, $6.50/child (3–11), $6.50/senior 65+, free/child under 3. Family rate for 2 adults & 1 or 2 children: $29.95. Behind-the-scenes tour: $25/person. Yearly family membership: $65 (2 adults & 2 children). Combination packages including aquarium admission and a bay cruise with the Gold and Blue Fleet: $19/adult, $11/child, and $15/senior. Visit the Web site for a $2 off coupon. Internet advanced ticket purchases also get a discounted rate.

Bathrooms: Yes.

Facilities: Stroller friendly.

Food: No, but plenty available close by at Pier 39.

What to Bring: Cash for parking, jacket.

Follow-Up Activities: 1) Birthday parties and sleepovers offered. 2) For school groups, tours are led by a naturalist. For feeding schedule, birthday party information, sleepovers, and special events schedule: select the "Programs" button on the top toolbar once you've entered the Web site.

Marine Mammal Center (Ages 2 +)
Marin Headlands
(415) 289-7325; 1065 Fort Cronkhite, Sausalito, CA 94965

<www.marinemammalcenter.org>

Description: This is a rehabilitation hospital for marine mammals, to help return them to the wild. As such, the animals that are in residence vary day by day and season by season. The best time to visit is in the spring, when northern elephant seals or their pups may be in residence. The summer and fall seasons tend to have sea lions in residence. Visit the Web site for current animal patient information: <www.marinemammalc enter.org/what_we_do/rehab/current_patients.asp>.

Hours: Daily: 10am–4pm. Closed Thanksgiving, Christmas, and New Year's Days.

Cost: Free. Donations appreciated.

Bathrooms: Yes.

Facilities: Stroller friendly.

Food: No.

What to Bring: Warm jacket, picnic lunch, and sunglasses.

Follow-Up Activities: 1) Close to the Bay Area Discovery Museum. 2) Educational programs for groups and schools.

Monterey Bay Aquarium (All Ages)

(831) 648-4800; 886 Cannery Row, Monterey, CA 93940
<www.montereyaquarium.org>

Description: This aquarium is deservedly world famous, visited by people from all over the world and featured in a Star Trek movie. There are many exhibits of the different environments within Monterey Bay. *The Kelp Forest* exhibit shows the interaction between fish and the kelp forest. *The Mysteries of the Deep* exhibit showcases the exotic life found in the deep sea in the Monterey Canyon, just off shore. *The Splash Zone* is a wonderful exhibit for toddlers to elementary school age children with its colorful coral reef animals and interactive displays; it has an interactive educational water play area for little ones. Don't miss the little *tank of sea dragons*, cousins of sea horses, on display at the Splash Zone next to the play area. There are *two touch pools*: one at the Splash Zone exhibit for toddlers, and a set of big touch pools on the first floor with bat rays. There is an *Outer Bay* exhibit with speedy tunas. When the tunas take off, the burst of speed is absolutely breathtaking. Don't miss the animal feedings at the otter exhibit, the penguin exhibit, and the Kelp Forest exhibit. The courtyard/outside decks of the aquarium provide gorgeous views of the Monterey Bay and telescopes for viewing otters, sea lions, and other wildlife on the bay. If you're lucky you might even spot some dolphins and whales.

Hours: 10am–6pm daily. *Summer and holiday hours:* 9:30am–6pm. Closed Christmas Day. Feeding at the *Kelp Forest exhibit:* 11:30am & 4pm. Daily *sea otter feeding:* 10:30am, 1:30pm, 3:30pm.

Cost: *Parking fees:* depend on the lot or street metered parking. Bring quarters for metered parking on the street. I recommend parking at Cannery Row Parking Garage <**www.monterey.org/parking/crgmap.html**> on Wave Street, between Hoffman Ave and Prescott Avenue *Admission:* $17.95/Adult, $14.95/Student (age 13–17) with student ID or Senior (age 65+), $7.95/Child (age 3–12) or Disabled. *Membership:* $85/year includes 2 adults and children or grandchildren ages 3–12. *Discount Membership:* $35/year per individual, excludes children. Only seniors 65+ and students with ID qualify. You may want to consider purchasing a family membership. Just coming to the aquarium twice will equal the cost of the membership if you have 2 adults and at least one child age 3 or older. One great benefit of membership is the members' entrance. The members' entrance allows you to bypass long admission lines on busy summer weekends. You also get 10% off merchandise at the stores.

Bathrooms: Great bathrooms with baby changing tables.

Food: Wonderful cafeteria, restaurant, and snack bar with hot entrees and fabulous oceanfront views.

What to Bring: The coast can be windy and foggy in the summertime, so be sure to bring a sweatshirt/jacket just in case. You can bring a picnic lunch and eat outside on the deck, if you'd like. I recommend parking in a lot, but bring quarters if you're considering metered street parking.

Follow-Up Activities: 1) Teens ages 14–17 can volunteer during the summer and learn lots about marine life. 2) For a virtual tour of the aquarium, and more ocean facts, visit the "E-Quarium" for kids at: **<www .montereybayaquarium.org/lc/kids_place/kidseq_equarium.asp>**. 3) They have programs for teachers and schools, too. 4) There's a trail along the coast directly in front of the aquarium that takes you past Pacific Grove to Asilomar State Beach. Lovers' Point Park and the adjacent beach are located in Pacific Grove, just a short drive away. If you have more time, consider renting bikes or just strolling down the trail. Adventures by the Sea rents bikes (831) 372-1807. You can access the trail just outside of the aquarium at the intersection of Wave Street and David Avenue. At that intersection, Wave becomes Ocean View Blvd. This is a very scenic coastal drive. In fact, we always leave the aquarium by this route and take Route 68 back to meet up with Hwy 1. Sometimes we catch the sunset along the way. The Tinnery Restaurant, located at Lovers' Point Park, has wonderful views overlooking the ocean and Lovers' Point Park. It's a great place for lunch and dinner, and family friendly.

Directions: *Getting There:* Get maps and directions from the aquarium's own Web site. *Come back the scenic way via coastal drive along Ocean View Blvd. to Pacific Grove:* If you parked at the Cannery Row Parking Garage on Wave Street, between Hoffman and Prescott Avenue, then as you exit the parking structure at Hoffman, turn left onto Hoffman. Make an immediate left onto Wave Street. Wave Street becomes Ocean View Blvd. Follow Ocean View Blvd along the coast. After Asilomar State Beach, Ocean View Blvd. becomes Sunset Drive/Route 68. Follow signs for Route 68. Turn Right onto Forest Ave/Route 68 to meet Hwy 1. Take Hwy 1 North to come back to the Bay Area.

Seymour Marine Discovery Center (Ages 2 +)
Long Marine Labs at UC Santa Cruz
(831) 459-3800; 100 Shaffer Road, Santa Cruz, CA 95060
<www2.ucsc.edu/seymourcenter>

Description: This is a small center that's worth visiting if you're in the Santa Cruz area. Hourly site tours are available from 1–3pm daily on a first come first served basis. You need to sign up at the admissions desk. The center also has Mammal Research Tours (75 minutes), which provide insight on Long Marine Lab scientists' research on dolphins, sea lions, seals, and blue whales. Advanced reservations are required, as space is limited to 12 participants. Check the Web site's "Learning Programs: Visitor" page or call 831-459-3799 for the schedule.

Hours: Tues–Sat: 10am–5pm, Sun: noon–5pm, Closed Monday.

Cost: Free admission on the first Tuesday of each month. $5/adult, $3/ student or senior (60+), $3/youth (6–16), free/child (5 and under).

Bathroom: Yes.

Facilities: Stroller friendly.

Food: No.

What to Bring: Picnic lunch, sunglasses, and jacket.

Follow-Up Activities: 1) There's an annual Father's Day guided tide pooling trip that requires advanced booking. Call Terri, the office manager, at (408) 459-3800 for information and reservations. 2) In January, there is an annual Whale Watching Trip with a biology professor from UC Santa Cruz in conjunction with Sanctuary Cruises. Call for more information. Refer to the "Whale-watching" section for additional information on Sanctuary Cruises. 3) Ocean Explorers: marine science weekly summer camps for children ages 7–14. Select "Learning Programs" then "Youth Programs" once you've entered the Web site's home page.

Six Flags Marine World (Ages 2 +)
(707) 643-6722; 2001 Marine World Parkway, Vallejo, CA 94589
<www.sfmwonline.com>

Description: This is a combination theme park, animal park, and marine life showcase. See animals in action in their wildlife theater shows and watch them do tricks and stunts. There are sea lion, birds in flight, dolphin, killer whale, tiger, and elephant shows. Hand-feed the giraffe at the giraffe feeding dock. Walk through the Butterfly Habitat with 500 free flying butterflies from all over the world, and learn about the life cycle of the butterfly. Ride an elephant at the Elephant Encounter. Visit hand raised animal babies from tiger cubs to monkeys. The best time to visit these babies is in the morning during the late spring. Don't miss the lorikeets at the Lorikeet Aviary where you can hand-feed these beautiful birds their nectar. The teenagers and older youths will welcome the thrill rides and water rides located throughout the theme park. Little ones will enjoy the Looney Tunes Seaport area with carousel, interactive water play, miniature train, and other rides designed for those 54" and under, accompanied by an adult.

Hours: Closed November through February. *March:* Weekends: 10am–8pm. *April:* Fri–Sun: 10am–8pm. *April 14-27:* Mon–Sun: 10am–8pm. *May:* Fri–Sun: 10am–9pm. *June–August:* Open daily. *September–October:* Open weekends only. Hours may vary. Check the Web site or call to verify times.

Cost: $10/parking. $43.99/general admission, $26.99/child 48" & under, free/child 2 & under. $53.99/2-day general admission, $36.99/2-day child admission, $42.99/2-day senior or disabled admission. *Season Passes:* $59.99/individual or $54.99/pass when purchasing 4 or more passes. $10 extra per person for a "fast pass," which can come in handy on crowded summer weekends with long lines for the thrill rides. These fast passes allow you to bypass the long lines, with a total limit of 5 rides for each pass. Sometimes there are 50% discount promotions on the Web site as well as buy-one get-one general admission free coupons from local grocery stores. Special programs such as the Sea Lion Training Session, Dolphin Discovery (for ages 9+), Sunset Safari cost extra and require advanced reservations. Many of the pony rides, elephant rides, etc. also cost a bit extra. Plan on spending extra for these events.

Bathrooms: Yes.

Facilities: Lockers, stroller & wheelchair rental. Stroller friendly, but strollers are not allowed inside shows, rides, and exhibits, so plan accordingly. Many rides require a minimum of 42 inches in height.

Food: Yes. Outside food is not allowed, except for baby food.

What to Bring: Swimsuit/change of clothes if you're planning to go on a water ride or have the kids play in the water works area. Don't forget your sunscreen, sunglasses, hat, and lots of extra cash for parking, food, and animal rides.

Follow-Up Activities: Week-long Summer Seafari Camp for kids 4-12.

Steinhart Aquarium (All Ages)
California Academy of Sciences, Golden Gate Park
(415) 750-7145; 55 Concourse Drive, San Francisco, CA 94118 (Reopens 2008)

Temporary Location: 875 Howard Street, San Francisco, CA 94103
<www.calacademy.org/aquarium>

Description: The Steinhart Aquarium includes exhibits on a living coral reef, tropical sharks, seahorses, a touch pool, a fish roundabout, reptiles and amphibians, and a penguin colony. See full entry in Chapter 4: Science Museums.

Tide Pools

Tide pooling is best done in the spring and summer, when there's a longer period of time to view the tide pools when tides are at their lowest. This is a wonderful and fun outing, but must be done with care. Please keep in mind that you will be walking over slippery rocks and doing some rock climbing to view these tide pools. The terrain can be very slippery. Babies in backpacks are not advised because you can really hurt yourself or the baby should you slip and fall. I would definitely recommend visiting with 2 adults if you have a little one less than 5 years old. It's helpful to have an extra pair of hands to help the little one navigate the rocks.

You can learn how to read the tide charts from Coyote Pointe Museum's Web site on tide pools: <www.coyoteptmuseum.org/education/tide_info.htm>. For more specific geographic tide information, go to <http://ceres.ca.gov/ocean/index.html>. In the "Information Indexes" box, click on the "Coastal Counties" under the "By Geographic Area" section, find your county, and click on the "Tides and Ocean Currents" link in the "Coastal Conditions" box. Tide tables can also be purchased from the Crab Cove Visitor Center for 35 cents.

Asilomar State Beach (Ages 3+)

(831) 372-4076; 800 Asilomar Boulevard, Pacific Grove, CA 93950
<www.parks.ca.gov/default.asp?page_id=566>

Description: This beautiful, scenic beach is right off Ocean Blvd in Pacific Grove. During low tide you can do tide pooling here. The Asilomar Conference grounds (831-372-8016) are located just across Ocean Boulevard, within a short walk of the beach. There's a gift shop and restaurant.
Hours: 8am–5pm.
Cost: Free.
Bathrooms: Yes, at the conference center, a bit of a walk from the beach.
Facilities: Not stroller friendly on the beach.
Food: Not on the beach. Conference center has a restaurant.
What to Bring: Sunscreen, sunglasses, jacket, and shoes with good traction.
Directions: For map and directions to the beach:
<www.asilomarcenter.com/planyourvisit/directions.html>.

Agate Beach County Park (Ages 3+)

(415) 499-6387; (415) 507-2818
End of Elm Road at Ocean Parkway, Bolinas, CA
<www.co.marin.ca.us/depts/pk/main/pos/pdagatebch.cfm>

Description: Located within the Duxbury Reef State Marine Sanctuary, Agate Beach provides almost 2 miles of shoreline for tide pooling during low tide. No collecting allowed.
Hours: Dawn to dusk.
Cost: Free. No parking fee.
Bathrooms: Portables only.
Facilities: Not stroller friendly.
Food: No. Bolinas or Pointe Reyes Station is the closest for food.
What to Bring: Picnic lunch, sunscreen, sunglasses, hats, and jacket. Don't forget to wear shoes with good traction. Rocky shore can be very slippery!
Follow-Up Activities: For naturalist programs information for Marin, call (415) 499-3647.

Fitzgerald Marine Reserve (Ages 3+)

(650) 728-3584; California & North Lake Streets, Moss Beach, CA 94038
<www.eparks.net/Parks/Fitzgerald/index.htm>

Description: This reserve is rich in marine life diversity along the rocky reef habitat. During low tides, you can see marine life in the ten habitats found along the 3 miles of the Reserve's coastline.

Hours: Daily, including holidays: 8am–5pm. Open later, depending on season. For groups of 20+, reservations are required with Coyote Point Museum: (650) 340-7598.

Cost: Free.

Bathrooms: Yes.

Facilities: Not stroller friendly.

Food: No. Picnic tables by the entrance.

What to Bring: Wear walking shoes with good traction (rocky shore is very slippery), sunscreen, sunglasses, extra change of shoes/clothes, beach gear, and sand toys.

Follow-Up Activities: 1) On weekends, during low tide, a roving naturalist will provide information about the marine life found here. Call ahead of time to see when these programs are scheduled. 2) "Jr. Ranger" program for children 9–12 years old during the summer time. 3) Nighttime tide-pooling event in December/January. Call for specific details.

Natural Bridges State Beach (Ages 3+)

(831) 423-4609; 2531 West Cliff Drive, Santa Cruz, CA
<www.santacruzstateparks.org>
<www.parks.ca.gov/default.asp?page_id=541>
For tide information at Natural Bridges, visit <www.santacruzwharf.com> and click on the "Tides" icon.

Description: During low tide, the tide pools at the northern end of the beach are wonderful to view. There are sea anemones, mussels, sea snails, starfish, and a few hermit crabs. It does require some rock climbing. We went with our one-year-old in a baby backpack carrier. While doable, it's not recommended for your safety because of the slippery rocks.

Hours: 8am–sunset.

Cost: $5 parking.

Bathrooms: At the beach and at the Visitor Center. There are also changing rooms and outdoor showers to wash off the sand.

Facilities: Not stroller friendly at the beach.

Food: No. Picnic tables.

What to Bring: Sunscreen, sunglasses, extra change of clothes and shoes, beach gear, and sand toys. Wear comfortable shoes that provide good traction. Climbing the rocks can be very slippery.

Follow-Up Activities: 1) Monarch butterflies are in residence in the winter. See Chapter 3: Bees, Butterflies, and Bugs for more details. 2) Close to the UCSC Seymour Marine Labs. 3) Close to Wilder Ranch State Park, an historic dairy ranch of the 1900s.

Whale-Watching Cruises

California's coastline is on the migratory path of many species of whales. Whale-watching can be done year round: from December to April, California gray whales are in our waters; from May to October, humpbacks, orcas (killer whales), minkes, and blue whales are passing through. Dolphins, otters, seals, and other marine life can be seen as well during a cruise.

Whale-watching cruises depart from San Francisco, Half Moon Bay, Santa Cruz, and Monterey. They vary in price and length of the trip. Some operate year-round, while others only operate in the winter. Some have food onboard, while others provide no food at all. Some have the facilities to accommodate all ages, while other companies have minimum age requirements, or at least age recommendations. If you have any doubts about bringing a little one on a cruise, call the companies and speak with them directly, to make sure all your concerns are addressed before you make reservations and commit to a cruise.

Dress warmly and in layers, regardless of the season. Consider bringing warm gloves and a scarf. Wear flat shoes with good traction. Don't forget your sunglasses, sunscreen, hat, camera with film, video camera and battery backups, and binoculars. If you get seasick, consider purchasing non-drowsy over-the-counter medication, and check with your doctor.

Chardonnay Sailing Charters
(Facility recommends 8+)
(831) 423-1213; 790 Mariner Park Way, Dock FF, Santa Cruz, CA 95062
<www.chardonnay.com>

Description: This company provides many cruises on Monterey Bay, departing from Santa Cruz. These cruises include whale-watching, fireworks on July 4th, and others. Naturalist onboard provides narration and answers questions on whale-watching cruises.
Schedule: January–March, tours to see California gray whales. The whale-watching cruises are three hours in length and depart on Saturday and some Sunday mornings.
Cost: $39.50/adult, $29.50/child under 12, includes continental breakfast and champagne.
Bathrooms: Yes.
Facilities: Not stroller friendly.
Food: Yes.

Chris' Whale Watching Trips (Ages 8+)
(831) 375-5951; 48 Fisherman's Wharf, Monterey, CA 93940
<www.chrisswhalewatching.com>

Description: The primary focus is on fishing trips, but also offer whale-watching trips. In the past this company offered whale-watching trips from December to April; now they are offered year-round. Look at the Web site for pictures of the small boats.
Schedule: Daily trips with 2-hour narrated tours December–April. May–November trips last 3 to 3 ½ hours and cost a bit more.
Cost: $18/adult, $12/child. May–November: $25/adult, $15/child
Bathrooms: No.
Facilities: Not stroller friendly.
Food: No.

Monterey Bay Whale Watch (All Ages)
Departs from Sam's Fishing Fleet
(831) 375-4658; 84 Fisherman's Wharf #1, Monterey, CA 93940
<www.montereybaywhalecruise.com>

Description: Marine biologist accompanies each trip. *Winter & Spring*

Trips: gray whales, dolphins, and killer whales. *Summer & Fall Trips*: humpback whales, blue whales, dolphins, and killer whales.

Schedule: *Winter & Spring Trips:* Mon–Thur: 10am, Fri–Sun: 10am & 1:30 pm, 3 hours long trips. *Summer & Fall Trips:* Daily trips depart at 9am and return between 1 and 3pm, 4- to 6-hour trips.

Cost: *Winter & Spring Trips* (December 14–April 30): $27/adult, $18/child 12 and under, free/child up to 3 years old. *Summer & Fall Trips* (May 1–December 1): $42/adult, $35/child 12 and under, free/child up to 3 years old.

Bathrooms: Yes.

Facilities: Stroller friendly, but too crowded to allow on weekends. Baby carriers recommended.

Food: Yes, but you can still bring your own food and drinks.

Monterey Sport Fishing & Whale Watching Cruises (Min. Age: 3+)

(831) 372-2203; 96 Fisherman's Wharf #1, Monterey, CA 93940
<www.montereywhalewatching.com/frameset.html >

Description: *__Expectant moms and infants are not allowed on the whale-watching trips.__* Nature or Sunset Cruise recommended for kids younger than three years old, because the cruise stays within Monterey Bay where the waves are calm.

Schedule: *December–April*: California gray whales. Departs every hour 9am–3pm, on the hour. Trip lasts 1½–2 hours. *May–October*: Daily departures at 10am, 11am, 1pm, and 2pm. Each trip lasts 3 hours.
Mid-April–October: 45-min. Coastal Nature Tour or Sunset Cruise. Call for times and reservations.

Cost: *December–April*: $18/adult, $12/child under 12. *May–October*: $25/adult, $20/child under 12. Sunset Cruises also offered during this time. *Mid-April–October:* Coastal Nature Tour or Sunset Cruise: $9.95/adult, $7.95/child under 12.

Bathrooms: Yes.

Facilities: Stroller friendly.

Food: Snacks and drinks. You're welcome to bring your own picnic lunch.

Oceanic Society (Min. Age: 10+)

Adults must accompany those 15 and under.
(800) 326-7491; (415) 474-3385 for reservations and further details.
Fort Mason, San Francisco, CA 94123
<www.oceanic-society.org/pages/wwa.html>

Schedule: Whale cruises with expert naturalists departing from San Francisco (6½ hours), Half Moon Bay (3 hours), and Bodega Bay (3 hours) every Sat & Sun from December to mid-May. Bring your own food and drinks. Tours go rain or shine!
Cost: For San Francisco: $52/adult, $50/youth (7–15) & senior 60+. For Half Moon Bay or Bodega Bay: $34/adult, $32/youth (7–15) & senior (60+). For trips to Farallon Islands (8 hours): $69/person. Trips depart at 8:30am on Sat & Sun June—November. Some Friday and Monday departures at slightly lower cost. Visit the Web site for departure dates and cost information.

Sanctuary Cruises (All Ages)

(831) 643-0128; (831) 917-1042;
Moss Landing Harbor, "A" Dock, Moss Landing Road, Moss Landing, CA
<www.sanctuarycruises.com>

Description: Gray whales are migrating in the winter. Cruise representative said that the best time to whale watch is in March/April, when the humpback whales are migrating, because these whales put on a good show. This company provides whale-watching cruises for Seymour Marine Labs and the Monterey Bay Aquarium.
Schedule: Wed–Sun departing at 9:30am and returning in 3 to 5 hours. Reservations required.
Cost: 3- to 5-hour whale-watching trips are $37.50/adult, $27.50/child 12 and under, free/child under 2. Check the Web site for discounts.
Bathrooms: Yes.
Facilities: Stroller friendly.
Food: Food available onboard. You may what to bring your own lunch or crackers to help counteract seasickness. You can also purchase onetime use cameras and rent a band to counteract seasickness.
What to Bring: Dress in layers and bring a warm jacket. Cash for food. Picnic lunch is OK.

Chapter 2
Plant Kingdom

In this age of technology, children often get shortchanged in their under-standing of biology. Apples and carrots come out of a bag that Mommy brought home from the grocery store. The plants that produce them have become completely detached. Even as an adult, I had never seen a pine-apple plant until I went to Hawaii. I had always imagined that pineapples came from something like a palm tree. Farms, orchards, gardens, and ar-boretums help us make the connection between the product and the producer. Where do apples come from? Is it from a plant, a shrub, or a tree? Do carrots grow on trees, too? This section provides information on organic gardens, flower gardens, botanical gardens, arboretums, farms, and orchards.

Here are some gardens to put the apples back on the apple tree, the grapes on the vine, and the artichokes on the plant.

Organic Gardens

Ardenwood Farm (All Ages)
(510) 796-0663; 34600 Ardenwood Boulevard, Fremont, CA 94555
<www.ebparks.org/parks/arden.htm>
<www.fremont.gov/recreation/ardenwoodpark>

See full entry in Chapter 1: Animal Kingdom—Farms section.

Children's Discovery Museum (All Ages)
(408) 298-5437; 180 Woz Way, San Jose, CA 95110
<www.cdm.org>

See full entry in Chapter 4: Science Museums.

Cupertino Community Gardens (All Ages)
(408) 777-3149; 22221 McClellan Road, Cupertino, CA 95014

See the McClellan Ranch Park entry in Chapter 1: Animal Kingdom—Farms section.

Emma Prusch Farms (All Ages)
Community Gardens: Cornucopia & El Jardin.
<www.sjcommunitygardens.org>

For full entry, see Emma Prusch Farm in Chapter 1: Animal Kingdom – Farms section. See the list of community gardens in the San Jose Community Gardens.
Bathrooms: Portables in the field.

Hidden Villa (All Ages)
(650) 949-8644; 26870 Moody Road, Los Altos Hills, CA 94022
<www.hiddenvilla.org>

See full entry in Chapter 1: Animal Kingdom – Farms section.

San Jose Community Gardens (All Ages)
<www.sjcommunitygardens.org>

These gardens are assigned to San Jose residents on a first come first served basis, allowing residents to grow a wide range of plants from vegetables, flowers, herbs, and fruits organically. The plots range from 10' x 10' to 20' x 30.' Call (408) 277-2575 for additional information if you'd like to start your own plot.
- Alviso (N. 1st & Tony P. Santos)
- Berryessa (Flickinger & Doxey)
- Calabazas (Blaney & Danridge)
- Cornucopia (S. King & Story) (at the Emma Prusch Farm park)
- Coyote (Tully at Galveston)
- El Jardin (S. King & Story) (at the Emma Prusch Farm park)
- Green Thumb (Rhoda & Roewill)
- Hamline (Hamline & Sherwood)
- Jesse Frey (Alma & Belmont)

- La Colina (Allegan Circle)
- Laguna Seca (Manresa & Bayliss)
- Las Milpas (E. Jackson & 22nd)
- Mayfair (Kammerer and Sunset)
- Nuestra Tierra (Tully & La Ragione)
- Wallenberg (Curtner & Cottle)
- Watson (E. Jackson & 22nd)

U.C. Santa Cruz Farm & Garden (All Ages)
CASFS, UC Santa Cruz
(831) 459-4140; (831) 459-3240; 1156 High Street, Santa Cruz, CA 95064
<http://zzyx.ucsc.edu/casfs/community/tours.html>

Description: This organic garden and farm is open year-round. There are Kids Tours with hands-on activities in the new Garden Classroom from April–June. In the fall, there's a Life Lab Science Program.
Hours: Daily: 8am–6pm. *Kids' Tours* for school groups: Tues, Thur, & Fri April–early June. Call (831) 459-2001 to schedule a tour.
Cost: Free.
Bathrooms: Yes.
Facilities: Stroller friendly.
Food: No.
Follow-Up Activities: 1) Harvest Festival at the Farm: an annual celebration at the farm with hayrides, food, music, tours, and kids' events. Held usually on Saturday in mid-October 11am–4pm. Free for members and kids 12 and under, $5 for non-members. 2) Check calendar of events for current info: <http://zzyx.ucsc.edu/casfs/community/calendar.html>.

Gardens & Arboretums

Bonfante Gardens Family Theme Park (All Ages)
(408) 840-7100; 3050 Hecker Pass Highway, Gilroy, CA 95020
<www.bonfantegardens.com >

Description: The theme park was built specifically to showcase the circus trees with their intricate trunk designs that were created by using grafting techniques. Unfortunately, the closely guarded technique has been lost, so these trees are unique. This park is beautifully landscaped with gardens intermingling with the rides. There are waterfalls and gardens of orchids and camellias. The theme park provides the best combination of transportation examples. It has paddle boat and other boat rides, replica antique cars of the 1920s and 1950s, a mini-train that goes around the perimeter of the park, a monorail through the orchid garden, a restored antique 1920s carousel, and a mini-air balloon ride.

Hours: Closed in the winter. Opening in April: 10am–5pm. Hours vary based on the season. Visit the Web site or call for current information.

Cost: $7/parking fee. Admission: $21.95/child 3+ or senior 65+, $29.95/adult. Season passes: $49/person. Look for discount coupons from Nob Hill and AAA (Automobile Association of California). In 2003, Paramount's Great America sold a VIP Pass that included free admission to Bonfante Gardens.

Bathrooms: Yes, but baby changing stations are outside the bathrooms.

Facilities: Day use lockers available. Stroller friendly.

Food: Many cafés to choose from (from burgers and hot dogs to Mexican food).

What to Bring: Sunscreen, sunglasses, hat, cash for food and drinks, quarters for locker use, extra change of clothes for water play and perhaps swimsuits for the little ones (water play fountain area), extra pair of shoes or water shoes for getting wet.

Follow-Up Activities: Educational programs for groups and school field trips relate to trees, water management, the life cycle, agriculture, and nature.

Conservatory of Flowers (All Ages)

Golden Gate Park

(415) 666-7001; Physical location:JFK Drive, San Francisco
Admin: 501 Stanyan Street, San Francisco, CA 94117
<www.conservatoryofflowers.org>

Description: This well-known landmark of San Francisco Golden Gate Park has been undergoing major restoration. It reopened in late September 2003. The plant collection includes the native plants of Africa, Australia and the Pacific, Asia, and Central and South America. There are educational programs geared for school groups and future plans for family programs also. Call for details or check the Web site.

Hours: Tues–Sun: 9am–5pm, last entry is at 4:30pm.

Cost: $5/adult; $3/youth 12-17, seniors 65 & over, and students with ID; $1.50/child 5–11; free/child 4 and under.

Bathrooms: Located in a brand new facility next door.

Facilities: Stroller friendly.

Food: No. Picnic on the lawns outside. No food allowed in the Conservatory.

What to Bring: Picnic lunch, blanket to sit on, and sweater in case of cool weather.

Follow-Up Activities: Stowe Lake, California Academy of Sciences, and Strybing Arboretum are all located within Golden Gate Park.

Filoli Gardens (Ages 5+)
(650) 364-8300 x507; 86 Cañada Road, Woodside, CA 94062
<www.filoli.org>

Description: This is a gorgeous formal garden and mansion. The best time of year to visit is in April when almost everything (tulips, camellias, dogwoods, rhododendrons, and too many others to list) in the gardens is in bloom, except the roses.

Hours: Closed November–January. Open February–October. Tues–Sat: 10am–3pm, last admission at 2pm.

Cost: $10/adult, $5/student w/ ID, $1/youth 7–12, free/child under 7.

Bathrooms: Yes.

Facilities: Stroller friendly.

Food: Small café at main entry building. Picnics not allowed at Filoli. Edgewood Park or Pulgas Water Temple is ¼ mile north on Cañada Rd.

What to Bring: Sunscreen, sunglasses, camera, and picnic lunch.

Follow-Up Activities: 1) Bring a picnic and lunch at Pulgas Water Temple to let the kids run and get out their energy. 2) In March/April there is an annual East Egg Hunt event. 3) In early December, there are Parent and Child Luncheon Parties ($30 per person). These feature a magician, a ventriloquist, dancers, and visits with Santa and Mrs. Claus. 4) *David C. Daniels Nature Center* is close by at Alpine Road, Woodside, CA. (650) 691-1200. Its Web site is **<www.openspace.org/preserves/preserve_ hightlights.html>**. The Nature Center is open mid-March–November: Sat & Sun noon–5pm. There's a hands-on lab with microscopes to view microscopic life, wildlife skulls, and animal pelts that children can touch.

Gamble Garden (All Ages)

(650) 329-1356; 1431 Waverley Street, Palo Alto, CA 94301
<www.gamblegarden.org>

Description: Beautiful, serene garden to stroll through. There are flowering annuals, perennials, herbs, and vegetable beds, too. *Teas:* Teas include savories, sweets, and tea.

Hours: *Office & House:* Mon–Fri: 9am–noon. *Gardens* open daily during daylight hours. *Teas* are held every third Wednesday of the month 2–4pm at the Main House. *Optional guided tour:* Also on the third Wednesday of the month, starts at 3:15pm. Reservations made for groups of 2–10, with paid reservation. Reserve early to avoid disappointment.

Cost: Free. $3 for docent-led tours. Teas cost $15/person. The Children's Puppet Shows in December cost extra.

Bathrooms: Yes.

Facilities: Stroller friendly.

Food: No.

Follow-Up Activities: 1) "Roots and Shoots program" teams up senior volunteers with third-grade students. These teams work together by weeding, watering, and learning about seed and plant propagation, transplanting, composting, mulching, pest control, etc. 2) Children's Puppet Shows designed for children ages 3–6, are in early December. There are only three performances. Light refreshments are served. 3) Holiday tea parties in December. Reserve early to avoid disappointment.

Gardens at Heather Farms (All Ages)

(925) 947-6712; 1540 Marchbanks Road, Walnut Creek, CA 94598
<www.gardenshf.org>

Description: These beautiful gardens include a children's garden, a sensory garden with 75 fragrant herbs, a butterfly garden with milkweed plants for monarch butterflies, a rose garden, a composting demonstration area, a water conservation garden, and much more. For a virtual tour, visit the Web site: <www.gardenshf.org/GardenStroll.html>.

Hours: Daily sunrise–sunset.

Cost: Free.

Bathrooms: Yes.

Facilities: Stroller friendly.

Food: No. Snack bar is located at the Clarke Memorial Swim Center.

What to Bring: Sunscreen, sunglasses, picnic lunch, and swimming gear if you plan on swimming at the pool.

Follow-Up Activities: 1) Docent-led tours available to groups. Tours cost $4/person with a minimum of $30/group. 2) School programs for preschool through 5th grades. Call (925) 947-6712 from Mon–Thur for additional information and reservations. 3) Located in the same park, the Clarke Memorial Swim Center has an Olympic sized pool, a diving pool, and a shallow wading pool. It is located at 1750 Heather Drive, Heather Farm Park, Walnut Creek. Open Mon–Fri: 5:30am–5pm & 7pm–9pm, Sat & Sun: 10am–5pm. *Recreational swimming:* daily 1–4:45pm. *Cost:* $3/adult, $2.50/child 7–15, $1.75/child 6 & under. Phone: (925) 943-5856.

Hakone Gardens (Ages 3+)

(408) 741-4994; 21000 Big Basin Way, Saratoga, CA 95070
<www.hakone.com>

Description: Nestled in the Saratoga foothills, these serene gardens include hiking trails and gardens with a koi pond. Unfortunately, feeding the koi is not encouraged here.

Hours: Mon–Fri: 10am–5pm, weekends: 11am–5pm. *Docent Tours:* April–September: 1–4pm.

Cost: Free admission. $5 parking fee.

Bathrooms: Yes.

Facilities: Not stroller friendly. Bring baby in baby carrier.

Food: No. Picnic tables available.

What to Bring: Picnic lunch, camera, and cash for parking.

Follow-Up Activities: 1) Classes available through the Saratoga Recreation Department <www.saratoga.ca.us/recreation>. 2) Close to Sanborn Park, where the Youth and Science Institute is located and has a Visitor Center.

Japanese Friendship Garden, Kelly Park (All Ages)

(408) 277-5254; 1300 Senter Road, San Jose, CA 95112
<www.ci.san-jose.ca.us/cae/parks/kp/jfg.html>

Description: This beautiful garden is located within walking distance of Happy Hollow Zoo and Park and the History Park, San Jose at Kelly Park. There are two gardens, an upper garden and a lower garden. Each garden has its own koi pond. Meandering paths and curved bridges provide a nice respite from the crowds and noise of Happy Hollow.

Hours: Daily 10am–sunset.

Cost: Free entrance to the garden. Parking fee: $5 on weekends and daily from Memorial Day to Labor Day.

Bathrooms: Portable just outside the front gate of the garden.

Facilities: Stroller friendly, except in a couple of steep sections.

Food: No. Picnic tables.

What to Bring: Picnic lunch and drinks. Quarters to buy food to feed the koi. Cash for parking. Don't forget the sunscreen, sunglasses, and hat.

Follow-Up Activities: Happy Hollow Park and Zoo and the History Park, San Jose are also within Kelly Park.

Japanese Tea Garden (All Ages)
Central Park, San Mateo
(650) 522-7409; (650) 522-7400; 50 East 5th Avenue, San Mateo 94403
<www.cityofsanmateo.org/dept/parks/locations/teagarden.html>

Description: This Japanese Tea Garden was designed by the landscape architect of the Imperial Palace of Tokyo. It is located within San Mateo's Central Park. Central Park is also home to a mini-train, Bianchi Railway, and a children's playground.

Hours: Weekdays: 10am–4pm, weekends: 11am–4pm.

Cost: Free.

Bathrooms: Yes.

Facilities: Stroller friendly.

Food: No. Picnic tables and nearby restaurants.

What to Bring: Picnic lunch, sunscreen, sunglasses, and plenty to drink.

Follow-Up Activities: See Chapter 6:Transportation Favorites—Mini-Trains section for information on Bianchi Railway.

Japanese Tea Garden (Ages 3+)
Golden Gate Park
(415) 752-4227; (415) 752-1171 Teahouse; Between John F. Kennedy Dr. & Martin Luther King Jr. Drive, San Francisco, CA 94122

Description: One of the most beautiful Japanese Tea Gardens in the Bay Area. This is a large garden with a waterfall and koi pond. There's also a teahouse for snacks and tea, of course.

Hours: 8:30am–5pm.
Cost: $3.50/adult, $1.25/senior 65+ or child 6–12, free/child under 6.
Bathrooms: Yes.
Facilities: Stroller friendly.
Food: Teahouse has a few Japanese snack items and tea.
What to Bring: Jacket, cash for entry and teahouse, and quarters for metered parking and to purchase food for the fish.
Follow-Up Activities: The California Academy of Sciences is located just across the plaza and the Strybing Arboretum is across the street.

Quarryhill Botanical Garden (Ages 5+)
(707) 996-3802; PO Box 232, Glen Ellen, CA 95442
<www.quarryhillbg.org>

Description: This botanical garden is dedicated to the conservation and preservation of Asian plants and flowers.
Hours: Docent-led tours available on the 3rd Saturday of the month from March to October, by appointment only. Tours start at 10am and last 1½ hours. Groups of less than 25 can make reservations with 2 weeks notice. Groups of over 25 require 1 month advanced reservation.

The Ruth Bancroft Garden (All Ages)
(925) 944-9352; (925) 210-9663;
1500 Bancroft Road, Walnut Creek, CA 94598
<www.ruthbancroftgarden.org>

Description: This garden has a great collection of succulents, cacti, yucca, and low water consumption plants. It is recognized as a premier private garden that showcases the design possibilities of a water wise garden.
Hours: Closed in the winter. The garden is open only during scheduled tour times. *Docent-led tours:* mid-April to mid-July, tours on Fri & Sat at 9:30am & 1pm. Mid-July—mid-October, tours on Fri & Sat at 9:30am and on Sat at 6pm. September–October: at 9:30am and on Sat at 5pm. From November–March, 2004, tours only on 1st and 3rd Sat. at 10am. Call to make reservations. *Self-guided tours:* Mid-April–July: tours on Fri & Sun 5–7pm only; July–August: tours on Fri & Sun 6–8pm only, September–October: tours on Fri & Sun 5–7pm only. Hours may change. Please check the Web site or call prior to your visit. Reservations required for all tours and most events.

Cost: $5/person, free for children.
Bathrooms: Portables only.
Facilities: Stroller friendly.
Food: No. Picnicking not allowed.
What to Bring: Sunscreen, sunglasses, hat, and cash for entry. Bring picnic lunch and picnic at Heather Farms. See Heather Farms entry in Chapter 2: Plant Kingdom—Gardens & Arboretums section.
Follow-Up Activities: Part of the Annual Garden Tour in early May. The annual tour includes 8 area gardens and costs $30/person in advance and $35 at the door. For tickets, call (800) 594-TIXX.

Strybing Arboretum & Botanical Gardens (All Ages)
Golden Gate Park
(415) 661-1316; 9th Avenue, San Francisco, CA 94122
<www.strybing.org>

Description: This is one of the more extensive gardens and arboretums, with plants from Chile, New Zealand, Australia, Asia, and South Africa's Cape Province. It also includes California native plants and a fragrance garden.
Hours: Open daily. *Weekdays:* 8am–4:30pm. *Weekends and holidays:* 10am–5pm. Free guided walks daily at 1:30pm.
Cost: Free.
Bathrooms: Yes.
Facilities: Stroller friendly.
Food: No.
What to Bring: Jacket, quarters for metered street parking, sunscreen, sunglasses, and picnic lunch.
Follow-Up Activities: 1) Japanese Tea Garden and the California Academy of Sciences are located within walking distance. 2) For events schedule, select the "Events" icon on the home page. 3) There is a "Summer Family Days" program for children from 5 to 10 years old, and another program for preschoolers. Select the "Youth Education" button on the Web site's home page for information on classes and programs for kids. For dates and registration information, call (415) 661-1316, ext. 307.

Sunset Magazine's Demonstration Gardens (All Ages)

(650) 321-3600; 80 Willow Road, Menlo Park, CA 94025

<www.sunset.com/sunset/AboutSunset/FAQs/FAQs.html#TouringSunsetAnchor>

Description: The best time to visit this garden is in the spring. Since the gardens are replanted 3 times a year, it is a nice year-round garden to visit.

Hours: Mon–Fri: 9am–4:30pm. Closed on holidays.

Cost: Free.

Bathrooms: Yes.

Facilities: Stroller friendly.

Food: No, but you can picnic here.

What to Bring: Picnic lunch, sunscreen, sunglasses, and hat.

Follow-Up Activities: Tours are available for schools, grades 2–5, by reservations only. Call (650) 324-5400 for reservations.

Botanic Garden, Tilden (All Ages)

Tilden Nature Preserve Regional Parks

(510) 841-8732; Wildcat Canyon Road at Shasta Road, Berkeley, CA 94701

<www.nativeplants.org>; <www.nativeplants.org/about.html> for the map

Description: This botanical garden features native California plants, with 10 different sections to display the diversity of the California climate and environment. See full entry under Tilden Park in Chapter 1: Animal Kingdom—Farms section.

Hours: 8:30am–5pm. Garden tours begin at 2pm on Saturday and Sunday. Closed New Year's Day, Thanksgiving, and Christmas. Visitor Center lectures and slide shows scheduled on Saturdays 10:30am–noon, usually from November through February, as part of the Wayne Roderick Lecture Series. For a schedule of topics: <**www.nativeplants.org/wayne.html**>.

Cost: Free.

Bathrooms: Yes.

Facilities: Stroller friendly.

Food: No.

What to Bring: Picnic lunch, sunscreen, sunglasses, and hat.

U.C. Berkeley Botanical Garden (All Ages)

(510) 643-2755; 200 Centennial Drive, Berkeley, CA 94720
<http://shanana.berkeley.edu/garden>

Description: Set in the Berkeley hills, this huge botanical garden has an extensive collection of plants from various habitats all over the world and from fern grottos to deserts.

Hours: Daily 9am–5pm. Closed 1st Tuesday of each month, Thanksgiving, Christmas Eve, Christmas Day, New Year's Eve, New Year's Day, and Martin Luther King Jr. Day. Summer hours (Memorial Day–Labor Day): Wed–Sun: 9am–8pm . Docent-led tours at 1:30pm on Sat & Sun.

Cost: *Thursdays:* Free. All other days: $3/adult, $1/child 3–18, UC students free. Parking 50 cents/hour.

Bathrooms: Yes.

Facilities: Only one trail in the canyon is stroller friendly. Bring baby in baby carrier.

Food: No.

What to Bring: Sunscreen, sunglasses, picnic lunch, and cash for parking.

Follow-Up Activities: 1) Educational tours for class groups. 2) Close to Lawrence Hall of Science. See Chapter 4: Science Museums.

U.C. Santa Cruz Arboretum (All Ages)

(831) 427-2998; 1156 High Street, Santa Cruz, CA 95064
<www2.ucsc.edu/arboretum>

Description: There is a wonderful collection of South African proteas as well as plants from South Africa, Australia, New Zealand, and North America. Also featured are plants native to California and to the nearby islands off the California coast.

Hours: Daily 9am–5pm. *Docent-led Tours*: Thur–Sat from mid-April through May 31, at 10 am. Closed Thanksgiving and Christmas.

Cost: Free.

Bathrooms: Yes.

Facilities: Stroller friendly.

Food: No, but you can picnic here.

What to Bring: Sunglasses, sunscreen, picnic lunch, and camera.

Follow-Up Activities: Santa Cruz Mission, Natural Bridges State Beach, Seymour Marine Labs, and Santa Cruz Beach Boardwalk are all nearby.

Fruit Farms & Orchards

To help prepare little ones, consider reading the picture book, *Little Apple: A Book of Thanks* by Brigitte Weninger and Anne Möller for a wonderful introduction to how apples come from the tree and how the tree comes from the apple seed.

The following berry farms along the coast and the fruit farms in Brentwood allow you to pick your own fruit. Prepicked items are sometimes available for sale. Fruit ripens differently based on the local climate, season, and variety of fruit.

Below is a general guideline on the approximate times for different fruits to ripen. Keep in mind that different varieties of the same fruit ripen at different times. Each variety may last just a few weeks. This table provides a rough timeline to help you with your planning. Call the various farms that you're interested in visiting ahead of time to ensure ripeness and availability.

Month	Fruit
May	Cherries, strawberries (best for preschoolers—no thorns)
June	Nectarines, plums, apricots, boysenberries, olallieberries, strawberries, peaches
July	Nectarines, peaches, plums, apricots, raspberries
August	Asian pears
September	Apples
October	Apples, pumpkins
Nov/Dec	Kiwis

Items to Bring With You

1) Cash to purchase the fruit you pick. 2) Containers to hold your picked fruit. Bigger containers for bigger fruit such as apples and peaches, etc. Sealable plastic containers are good choices for berries. If you're planning to pick blackberries or raspberries, consider bringing something to line your car to prevent staining. 3) Gloves for berry picking, especially for raspberries and blackberries. The vines have thorns. 4) Don't forget your

sunscreen, sunglasses, and hat. 5) Pack lots of drinks for the return trip. Picking berries in the sun makes for thirsty kids. 6) Handy wipes to clean hands off after picking berries. If you're lucky, there will be a place where you can wash your hands, but it's best to be prepared. 7) A light jacket or sweater if the farm is along the coast, since the coast can be overcast or foggy. 8) You might also want to bring an extra change of clothes and shoes for the kids. Being in the fields can get shoes and clothes muddy. 9) Generally speaking, fruit picking is done in the fields. Strollers don't work very well over bumpy, and sometimes muddy, fields. I would recommend putting babies in baby backpacks or baby carriers. 10) Most farms have portable bathrooms in the fields; some have nice, standard bathrooms by the store or picnic area.

Making Jam with Your Harvest

Jam making is relatively easy and definitely worth the trouble. Homemade jams are very flavorful! If you'd like to make jam, plan on purchasing canning jars, *SureJell* fruit pectin ahead of time, and have lots of sugar on hand. Depending on the fruit, you may also need some lemons. When you get home, load up your dishwasher with the canning jars and wash them while you're preparing the fruit and the jam. You need about 5 cups of prepared fruit for a package of *SureJell*. Follow the instructions in the recipe that comes with the *SureJell* packet to make your jam. It's a tasty treat! Plan about 1 to 1½ hours for making jam. This includes preparing your fruit and cooking the jam. This is a great gift idea for Christmas that the kids can give to friends and relatives.

Additional Resources

For a map of the farms in the Santa Clara/Santa Cruz Counties and surrounding area, send a self-addressed stamped envelope to: Country Crossroads, Santa Clara County Farm Bureau, 605 Tennant Avenue, Suite B, Morgan Hill, CA 95037. Alternatively you can send your request to Santa Cruz County Farm Bureau, 141 Monte Vista Avenue, Watsonville, CA 95076. Their phone number is (408) 776-1684.

The Harvest Trails Map to farms in San Mateo County can be obtained by calling (650) 726-4485 or sending a self-addressed stamped envelope to San Mateo County Farm Bureau, Harvest Trails Map, 765 Main Street, Half Moon Bay, CA 94019.

Marin County's Marin Agricultural Land Trust has a Web site, <www.malt.org>, which provides information on organic farming and agriculture. The member farms sponsor hikes and tours throughout the year. These tours include Hog Island Oyster Farm and dairy, ranch, and farm tours. Don't miss these popular programs! Check the "Hikes and Programs" then the "Hikes and Tours" section on the Web site <www.malt.org/hp/hikestours.html> for calendar with dates, times, and places to meet.

For the Sonoma County Farm Trails map, call 1-800-207-9464 or (707)571-8288 or e-mail your request to: farmtrails@farmtrails.org. The Web site is <www.farmtrails.org>. For the Sonoma County harvest calendar: <www.farmtrails.org/html/harvest_calendar.html>.

Farther afield, *Central Valley* farms have the *Harvest Trails* publication that provides information on farms, a harvest calendar, and maps. The Web site is <www.co.stanislaus.ca.us/spendtheday/HarvestTrails.pdf>. Alternatively, visit the home page: <www.spendtheday.org>, then type in "Harvest Trails" in the "Search" box.

Napa, Yolo, and Solano counties will be publishing a Web site and a map and directory to be called *Napa–Yolano Harvest Trails*.

The Small Farm Center at UC Davis has a wonderful database on its-Web site that provides information on California Agri-Tourism farms that are open to the public and those which provide educational experiences. The Web site is <www.calagtour.org>. Here's a direct link to the database: <www.calagtour.org/AgTour.ASP>.

Coastal Berry Picking Farms

I would recommend strawberries for little ones since there are no thorns. Boysenberries or blackberries are fairly easy to pick for little ones, too. Raspberries definitely require gloves and some skill. Part the raspberry plant to look for raspberries in the center of the plant.

CoastWays Ranch (Ages 3+)
(650) 879-0414; 640 Cabrillo Highway, Pescadero, CA 94060
<www.well.com/user/dmsml/coastways>

Description: This ranch has boysenberries, olallieberries, and loganberries. Pumpkin and winter squash season: October. Kiwi fruit season: November–December. Christmas tree season: November–December, starting the day after Thanksgiving.
Schedule: Olallie blackberries season: late May–July 9am–5pm.
Cost: Ranges around $1.37/pound for the berries.
Bathrooms: Portables.
Food: No.

Emile Agaccio Farms (Ages 3+)
(831) 728-2009; 4 Casserly Road, Watsonville, CA 95076

Description: Blackberries and raspberries.
Schedule: Olallieberries season: May–June. Raspberry season: May–July.
Cost: No entrance fee. Olallieberries are around $1.30/lb and the raspberries are around $2/lb, depending on market conditions.
Bathrooms: Portable restrooms in the fields.
Facilities: Not stroller friendly.
Food: No, picnic tables by the fruit stand.

Gizdich Ranch (Ages 3+)
(831) 722-1056; 55 Peckham Road, Watsonville, CA 95076
<www.gizdichranch.com/gizhome2.html>

Description: Gizdich Ranch has a variety of berries for you to pick: strawberries, boysenberries, marionberries, olalliberries, and raspberries. In October, apples are available.
Schedule: Open 9am–5pm (May and August: strawberries; June: boysenberries, marionberries, ollalieberries; July: raspberries; September/October: apples). The Apple Butter Festival in October has apple butter making and canning as well as hayrides and a pumpkin patch.
Cost: Prices for berries are ~ $1.50 per pound. You need cash to purchase the berries you pick and anything else you'd like such as juices, lunch, jams, or pies. Cardboard trays are $1 each.
Bathrooms: Yes. There are portables on the fields and nice bathrooms at

the café and picnic area.

Facilities: Not stroller friendly, bring a baby carrier instead.

Food: Café has sandwiches and box lunches. Picnic area is available if you'd like to bring your own lunch. Homemade pies and fresh-squeezed juice are sold at the café. Fresh pressed apple cider is especially good, but be careful of giving the juice to little ones since it is not pasteurized. You can also purchase freshly picked fruit, homemade jam, and honey at the main store.

Directions: Berry farms are located at the corner of Lakeview and Carlton. Look for signs. Watsonville is 20 min. south of Santa Cruz.

Phipps Ranch (Ages 3+)

(650) 879-0787; 2700 Pescadero Road, Pescadero, CA 94060
<www.phippscountry.com>

Description: In addition to strawberries and blackberries, Phipps Ranch also has a barnyard of animals. These animals include rabbits, goats, geese, chickens, ducks, turkeys, donkeys, pigs, and some exotic birds. Check the Web site before your trip for directions and weather. It is on the coast by Half Moon Bay, and the weather can be foggy and cool.

Schedule: Strawberry season: mid-May–end of September (call to check on season). Olallieberry season: Jun–July (call to check on season).

Cost: The strawberries and olallieberries are $1/lb. However, there is an entrance fee of $1/child 5–9, $2/person ages 10–59, free/child younger than 5 or senior 60+.

Bathrooms: Portables.

Facilities: Strollers OK.

Food: No. Picnic lunch OK.

Brentwood's Fruit Orchards

Many farms have planted lower limbed trees that make picking accessible to all, even a toddler. Ladders are generally not necessary.

The following Web site provides a comprehensive collection of farms in the Brentwood area. The following farms allow you to pick your own fruit or you can purchase from the farms directly: <www.harvest4u.com>.

For the area map of the Brentwood farms: <www.harvest4u.com/images/HT_2002_map.pdf>.

Bacchini's Fruit Tree

(925) 634-3645; 2000 Walnut Boulevard, Brentwood, CA 94513
<www.brentwoodfruit.com>

Description: Apricots (Flavor Giant, Katy, and Patterson), peaches (Arctic Snow), plums, and pluots (cross of plum and apricot) in May and June. Orchard is designed with lower limbed trees so ladders will not usually be needed.
Hours: Daily in season 8am–4pm. Closed in the winter.
Bathrooms: Portables.
Food: No.

Brentwood Garden Ranch

(925) 513-6655; 175 Eureka Avenue, Brentwood, CA 94513 (end of Eureka Avenue off Walnut Blvd)

Description: Cherries: Bing and other varieties available.
Hours: Cherry season starts in late May.
Bathrooms: Portables.
Food: No.

Canciamilla Ranch

(925) 634-5123; 401 Eureka Avenue, Brentwood, CA 94513 (next to Seko Ranch)

Description: Peaches, nectarines, and plums, beginning in late May. Peach varieties available: Spring Gold, Springcrest, and Babcock white peaches. Nectarine varieties available: Juneglo, Fire Bright, Independence, Fantasia, and assorted white nectarines. Plum varieties available: Satsuma and Santa Rosa.
Hours: May–August: Daily 8am–6pm.
Bathrooms: Portables.
Food: Picked fruit, dried fruit, walnuts, flavored honey, drinks, and ice cream are for sale. Picnic area available.

DC's Extraordinary Cherries
(925) 516-4495; Marsh Creek Road, Brentwood, CA 94513
(1 mile west of Walnut Blvd)

Description: Cherry varieties available: Bing, Utah Giant, Sweet Anne, Rainier (white), and Van. Claims to have a unique planting that makes it easy to pick and does not require ladders. Toddlers and handicapped can pick here.
Hours: Around Memorial Day to mid-June, Mon–Fri: 9am–5pm, Sat & Sun: 8am–5pm.
Bathrooms: Portables.
Food: No.

The Farmer's Daughter Produce
(925) 634-4827; Marsh Creek Rd and Walnut Boulevard, Brentwood, CA 94513

Description: Cherries, apricots, freestone and cling peaches, nectarines, plums, white peaches, and white nectarines are available.
Hours: Season is May to September 1. Mon–Fri: 8am–5pm, Sat/Sun: 8am–6pm.
Bathrooms: Portables.
Food: Fruit and produce stand. Cold drinks available.

The Gerry's Fruit Bowl
(925) 634-3155; Marsh Creek Road and Walnut Boulevard, Brentwood; Marsh Creek Road and Orchard Lane, Brentwood 94513

Description: *Apricots:* June–July; *Peaches:* June–August 15 (Red Top, Suncrest, Elegant Lady, O'Henry, Elberta, cling peaches); *Plums:* late June; *Nectarines:* July; *Summer Rose Apples:* mid-July; *Asian pears:* mid-July to mid-August.
Hours: Open first week of June, daily in season: 8am–5pm.
Bathrooms: Portables.
Food: No.

Gursky Ranch Country Store
(925) 634-4913
1921 Apricot Way, Brentwood, CA 94513 (½ mile west of Fairview Ave)
<http://home.pacbell.net/roygur/>

Description: Roy and Lynn Gursky own this "pick your own" walnuts orchard. The season is late fall/early winter. These walnut trees have been specially grown so that someone in a wheelchair can pick them. The store also sells 10 other kinds of nuts (either in-shell or meats), candied fruits and nuts (from plain to gourmet), honey, garlic items, flavored vinegars, olive oil, soup mixes, fruit butters, preserves, etc. You can also purchase dried fruits, gift baskets, and boxed selections of other gourmet nut and fruit items.

Hours: October–December 24th daily: 9am–5pm. After Christmas, open on Saturdays only: 9am–3pm.

Lopez Ranch
(925) 634-4433
Marsh Creek Road, Brentwood, CA 94513; 1 ¼ miles west of Walnut Blvd.

Description: Bing and White Rainier cherries, white peaches, plums, nectarines, and apples including Mutsu, Gala, Granny Smith and Fuji varieties.

Hours: Open daily late May to September: 8am–5pm.

Bathrooms: Portables.

Food: No.

Maggiore Cherry Ranch (Ages 5+)
(925) 634-4176; Fairview and Apricot Way, Brentwood, CA 94513
2nd Site: Walnut Blvd. and Eureka, Brentwood, CA

Description: Bing and Corales cherries: Memorial Day weekend in May to mid-June. Note: Keep in mind that children are not allowed on ladders.

Hours: Daily late May to the end of June: 8am–5pm.

Bathrooms: Portables.

Food: No. Picnicking OK. About 1mile from downtown Brentwood, where there are restaurants.

McKinney Farms (Ages 5+)
(925) 634-7350; 25221 Marsh Creek Road, Brentwood, CA 94513
(¾ mile west of Hwy. 4) or right on Marsh Creek from Vasco Road

Description: White peaches (Freestone and cling peaches), apricots

(Blenheim and Katy), nectarines, white nectarines, and plums. The orchards have been planted for picking and do not require ladders. There are also fresh picked vegetables, fruits, melons, dried fruit, and refreshments.
Hours: Open daily May to end of June: 9am–4pm.
Cost: $1/lb, depending on market conditions.
Bathrooms: Portables.
Food: No. Picnicking OK.

Moffat Ranch (Ages 5+)
(925) 634-3049; 1870 Walnut Boulevard, Brentwood, CA 94513
(just north of Marsh Creek Road)

Description: Peaches (Suncrest, Faye Elberta, Rio Oso, Pink Lady) and nectarines (Fantasia and July Red). Bring containers. Most varieties last approximately two weeks. Ladders provided.
Hours: Open daily during season: 8am–5pm mid-July—August.
Cost: ~$1–$1.50/lb, depending on market conditions.
Bathrooms: Portables.
Food: No. No picnicking allowed. ~2 miles to downtown Brentwood.

Papini Farms
(925) 516-1391
301 Sellers Avenue, Brentwood, CA 94513 (Cross Street: Marsh Creek Rd)

Description: Cherries (Bing and Rainier), early variety Springcrest peaches, apricots (Tilton, Patterson, and Lady Poppies), nectarines (white and yellow), white peaches, and plums (Santa Rosa and Queen Rosa). Buckets provided for picking and boxes for the fruit. Ladders provided, but ladders are only needed for the cherries.
Hours: Daily Memorial Day—mid-July: 8am–4pm.
Cost: ~$1/lb for apricots, peaches, plums, and nectarines, depending on market conditions. ~$1.50 to $2/lb for cherries.
Bathrooms: Portables.
Food: No. No picnicking allowed.

Pease Ranch
(925) 634-4646
Marsh Creek Road, Brentwood, CA 94513
(1 mile west of Hwy 4 or 2 miles east of Vasco Road and Walnut Blvd.)

Description: Cherries (Bing, Rainier, and Jubilee), boysenberries, olallieberries, and tayberries. Tayberries are a cross between boysenberries and raspberries. The best time for the cherries is one week before and one week after Memorial Day. Ladders available, but only for those over 12 years old due to insurance requirements.
Hours: Open daily mid-May–June: 8am–5pm.
Cost: ~ $1.50/lb for cherries and ~$1.75/lb for berries.
Bathrooms: Portables and hand washing area.
Food: No. Picnics OK and plenty of shade. Juice, soda, and mineral water for sale. ~5 miles to downtown Brentwood.

Pomeroy Farms
(925) 634-3080
Marsh Creek Road, Brentwood, CA 94513; west of Walnut Blvd. (Vasco Road)

Description: Cherries, nectarines, and peaches. White Rainier and Brooks cherries are located on Payne Avenue east of Walnut Blvd. Cherry season starts late May to mid-June. In June, nectarines and peaches (Springcrest and Flavorcrest) are available at the Patterson and Westley orchard, at the east end of Eureka Avenue, May 20—June 30. Walnuts and walnut meats available.
Hours: Season starts in late May and lasts through July.
Cost: NA.
Bathrooms: Portables.
Food: No.

Seko Cherry Ranch
(925) 634-3771; Eureka Avenue, Brentwood, CA 94513; off Walnut Blvd.

Description: Bing cherries for you to pick. Pre-picked Burlat and Mono cherries for sale.
Hours: Season is mid-May to mid-June: 8am–5pm.
Cost: ~$2/lb.
Bathrooms: Portables.
Food: No. No picnicking allowed.

Sharp Ranch

(925) 513-1517; 795 Hoffman Lane, Brentwood, CA 94513
(¾ mile South of Marsh Creek Road)

Description: Bing cherries.
Hours: Season starts mid-May. Open during season Fri–Sun: 8am–4pm.
Bathrooms: Portables.
Food: No.

Smith Family Farm

(925) 625-5966 or 625-3544 ; 4430 Sellers Avenue, Brentwood, CA, 94513
<www.smithfamilyfarm.com>

Description: Boysenberries, tomatoes (over 50 varieties), pumpkins, and
Christmas trees that you can pick yourself. It also sells and delivers toma-
toes to restaurants and stores.
Hours: June–October fruit stand open daily: 8am–5pm. On weekends,
U-pick boysenberries. Open in December for Christmas Trees.
Cost: $5.50/person for the farm tours for school groups.
Bathrooms: Portables.
Food: No.
Follow-Up Activities: Fall Pumpkin Harvest is held in October. In the
past, it featured hayrides, a pumpkin patch, live music, farm animals, hay
tunnel, scarecrows, a corn maze, and sunflowers. There's a picnic area and
a replica of a Coast Miwok Village. Farm tours for school groups are avail-
able in April, May, October, and November.

Tidrick Ranch

(925) 634-5115; 1800 Orchard Lane, Brentwood, CA 94513

Description: Bing cherries.
Hours: Memorial Day to mid-June: daily 7am–dusk.
Cost: ~$2/lb.
Bathrooms: Portables.
Food: Hot dogs and snacks only. Picnics OK.

Wolfe Ranch (Ages 5+)
(925) 634-1308; 2111 Concord Avenue, Brentwood, CA 94513;
700 Marsh Creek Road; 164 Payne Avenue
<www.peterwolfe.com>

Description: Cherries (Bing, White Rainier, and Van) from late May to the first part of June, peaches (Springcrest, Red Top, and Suncrest) from late May to late July, and apricots. Black Friar plums are available for picking at Payne Avenue. Prepicked apricots (Blenheim, Tilton, Patterson), loquats, heirloom tomatoes, and homemade honey for sale.

Hours: Memorial Day to mid-June. Open daily: 8:30am–4:30pm.

Bathrooms: Portables.

Food: No.

Chapter 3
Bees, Butterflies, & Bugs

Insects play an important role in the environment. Butterflies and bees are pollinators that help us farm; ants, earthworms, and termites help us decompose dead plant materials; spiders and ladybugs help keep other bugs under control.

Kids love bugs. They are fascinated with ladybug beetles, beautiful butterflies and dragonflies, bees, and spiders. Learning about insects and their life cycles provides a wonderful introduction to the world of science.

To learn about insects, visit the Insect Zoo in the San Francisco Zoo, which has bees, beetles, millipedes, centipedes, praying mantis, and other interesting bugs.

Learn how bees make honey, how they dance to communicate, and the important role they play as pollinators. San Francisco Zoo's Insect Zoo, the Randall Museum in San Francisco, and the Children's Discovery Museum in San Jose have see-through beehives.

Visit butterfly habitats at Natural Bridges, in Pacific Grove, and at Point Lobos State Reserve in Carmel to learn about butterflies, their life cycle, and their migration routes. Six Flags Marine World's walk-through Butterfly Kingdom allows you to experience butterflies flying all around you.

For a wonderful interactive exhibit to learn all about spiders, visit the Blackhawk Museum.

Butterflies:
Recommended books on butterflies:
The Very Hungry Caterpillar by Eric Carle (for toddlers and preschoolers)
Monarch Magic! Butterfly Activities & Nature Discoveries by Lynn M. Rosenblatt (for ages 4–12).
My Monarch Journal by Connie Muther (Parent-Teacher Edition) (for grades 1+). This book has detailed time lapse photos of the egg to caterpillar to butterfly stages, as well as areas for students to make observations and guided questions and discussion tips for parents and teachers. Best when used with a live egg to watch through the many stages of the monarch's life cycle.

For monarch butterflies, I highly recommend the Natural Bridges site. The visitor center is excellent, providing in-depth exhibits about these special butterflies, their migration routes, their life cycle, their habitats, and much more. Natural Bridges State Beach is easy to find; it provides easy stroller access between the parking lot, the visitor center, and the grove where the butterflies cluster on the eucalyptus trees. Finally, the on-site docents are extremely knowledgeable and provide an enriching experience.

Ardenwood Historic Farm in Fremont has butterfly and bird

programs on select days in the winter and early spring. See the full entry in Chapter 1: Animal Kingdom—Farms section.

Blackhawk Museum (Ages 2+) in Blackhawk specializes

in gorgeous classic cars and also has a fabulous exhibit on spiders. These interactive exhibits show how spiders molt in order to grow, the different types of silk spun by spiders and how they are used, the art and science of web spinning, the different types of webs spun by spiders, how spiders detect their prey, and more. This is a "don't miss" exhibit for all ages. See the full entry for Blackhawk Museum in Chapter 6: Transportation Favorites—Cars section.

CityBugs (Ages 4+)
<http://nature.berkeley.edu/citybugs>

The wonderful Web site has links to on-line bug museums, information on insects and spiders, teacher lesson plans, student games and activities, and an "ask the experts" section where you can e-mail your questions to UC Berkeley entomologists. There's also a bank of previously asked questions and answers. It participates in Cal Day at UC Berkeley, held annually in early April. For more details on Cal Day, see the entry in Chapter 10: Seasonal Events. Visit <www.berkeley.edu/calday> for current information on Cal Day.

Essig Museum of Entomology (Ages 4+)
UC Berkeley
(510) 643-0804; Room 211, Wellman Hall, UC Berkeley, Berkeley, CA 94720
<www.mip.berkeley.edu/essig/index.html>
Map: <www.mip.berkeley.edu/essig/wellman.jpg>

Description: Displays of bees, beetles, butterflies, etc. in the hallway of Wellman Hall. This museum is not generally open to the public. The collection is for research and sharing within the scientific community. However, school groups and individuals may arrange for tours. There are on-line exhibits. It also participates in Cal Day. For current information on Cal Day: <www.berkeley.edu/calday>.

Junior Nature Museum (All Ages)
McClellan Ranch Park in Cupertino has live insects on display. Displays vary week by week, depending on the season and availability. Call prior to visit for details. See entry in Chapter 1: Animal Kingdom—Farms section.

Natural Bridges State Beach (All Ages)
(831) 423-4609; West Cliff & Swanton, Santa Cruz, CA 95060
<www.parks.ca.gov/default.asp?page_id=541>

Description: The Visitor Center has exhibits on the migration routes and life cycle of the monarch butterfly. The park maintains a milkweed demonstration patch so visitors can view the larvae, caterpillars, and chrysalis. Milkweed is the only plant eaten by the monarch larva (caterpillar). Don't forget to pick up the brochure *The Monarch Butterfly* by the California State Parks. The bookstore located in the Visitor Center is great for children's books on butterflies and other insects. Allow approximately 1 hour for butterfly viewing. Don't forget to pick up your map to the Natural Bridges State Beach at the Visitor Center.

Hours: 8am–sunset. *Monarch Butterfly Tours*: Weekends mid-October to February. These docent-led tours are held at 11am & 2pm. The tours last for ~45 minutes. The Welcome Back Monarchs Day in October celebrates their migration to the Bay Area. The Migration Festival in February signals their departure.

Cost: $5 parking.

Bathrooms: Located at the Visitor Center and by the beach. There are dressing rooms and outdoor showers to wash off the sand.

Facilities: Stroller friendly to butterfly viewing area only.

Food: No. Picnic tables and barbecues are available.

What to Bring: Sweaters and jackets, binoculars for viewing butterflies, and camera or video camera if you'd like. Bring sand toys and beach gear if you're thinking about going to the beach afterward. Don't forget your sunscreen! If you go tide pooling here, be prepared to have an extra set of clothes and shoes, as you'll be climbing over some rocks and may get a bit dirty. Be careful of the slippery rocks! See Tide Pooling section in Chapter 1: Animal Kingdom—Marine Life for additional details.

Follow-Up Activities: 1) If it's a warm day, you may want to spend extra time at Natural Bridges State Beach and go tide pooling. 2) Consider visiting Seymour Marine Discovery Center, either before or after Natural Bridges, since it's just around the corner. To get there from Natural Bridges, as you're exiting Natural Bridge's entrance, turn left onto Swanton, away from the beach. Make a left onto Delaware. The Seymour Marine Labs Discovery Center entrance is at the end of Delaware. 3) Also, Santa Cruz Beach Boardwalk is close by. If you're thinking about going to Santa Cruz Beach Boardwalk, consider going to Natural Bridges in the morning, then spending the afternoon at the Boardwalk. 4) The Mountain Parks Foundation runs a summer day camp called the Ranger Explorers. It is held during June–August at various Santa Cruz County State Parks including Natural Bridges, Henry Cowell Redwoods State Park, and Wilder Ranch State Park. For more information, contact Mountain Parks Foundation (831) 335-3174 and visit the Web site in the spring (April) for summer camp information: <www.mountainparks.org>.

Magical Beginnings Butterfly Farms of Los Gatos (All Ages)

(408) 395-5123; (888) 639-9995 Toll free
114 Royce Street, Suite H, Los Gatos, CA 95030
<www.butterflyevents.com; www.magicalbeginnings.com>

1) Purchase butterflies for release at birthday parties or other events. Requires a minimum purchase of 16 butterflies at $10/butterfly.

2) Sponsors butterfly releases at various venues in the Bay Area usually in the fall. For most current information, call them in September or check the Web site:

<www.butterflyevents.com/butterfly_annualrelease.html>. In Los Gatos, usually the 3rd Sunday in October at the Los Gatos Hotel. In San Jose, at the Children's Discovery Museum (check with the Discovery Museum). At the Wild Bird Center in Walnut Creek: 1270A Newell Avenue, Walnut Creek, CA 94596. Call (925) 937-SEED or visit: <www.birdware.com>. Contact Magical Beginnings for additional information.

Monarch Grove Sanctuary (All Ages)

(831) 375-0982; (888) PG-MONARCH
Ridge Road & Lighthouse Avenue, Pacific Grove, CA 93950

Description: Friends of the Monarchs and the Museum of Natural History in Pacific Grove have docent programs to guide visitors.

Hours: Always open. During butterfly season from late October through February, docent-led tours are scheduled. *Weekdays:* noon–3pm. *Sat & Sun:* 10am–sunset. Special docent tours can be reserved in advance for groups.

Cost: Free.

Bathrooms: Portables.

Facilities: Stroller friendly.

Food: No.

What to Bring: Binoculars, camera or video camera, warm jacket, and picnic lunch.

Follow-Up Activities: 1) Learn about the migration of the monarch butterflies and their life cycle from the Pacific Grove Museum of Natural History. The Web site: <www.pgmuseum.org>. *The Pacific Grove Museum of Natural History* is located at 165 Forest Avenue, Pacific Grove, CA

93950. The phone number is: (831) 648-3116. Open Tues–Sun: 10am–5pm. Admission is free. 2) The Friends of the Monarchs' Web site has detailed information about the monarch's life cycle, migration, and habitat. The Web sites: <www.pgmonarchs.org/fomh.html> and <http://www.pgmonarchs.org/foml.html>.

Directions: Detailed map to the Monarch Grove Sanctuary via: <www.93950.com/monarchs.htm>. Or you can get directions from the Pacific Grove Museum of Natural History Web site: <www.pgmuseum.org> select "Monarchs", then select "Map & Directions;" for a detailed map to Monarch Grove Sanctuary: <www.93950.com/monarchs.htm>.

Point Lobos State Reserve (All Ages)

Point Lobos State Reserve is also host to wintering monarch butterflies. Ask the guard at the entrance gate to direct you to the butterflies. For full entry, see Chapter 1: Animal Kingdom—Nature Preserves section.

Santa Cruz Natural History Museum (All Ages)

(831) 420-6115; 1305 East Cliff Drive, Santa Cruz, CA 95062
<www.santacruzmuseums.org>

Description: This museum has wonderful children's exhibits. It has a bit of everything, from fossils and bees to the Ohlone Indians who lived in this area years ago. There's a touch pool with starfish and sea anemones. Kids can learn about the animals that lived in the Santa Cruz area and their natural habitats. The cement whale on the front lawn is a favorite climbing spot for kids.

Hours: Tues–Sun: 10am–5pm.

Cost: Free. Donation requested.

Bathrooms: Yes.

Facilities: Stroller friendly.

Food: No. Two restaurants within a couple of blocks' walk.

What to Bring: Picnic lunch. Don't forget your sunscreen and sunglasses. This museum is very close to the beach; bring beach gear if you want to go to the beach afterward.

Follow-Up Activities: 1) Close to Natural Bridges State Park, Seymour Marine Labs, and Santa Cruz Beach Board Walk. 2) Summer camps for kids 8–10. 3) Docent-led school tours for preschool to 6th grade are available with 4 weeks' notice. School tour times available: Tues–Fri at 9am,

10:15am, 11:30am, 12:45pm, or 2pm.

Directions: On the one-way street next to the museum, street parking on the side closest to the museum is by permit only. Stop in at the front to ask for a permit to park there.

Six Flags Marine World Theme Park (Ages 3+)

(707) 643-6722; 2001 Marine World Parkway, Vallejo, CA 94589
<www.sixflags.com/parks/marineworld>

Description: *Butterfly World* inside Six Flags Marine World Theme Park. For full entry, see Chapter 1: Animal Kingdom—Marine Life section.

Chapter 4
Science Museums

The physical world we live in is fascinating. Science museums provide interactive exhibits to help us learn about the physical world. These museums show us how physical work can be converted into energy and electricity, how the microprocessor works, how the ocean tides work, how the water cycle works on earth, and how the solar system and the universe work. Some of these museums cater to the learning style of very young children, some cater to school age children, and some to adults.

For current museum events in the Bay Area, visit the "Calendar of Events for Bay Area Museums" (through the San Francisco Visitor's Convention Web site <www.sfvisitor.org>—go to "Calendar of Events," then select "Museums").

How Come? by Kathy Wollard answers many questions from kids such as why the sky is blue, why giraffes have long necks, why bubbles are round, and more (Workman Publishing).

Bay Area Discovery Museum (All Ages)
East Fort Baker
(415) 331-2129; 557 McReynolds Road, Sausalito, CA 94965
< www.badm.org>

Description: The museum has many small buildings where the exhibits are housed. A changing exhibit area provides space for exhibits such as the Wizard of Oz, Arthur, Castles, etc; some of these exhibits also visit the Children's Discovery Museum in San Jose at different times. Like the Children's Discovery Museum, a small theater has plays and shows, even a marionette show from France every year. This museum has drop-in art and open ceramic studios on some Saturdays, a building exhibit space with changing projects, and a nature lab/study center in the basement of the entry building that provides hands-on interaction with different animal skins, skulls, and other materials. A play structure in another of the small buildings has a tunnel and a pretend fishing area.

Hours: Closed Monday. *Tues–Fri:* 9am–4pm, *Sat & Sun:* 10am–5pm.

Cost: $7/adult or child. Free for children under 1.

Bathrooms: Yes.

Facilities: Stroller accessible only between buildings. Strollers are not allowed inside the buildings.

Food: Yes, although on busy days it's very crowded, and places to sit and eat are limited. It's a good idea to pack a picnic lunch.

What to Bring: Warm jacket and windbreaker, especially in the winter. The museum is laid out as a series of small buildings. To go from area to area, you have to go outside to the next building. It's a good idea to bring a picnic lunch because the café gets overwhelmingly crowded. Don't forget to bring cash for the bridge crossing.

Follow-Up Activities: 1) Check the Web site for exhibit and special event schedules. There have been circus troupes, acrobats, Chinese New Year Celebrations, concerts, etc. 2) Birthday parties.

Bay Model Visitor Center (Ages 5+)
(415) 332-3870; (415) 332-3871; 2100 Bridgeway, Sausalito, CA 94965
<www.spn.usace.army.mil/bmvc/>
<www.baymodel.org>

Description: The Bay Model reproduces San Francisco Bay's and Sacramento Delta's rise and fall of tides, flow and currents of water, and mixing of freshwater and saltwater. Exhibits are on the estuary, wildlife habitats, and geography of the bay as well as the history of a World War II Sausalito shipyard.

Hours: *From Labor Day to Memorial Day:* Closed Sun & Mon. Tues–Sat: 9am–4pm. *From Memorial Day to Labor Day:* Closed Mon. Tues–Fri: 9am–4pm, Sat & Sun: 10am–5pm.

Cost: Free.

Bathrooms: Yes.

Facilities: Stroller friendly.

Food: No. Picnic tables available.

What to Bring: Picnic lunch, jacket, and cash for crossing the bridge.

Follow-Up Activities: For special events calendar:
<www.spn.usace.army.mil/bmvc/news/cal-cur/n-cal.htm>

California Academy of Sciences (All Ages)
Golden Gate Park
(415) 750-7145; 55 Concourse Drive, San Francisco, CA 94118 (reopening 2008)
Temporary Location: 875 Howard Street, San Francisco, CA 94103
<www.calacademy.org>

Description: 1) The Academy closed this location for several years of renovations on December 31, 2003. A temporary location in downtown San Francisco will be open to the public, but with scaled-down exhibits. The temporary location opens spring 2004. Check Web site for the latest information on the move. 2) The Academy of Sciences is a complex of three institutions that includes the Steinhart Aquarium, Natural History Museum, and Morrison Planetarium. The Natural History Museum includes exhibits of dinosaurs, African wildlife, California wildlife, earthquakes, insects, minerals, and changing exhibits. The Steinhart Aquarium has exhibits on the living coral reef, tropical sharks, seahorses, reptiles and amphibians, and a penguin colony. There is also a touch pool and a fish roundabout. The planetarium includes shows for young children. For more information on the planetarium, see the full entry in Chapter 5: Planetariums & Observatories. *Planetarium closed until 2008.*

Hours: Check Web site for current hours. Previous hours were: *Winter Hours:* 10am–5pm. *Summer hours (Memorial Day–Labor Day):* 9am–6pm. First Wednesdays of the month: open until 8:45pm. On Saturday mornings, there's Children's Story Time geared for children from 3–7 years old. These are held at 10:30am. Books are chosen from the Biodiversity Center Library based on monthly topics.

Cost: Free admission on the first Wednesday of each month. $8.50/adult; $5.50/youth (12–17), student w/ ID, or senior 65+; $2/child (4–11); free/ child 3 & under. *Planetarium tickets:* $2.50/adult, $1.25/youth (6–17) & senior 65+. San Francisco residents have additional "Neighborhood Free Days" depending on zip code and proof of residency in the form of a driver's license or utility bill. Check the Web site under "Admission" for the schedule or call (415) 750-7144.

Bathrooms: Yes.

Facilities: Stroller friendly.

Food: Cafeteria downstairs in the basement of the main entrance.

What to Bring: Quarters for metered parking and cash for food. Don't forget to bring a jacket, since San Francisco can be a bit cool, even in the summertime.

Follow-Up Activities: Many educational programs for families and schools. Visit the Web site: <www.calacademy.org/education/early_childhood_program> and <www.calacademy.org/education/course_catalog> for additional information. See Chapter 12: Science and Arts Education— Science Education section for more details of educational offerings.

Chabot Space & Science Center (Ages 5+)

(510) 336-7300; (510) 336-7373 Box Office
10000 Skyline Boulevard, Oakland, CA 94619
<www.chabotspace.org>

Description: Learn about the history of our space explorations; see our planet, our solar system, and the Milky Way. Learn about the sun and the various types of eclipses. There are also traveling exhibits.
Hours: Closed Mon. Tues–Thur: 10am–3pm, Fri–Sat: 10am–7:30pm, Sun: noon–5pm. *Theater & Planetarium Hours:* Fri–Sat: 7:30–9pm. *Free telescope viewing* on Fri & Sat. evenings. April–October: dusk–11pm (Daylight Savings Time) & November–March: 7–10pm. Open on certain holidays from 10am–5pm. Closed Christmas Day & Thanksgiving Day.
Cost: *General Admission:* $8/adult, $5.50/youth (4–12) or senior, *Plus 1 show:* $14.75/adult, $11/youth or senior, *Planetarium or Megadome Theater:* $8.75/adult, $6.50/youth or senior.
Bathrooms: Yes.
Facilities: Stroller friendly.
Food: Café on site.
What to Bring: Cash for food and planetarium tickets.
Follow-Up Activities: Many hands-on activities and lectures such as "Live from the Aurora," an interactive program with NASA scientists conducted live from Alaska, and lectures by professors and professionals from Jet Propulsion Labs, NASA, etc. For event details: <www.chabotspace.org/visit/events/aurora.asp>.

Children's Discovery Museum (Ages 2–10)

(408) 298-5437; 180 Woz Way, San Jose, CA 95110
<www.cdm.org>

Description: This is our favorite children's museum. We find it to be a safe and wonderfully engaging place for children as young as two. It has a permanent exhibit of transportation items including signal lights, an ambulance, a fire truck, and sometimes the Wells Fargo stagecoach. Interactive energy exhibits show how different kinds of work can be turned into electricity to power lights, a fan, and an airplane. There's a sound exhibit for kids to experience rhythm and how sounds "look" on the scope. There's also an exhibit for kids to interact with bubbles. The wonderful list goes on. Twice a year, special traveling exhibits such as Arthur's World, Richard Scary's Busy Town, Alice in Wonderland, Wizard of Oz, etc. come to Children's Discovery Museum. Call or check the Web site for the most current exhibit information. Don't miss the shows that correspond to the special traveling exhibit. Check show times under the "Information" icon under "Calendar" on the Web site. The shows usually ask the studio audience children to volunteer and participate. Don't miss the beehive and the old fashion laundry apparatus such as the clothes tub and clothesline located in the exhibit area next to the garden entrance. Upstairs, there's a cornhusk doll making station staffed with volunteers to help you create these dolls yourself. There's also a quiet toddler area upstairs for more hands-on play and reading. Allow 2 hours or more for your trip, depending on the age and attention span of your child. We've arrived at 11am and stayed until closing time.

Hours: Closed Mondays. Open Tues–Sat: 10am–5pm, Sun: noon–5pm. Check the Web site. It may open during some holidays such as Martin Luther King Day.

Cost: *Admission:* $7/child or adult, $6/senior (60+), free/infant under 1 year old. *Show:* $1/person. Purchase the show tickets from the "Post Office" beneath the stairs to the second floor. Cash only for the show tickets. *Parking:* Parking in the city owned lots varies from $3 to $7 per car, depending on the day and whether there are special events close by. If you plan to visit often, consider purchasing the family membership.

Bathrooms: Yes, including a family restroom.

Facilities: Day use lockers. Stroller friendly. ATM located next to the bookstore.

Food: Café.

What to Bring: Camera and cash for parking, lunch, and show.

Follow-Up Activities: 1) Art and science classes for all ages, including toddlers. 2) There also are summer camps. For descriptions of classes and schedule, you can call or go to the Web site and select the "Information" icon, then the "Parent/Child Workshop" icon (for ages 2–10), or the "calendar" icon for a full list of classes.

Directions: For a detailed map of the Children's Discovery Museum and the surrounding area in downtown San Jose, go to the Web site, and select "Information" icon, then the "Directions & Parking" icon.

Computer History Museum History Center (Ages 14+)

(650) 810-1010; 1401 N. Shoreline Boulevard, Mountain View, CA 94043
<www.computerhistory.org>

Description: This is a brand new facility located off Hwy 101 and Shoreline Blvd. See the very first computers (ILLIAC, JOHNNIAC & Cray) and the first Apple 1 computer at this museum. The museum documents the history of the microprocessor, the Internet, and eventually the timeline of computer history.

Hours: Open only during tours. Regular tours on Wed & Fri at 1pm. 1st and 3rd Saturdays of each month have tours at 1pm & 2pm.

Cost: Free.

Bathrooms: Yes.

Facilities: Stroller friendly.

Food: No, but restaurants are across the street.

Follow-Up Activities: An on-line exhibit and a free lecture series show the history of computing. Special tours can be arranged by calling (650) 810-1013.

Exploratorium (Ages 4+)
At the Palace of Fine Arts

(415) 563-7337; 3601 Lyon Street, San Francisco, CA 94123
<www.exploratorium.edu>

Description: This museum is all about interactive exhibits to demystify science and technology. The hands-on exhibits help the visitor experience and better understand physical forces such as momentum, light and optics, sound, and temperature. Upstairs, the Traits of Life exhibit provides actual examples of how plants use energy from the sun and produce the oxygen we breathe and how proteins are assembled from the code of life, DNA. The Tactile Dome is a whole new experience in touch and experience in the dark. It is extremely popular and requires advanced reservations. All the exhibits are made on site in the workshop. There's a theater that shows videos on various science and art topics to enhance the exhibits. Changing exhibits round out the museum's offerings. Don't miss the Web casts that provide more in-depth explorations that go beyond the walls of the museum. Topics include solar eclipse, mold science: cheese, biology of DNA, etc.

Hours: Closed Mondays. Tues–Sun: 10am–5pm. Closed Thanksgiving Day and Christmas Day. Open on Mondays for holidays such as Martin Luther King, Jr. Day; Presidents' Day; Memorial Day; and Labor Day.

Cost: Free admission on the first Wednesday of each month. *General admission:* $10/adult (18–64), $7.50/student (over 18 w/ ID) or senior, $6/disabled person or youth (5–17), free/child 4 & under. For those over 7 years old, the *Tactile Dome* includes general admission: $14/person. To purchase tickets to the Tactile Dome, call: (415) 561-0362. *Membership:* $70/year for a family of 2 adults & their children under 18. This membership is well worth considering because of its free admission to many museums in the Bay Area, including the Tech Museum, Zeum, Lindsay Wildlife Museum, Chabot Space & Science Center, Lawrence Hall of Science, Happy Hollow, etc. Look under the membership Web page for a full listing.

Bathrooms: Yes.

Facilities: Stroller friendly.

Food: Café.

What to Bring: Cash for food purchase.

Follow-Up Activities: Many classes and summer camps offered to older children of members. Members' classes often times take place on Sunday afternoons 1-3pm. These classes cost $35/class per child. See entry in Chapter 12: Science and Arts Education—Science Education section for details.

Intel Museum (Ages 8+)
Main Lobby, Intel Corporation's Robert Noyce Building
(408) 765-0503; 2200 Mission College Boulevard, Santa Clara, CA 95052
<www.intel.com/intel/intelis/museum>

Description: Intel Museum provides the history of the microprocessor and has exhibits showing how transistors and microprocessors work and how computer chips are made. Learn how Silicon Valley got its name. A virtual tour is on the Web site.

Hours: *Mon–Fri:* 9am–6pm, *Sat:* 10am–5pm. Closed Sunday.

Cost: Free.

Bathrooms: Yes.
Facilities: Stroller friendly.
Food: No.
What to Bring: No bags or backpacks are allowed inside the museum. There are also no coat check services. Please plan accordingly.
Follow-Up Activities: The wonderful Web site provides additional educational information on the transistor, chip design, etc.

Junior Center of Art and Science (Ages 2–9)
Lake Merrit/Oakland's Fairyland
(510) 839-5777; 558 Bellevue Avenue, Oakland, CA 94610
<www.juniorcenter.org>

Description: There is a drop in-art studio, a pottery studio, a Nature Room, a woodworking studio, and an exhibit on California Native Americans. The exhibit shows the tools, baskets, food, games, hunting techniques, and housing used by the American Indians. It is designed for schools and is usually reserved for them between 10:30am–2pm. Drop-in art and science activities are for children of all ages, including preschoolers.
Hours: *September–May*: Tues–Fri: 10am–6pm, Sat: 10am–3pm, *June–August*: Mon–Thur: 8:30am–5:30pm.
Cost: Free admission. Afterschool classes 4–6pm for children ages 5+. Registration is required. Pottery Studio: $7/hr for adults, $5/hr for kids plus cost of the ceramic item.
Bathrooms: Yes.
Facilities: Stroller friendly.
Food: No.
What to Bring: Dress for mess.
Follow-Up Activities: 1) Afterschool art and science classes. 2) Birthday parties. 3) Summer camps. 4) School programs available. 5) Next door to Children's Fairyland and Lake Merrit.

Lawrence Hall of Science (Ages 2+)
(510) 642-5132; Centennial Drive, Berkeley, CA 94720; (near Grizzly Peak Blvd.)
<www.lhs.berkeley.edu>

Description: The Lawrence Hall of Science is designed as a resource to provide hands-on activities for science and math education. It develops programs to make science and math fun and to share that knowledge with educators nationwide. A wide range of exhibits includes games and puzzles of different countries; an earthquake exhibit with an operational seismic recorder; and a Young Explorers Area with an insect zoo, puppet theater, blocks, and books. The Biology Lab has animals you can touch such as a chinchilla, a dove, a frog, a gecko, a lizard, a rat, turtles, and snakes. The Computer Lab is geared for children ages 5 and over, with age-appropriate software. The Planetarium includes shows for younger children during daytime hours. There is only one show for children 4–6 years old, titled *Flying High*. Other Planetarium shows allow only those 6 years or older. Planetarium tickets are sold at the Information Desk on a first come, first served basis.

Hours: Daily 10am–5pm. *Biology Lab*: Weekends & holidays 1:30–4pm. *Computer Lab:* Saturdays & holidays: 12:30–3:30pm. *Planetarium Shows*: Weekends & holidays: 1pm, 2:15pm, & 3:30pm. *Flying High*: weekends & holidays: 1pm.

Cost: $8/adult (19–61), $6/person (5–18, 62+) or disabled, $4/child (ages 3–4), free/child 2 & under. Planetarium show tickets are additional and cost $3/adult, $2.50/child 18 and under, with museum admission.

Bathrooms: Yes.

Facilities: Stroller friendly.

Food: Café open until 3:30pm daily. Menu on the Web site.

What to Bring: Cash for food.

Follow-Up Activities: Look in Chapter 12: Science and Arts Education— Science Education section under Lawrence Hall of Science for additional information on science classes and summer camps offered. Don't miss Cal Day in April. Other special events are posted on the Web site.

Directions: Look on the Web site under "About" icon for the "Directions" icon.

Mystery Spot (Ages 5+)

(831) 423-8897; 465 Mystery Spot Road, Santa Cruz, CA 95060
<www.mysteryspot.com>

Description: Come see this spot where strange phenomena occur, where tall objects seem short and balls seem to roll uphill. Are these merely optical illusions or strange natural forces? Scientists have brought their students to study this spot.

Hours: *Summer Hours (Memorial Day–Labor Day):* 9 am–last tour at 7pm. *Winter Hours:* 9am–last tour 4:30pm.

Cost: $5/adult, $3/child. Cash or check only for admission.
Bathrooms: Yes.
Facilities: Not stroller friendly; baby carrier recommended.
Food: No, some snacks only.
What to Bring: Picnic lunch and cash/check for admission.

NASA Ames Research Center (Min. Age: 10)
(650) 604-5000; Moffet Field, Mountain View, CA
<www.arc.nasa.gov>

Learning Tour available. See entry in Chapter 7: How Things Work – Site Tours section.

Oakland Discovery Center (Ages 6+)
Site 1: (510) 535-5657; 2521 High Street, Oakland, CA 94601
Site 2: (510) 832-3314; 935 Union Street, Oakland, CA 94067
<www.oaklandnet.com/parks/facilities/centers_oakland_discovery_e.asp>

Description: This recreation center provides afterschool hands-on activities in science and art projects. Activities include woodworking, telescopes, computers, rockets, electro-mechanics, physics, microscopes, and art.
Hours: *Summer:* Tues–Sat: 3–7pm, *September–June:* Tues–Thur: 3–7pm, Fri–Sat: 3–8pm.
Cost: Free.
Bathrooms: Yes.
Facilities: Stroller friendly.
Food: No.
What to Bring: Picnic lunch, cash for parking, sunscreen, and sunglasses.

Stanford Linear Accelerator Tour (Recommended Age: 11)
(650) 926-2204; 2575 Sand Hill Road, Menlo Park, CA 94025
<www2.slac.stanford.edu/vvc>

See full entry in Chapter 7: How Things Work – Site Tours section.

The Tech Museum of Innovation (Ages 7+)
(408) 795-6107; 201 South Market Street, San Jose, CA 95113
<www.thetech.org>

Description: The Tech Museum focuses on the innovation and technology that has made Silicon Valley world renown. Hands-on exhibits cover a range of topics, from biologically based innovations to microprocessors and robotics to space technologies that help us see and understand the universe better. Don't miss the IMAX Theater with shows that enrich your experience at the museum.

Hours: Tues–Sun: 10am–5pm. Closed Monday. Show times at the IMAX Theater vary, check the schedule at: **<www.thetech.org/imax/imax_showtimes.cfm>**.

Cost: *Admission:* $9/person (13–64), $7/child (3–12), $8/senior 65+. *Imax Theater Tickets:* $9/person (13–64), $7/child (3–12), $8/senior 65+. *Combination of Admission & Show:* $16/person (13–64), $13/child (3–12), $15/senior 65+.

Bathrooms: Yes.

Facilities: Stroller friendly.

Food: Café Primavera opens ½ hour *after* the museum opens and closes ½ hour *before* the museum closes.

What to Bring: Cash for parking and food.

Follow-Up Activities: 1) Summer camp programs on technology. See entry in Chapter 12: Science and arts Education—Science Education section. 2) On-line exhibits and archives on earthquakes, lasers, color, robotics, DNA, space and the Hubbell space telescope, and other technology topics.

Zeum, Yerba Buena Gardens (Ages 5+)
(415) 777-2800; (415) 247-6500 Carousel
221 Fourth Street, San Francisco, CA 94103
<www.zeum.com>

Description: Zeum combines traveling exhibits (such as the archaeology exhibit) with permanent exhibits that demonstrate various forms of media. The medium can be the art of book making and story telling with modern day technologies or it can be the most technologically advanced 3D modeling and animation. There are exhibits on sounds and special video effects, an animation studio, a production lab, and a learning lab to experiment with animation, 3D modeling, and video editing.

Hours: *Wed–Sun:* 11am–5pm. *Carousel Hours:* 11am–6pm. *Animation studio & Digital Sound Room* are sometimes reserved until 2:30pm for groups. Call ahead, as these vary day to day.

Cost: $7/adult, $6/students & seniors w/ ID, $5/youth (4–18). *Carousel:* $2/ticket, 2 rides per ticket. 4th & Mission parking lot for parking.

Bathrooms: Yes.

Facilities: Stroller friendly.

Food: Nearby.

What to Bring: Cash for parking and food.

Follow-Up Activities: 1) Workshops on weekends include theater workshops. Check the "Events Calendar" icon on the Web site. 2) Plays and exhibit films at the theater. Ticket prices vary, depending on the performance. 3) Birthday parties. 4) Learn about the world of archaeology on this Web site: <www.dignubia.org>.

Chapter 5
Planetariums
& Observatories

The sun, moon, and stars are an everyday part of our lives. Encourage your child's curiosity and help him learn about our solar system, the galaxies, and our universe. Planetariums simulate the night sky to help us visualize the constellations and learn how the sky changes with the seasons. Observatories provide telescopes for us to view the sky directly. It is possible to view the sun, with filtered telescopes to prevent eye damage. Foothill College in Los Altos Hills has a program on Saturday mornings to view the sun.

Cabrillo College Planetarium (Ages 4+)
Natural and Applied Sciences 700 building
(831) 479-6506; 6500 Soquel Drive, Aptos, CA 95003
<www.cabrillo.cc.ca.us/~rnolthenius/pltarium/planetarium.htm>

Description: Shows suitable for all ages, from preschool to high school. The show describes our solar system, how the sky changes as the earth rotates, a few constellations, asteroids, and comets.
Schedule: One-hour show available on Monday afternoons from 1–5pm. Reservations required.
Cost: $50/show per group.
Bathrooms: Yes.
Facilities: Stroller friendly.
Food: No.
Follow-Up Activities: Look through the *Summer Academy* class schedule for parent and student classes through the college. The Backyard Astronomy course for students in 6–12 grades is offered in the summer evenings with planetarium as well as telescope viewing at the Observatory

above Cabrillo College. Additionally, there is a summer whale-watching class and a computer robotics engineering course using Lego Dacta for students in grade 6 and up. Call the Community Education Office at Cabrillo (831) 479-6331 or visit the Web site and look under the *Summer Academy* catalog: <www.cabrillo.cc.ca.us/ce_ct/summeracademy/index.html>.

Directions: For a map of the campus: <www.cabrillo.cc.ca.us/instruct/instruct/facultyresource/cabrillomap0203.pdf>.

Chabot Space & Science Center (Ages 5+)
(510) 336-7300; (510) 336-7373 Box Office
10000 Skyline Boulevard, Oakland, CA 94619
<www.chabotspace.org>

For full entry information, look in Chapter 4: Science Museums.

Hours: Closed Mondays. Tues–Sun: 10am–5pm. *Spring Break Extended Hours:* Sat, March 30–Sat, April 6: Full facility open 10am–9pm daily. *Evening Planetarium & Theater Hours:* Fri–Sat: 6:45pm–10pm. *Free Telescope Viewing:* Fri–Sat evenings, weather permitting: November to March: 7–10pm, April to October: dusk–11pm.

Foothill Observatory, Foothill College (All Ages)
(650) 949-7334; 12345 El Monte Road, Los Altos Hills, CA 94022
<www.foothill.edu/ast/fhobs.htm>

Description: See the solar system, star clusters, nebulae, and even distant galaxies on Friday nights. Each viewing will be different, depending on the season and what's in viewing range. On Saturday mornings, see 2 layers of the sun through safe solar filters. Special viewing events are scheduled when there are eclipses, comets, supernova, etc. Check the Web site for these special events.

Hours: Weekly programs. Every Friday night: 9–11pm. Every Saturday morning: 10am–noon. Closed on cloudy days.

Cost: Free for the observatory. Parking is $2 from the parking lot ticket machines.

Bathrooms: Yes.

Facilities: Stroller friendly.

Food: No.

What to Bring: You'll need 8 quarters for parking and jackets for evening events.

Directions: For a map: <www.foothill.edu/ast/fhmap.htm>.

Minolta Planetarium (Ages 5+)
De Anza College
(408) 864-8814; 21250 Stevens Creek Boulevard, Cupertino, CA 95014
<www.planetarium.deanza.fhda.edu/pltwww/ghome.html>

Hours: The planetarium is located in the back of the campus, by the track and swimming pool area. Shows are on selected Saturday evenings at 7pm September–April. During the rest of the year, there are shows for school groups on weekday mornings. Individual families can attend by saying they're "walk ins" to find out when the next show is scheduled.

Cost: $2 parking at De Anza College. Tickets: $6/adult, $5/child under 12. Ticket purchase starts at 6pm. For "walk-in" shows, admission is $3.50 per person. Bring cash or check for entry fee.

Bathrooms: Yes.

Facilities: Stroller friendly.

Food: No.

What to Bring: 8 quarters for parking lot ticket machines, and cash or check for admission fee.

Follow-Up Activities: Telescope viewing available after each presentation as the weather permits in the evenings.

Morrison Planetarium (Ages 3+)
California Academy of Sciences, Golden Gate Park
(415) 750-7145; 55 Concourse Drive, San Francisco, CA 94118 (reopening 2008)
<www.calacademy.org/planetarium>

Description: *Due to reconstruction, the planetarium will be closed until the new building is completed in 2008.* Planetarium shows help us better understand the sun, moon, stars, constellations, and planets in our solar system. Special event shows on topics of current interest. One show is on the stars over San Francisco—now versus those 50 years ago. For full entry of the California Academy of Sciences, look in Chapter 4: Science Museums.

Schedule: Schedule varies, but usually on Sat & Sun: noon–4pm. "Free First Wednesdays" have shows noon–6pm. Check Web site or call for current information.

Cost: $2.50/adult, $1.25/youth or senior.

What to Bring: Jacket and cash for the show.

Follow-Up Activities: 1) Astronomy Day in early May is a special event featuring solar viewing, making a star wheel project, planetarium shows, and other activities. 2) Concerts and lectures on astronomy are held here. 3) San Francisco Amateur Astronomers meet here on the third Wednesday of each month. These meetings are open to the public. Look under "Special Events" on the Web site.

San Jose Astronomical Association (Ages 5+)

(408) 559-1221

<www.sjaa.net>

This organization is a group of amateurs who have star-gazing parties. These are open to the public. Go to the Web site to get the event calendar and meeting details.

UCO/Lick Observatory (Facility Recommended Ages 8+)

(408) 274-5061; Top of Mount Hamilton Road, San Jose, CA

<www.ucolick.org>

Description: Perched on the summit of Mount Hamilton, this site has beautiful views of the entire Bay Area on a clear day. While it is open to visitors on weekdays from 12:30–5pm and on weekends from 10am–5pm, telescope viewing by the public is limited only to a few special days during the summer. The summer program for the public to observe the stars includes history and astronomy lectures with each viewing. Check the Web site for dates, times, and ticket information.

Schedule: Usually held on a weekend each month from July—September in the evenings at 7:45pm.

Bathrooms: Yes.

Food: No.

What to Bring: Warm jacket.

Follow-Up Activities: On a sunny day, go down the other side of Mt. Hamilton to Livermore. This is a gorgeous drive. Bring a picnic lunch and a good map of the area, including Mt. Hamilton and the Livermore area. Have plenty of gas in the car, and spend a day exploring this "uncivilized" area. Not recommended for families with very young children.

William Knox Holt Planetarium (Min. Age: 4)
Lawrence Hall of Science
(510) 642-5132; Centennial Dr. & Grizzly Peak Boulevard, Berkeley, CA 94720
<www.lhs.berkeley.edu/Planetarium>

Description: *Flying High* is appropriate for children 4–7 years old and is scheduled at a convenient, early afternoon time on weekends. *Saving the Night* and *Constellations Tonight* are for children ages 6 and up. Except for *Flying High*, children under 6 are not allowed; most shows are for those 8 years and older. For full entry information, see Chapter 4: Science Museums.

Hours: Shows are presented on weekends, most holidays, and daily during the summer.

Cost: There is an additional fee of $3/adult and $2.50/child ages 18 and under for the planetarium.

Follow-Up Activities: It publishes a set of science education books and kits, for home schoolers, teachers, and day care providers. These books and kits are geared for different levels, from preschool through grade 12. Check the Web site under the "Shop" icon.

Chapter 6
Transportation Favorites

Kids love boats, cars, planes, and trains. They love to ride them, play with them, and learn about them. These vehicles come in many shapes and sizes. This chapter has specific sections on each of these types of transportation.

Boats

Boats come in a variety of sizes, functions, and materials: from rowboats, canoes, and paddleboats, to sailboats, ferryboats, aircraft carriers, submarines, and more. Pick a sunny day and rent a paddleboat or rowboat on one of the many recreational lakes in the Bay Area; take a bay cruise or ferry ride, and enjoy the experience of being on the water. Visit the maritime museums both afloat and on solid ground to experience the range and sizes of boats. For an answer to "Why do boats float?" visit this Web site: <**www.sciencenet.org.uk/database/Physics/Original/p00203d.html**>.

Paddleboat & Canoe Rentals

A wide selection of lakes and parks have inexpensive small boat rentals readily available. Some are open for business solely in the summer while others are open year-round, weather permitting.

Bonfante Gardens Family Theme Park (Ages 3+)
(408) 840-7100; 3050 Hecker Pass Highway, Gilroy, CA 95020
<www.bonfantegardens.com>

Description: One great place to introduce all these modes of transportation for the littlest ones is Bonfante Gardens Theme Park in the foothills of Gilroy, just before Hecker Pass. Originally built and designed for its beautiful gardens and unique circus trees, it has rides that feature boats, trains (both a miniature train and a monorail), vintage cars, and simulated airplane and hot air balloon rides. See full entry in Chapter 2: Plant Kingdom—Gardens & Arboretums section of this book.
Hours: Open spring–fall.
Cost: $29.95/adult, $21.95/child 3+, free/child under 3. Look for discount coupons from Nob Hill. AAA discounts also available. You may want to consider a season pass for older preschoolers.
Bathrooms: Yes, throughout the park.
Facilities: Day use lockers. Stroller friendly.
Food: Many concessions throughout the park offering hamburgers, pizzas, Mexican food, etc. Outside food is not allowed in the park. You may bring water and fruit into the park.
What to Bring: Sunscreen, sunglasses, water bottles, and an extra change of clothes and shoes.

Lafayette Reservoir (Ages 3+)
(925) 284-9669; 3849 Mt Diablo Boulevard, Lafayette, CA 94549
<www.lafayettechamber.org/pages/reservoir.htm >
<www.ebmud.com/services/recreation/east_bay/lafayette>

Description: Located off Hwy 24, this reservoir allows fishing and boating.
Hours: Ranges 6am–9pm, depending on the season.
Cost: $5 park entry fee. Rowboats and pedalboats are available for rent on an hourly, half-day, or full-day basis from the activity center. Rowboat and pedal boat rentals: $15/hour, $22.50/90minutes (rowboat only), $25/half day, $35/full day, $30 deposit. Seniors and the disabled get 50% off rentals.
Bathrooms: Yes.
Facilities: Stroller friendly.
Food: No. Picnic tables available.

What to Bring: Picnic lunch, drinks, sunscreen, and sunglasses. Wear comfortable shoes with good traction.

Lake Almaden (Ages 3 +)

(408) 277-5130; 6099 Winfield Boulevard, San Jose, CA 95120
<www.ci.san-jose.ca.us/cae/parks/alp>
Map of Lake Almaden: <www.ci.san-jose.ca.us/cae/parks/alp/map.jpg>

Description: Besides boating, this lake has a sandy beach and swim area with lifeguards on duty.

Hours: Year-round 6am–½ hour after sunset. Boat rentals and swimming area are open Memorial Day–Labor Day.

Cost: $4 parking fee collected April–October. Pedal boats and kayaks available for rental. Boat rental: $6/ first ½ hour, $10/ first hour, $8/each additional hour, $3 late fee for each 15-minute increment. Check the Web site: <**www.parkhere.org/infofees.htm**> for most current fees.

Bathrooms: Yes.

Facilities: Stroller friendly.

Food: Snack bar. Closed in the winter.

What to Bring: Sunscreen, sunglasses, beach gear, and water bottles.

Lake Chabot (Ages 3 +)

(510) 892-2177; 17936 Lake Chabot Road, Castro Valley, CA 94546
(510) 582-1230; P.O. Box 2213, Castro Valley
Lake Chabot Fishing Outfitters: (510) 247-2526
<www.norcalfishing.com/chabot.html>
For a brochure, call Urban Park Concessionaires at (925) 426-3060

Description: Boat tours of the lake are available on weekends and holidays.

Hours: *Park* hours are sunrise–sunset. *Marina & café*: Mon–Thur: 6am–5:30 pm; Fri, Sat, & Sun: 6am–6:30pm. *Boat tours:* Weekends & holidays through October, departing the marina at 11am, noon, 1pm, & 2pm.

Cost: $4 parking fee. Daily fishing access permit: $4, 2-day California state fishing license $11.05, California state fishing license $30.45. Boat rental ½ price on Weds. *Boat rentals:* Rowboats, canoes, & single kayaks: $15/hr; pedalboats & 2-person kayaks: $18/hr., $40 deposit. Extended ½-day and full-day rentals available. *Sightseeing boat tour*: $4.25/adult, $3.75/child (12 and under).

Bathrooms: Yes.

Facilities: Stroller friendly.

Food: Lake Chabot Marina Café serves breakfasts, lunches, snacks, and drinks.

What to Bring: Sunscreen, sunglasses, hats, and camera.

Lake Cunningham Park (Ages 3+)

(408) 277-4319; 2305 S. White Road, San Jose CA 95148

<www.ci.san-jose.ca.us/cae/parks/lcp>

Description: This lake has boating, fishing, and sailing in the spring and summer and bird watching in the winter.

Hours: 8am–½ hour after sunset. *Marina:* Spring weekends, daily during the summer (Memorial Day–Labor Day).

Cost: Parking fee: $4 collected on weekends and holidays, and daily during the summer through Labor Day. Paddleboat, sailboat, and rowboat rental: $6/first ½ hour, $10/first hour, $8/each additional hour. Check Web site for the most current fees: <www.parkhere.org/infofees.htm>.

Bathrooms: Yes, by the marina.

Facilities: Stroller friendly.

Food: Snack bar. Picnic tables.

What to Bring: Sunscreen, picnic lunch, sunglasses, change of clothes, and towels in the summer. Binoculars for bird watching in the winter.

Follow-Up Activities: 1) Sailing classes and summer sailing camps are offered. Call the park for additional information. 2) In the winter, Lake Cunningham Park is home to great blue herons, snowy white egrets, white pelicans, and Canadian geese. 3) Raging Waters Theme Park is located right next door.

Lake Del Valle (Ages 3+)

(925) 373-0332; 6999 Del Valle Road, Livermore, CA 94550

<www.ebparks.org>; Boat rental: <www.norcalfishing.com>

Description: In the summer, there are boat tours at the lake 1–2: 30 pm. Ticket sales start at 11am at the marina. Tour accommodates a maximum of 23 people. Fishing and swimming are allowed. For kids under age 16, no permits are required. For those 16 and up, a valid CA fishing license and daily fishing access permit are required. These can be purchased at the boating center. Call (925) 248-3474 for additional information.

Hours: Sunrise to sunset.

Cost: $5 parking fee. Paddleboats: $18/hr, canoes & rowboats: $15/hr. All require $20 deposit and ID. Motorboats and extended ½- and full-day rentals available at higher cost. *Del Valle Boat Rentals:* (925) 449-5201.

Bathrooms: Yes.

Facilities: Stroller friendly.

Food: Two snack bars available. East Beach Snack Bar is open from April through September. Rocky Snack Bar is open from May through Labor Day.

What to Bring: Sunscreen, sunglasses, swimsuit, and shoes appropriate for the water.

Follow-Up Activities: During the summer weekends from May to September, the Visitor Center has naturalist programs for all ages on a drop-in basis. Most of these programs are free. For additional information on the Naturalist Programs, call Sunol at (925) 862-2601. For additional information about Sunol, see the Nature Preserves section.

Lake El Estero (Ages 2+)
(831) 375-1484 Boat Rental; (831) 646-3860 Playground
Del Monte Avenue & Camino El Estero, Monterey, CA 93940

Description: The lake and Dennis the Menace Playground are both lo-cated at the El Estero Park. The lake allows for boating and fishing; it is stocked with rainbow trout, Sacramento perch, and blackfish, etc. Fishing piers are located on Pearl Street.

Hours: *Park:* Tues–Sun: 10am–dusk. Closed Monday except on holidays. *Boating* concession: 10am–4pm, with the last boat out at 3:30pm.

Cost: Boat rentals at Lake El Estero cost $8/half hour, $13/hour. For ad-ditional boating information, call El Estero Park at (831) 375-1484.

Bathrooms: Yes.

Facilities: Stroller friendly.

Food: Snack bar outside of the Dennis the Menace Playground on Pearl Street.

What to Bring: Picnic lunch and cash for food and rides.

Follow-Up Activities: *Dennis the Menace Playground* is adjacent to the Lake El Estero Park boating area on Pearl Street. This unusual playground has a steam mini-train, a swinging rope bridge, and a maze.

Lake Elizabeth in Central Park (Ages 2+)

(510) 791-4340; 40000 Paseo Padre Pkwy, Fremont, CA 94538
<www.ci.fremont.ca.us/Recreation/Boating>

Description: This is a pretty city park with a swimming lagoon, children's playgrounds, baseball fields, and a 2-mile trail that circles the lake. Be careful of the resident geese, especially with little ones, since the geese can be aggressive.

Hours: Sunrise–10pm.

Cost: Kayaks: $8/hour, small paddleboat or canoe: $15/hour, large paddleboat or canoe: $17/hour, El Toro Sailboat: $12/hour, Topper Sailboat: $12/hour.

Bathrooms: Yes.

Facilities: Stroller friendly.

Food: 3 concession stands located in various parts of the park.

What to Bring: Sunscreen, sunglasses, swim gear, beach towel, and umbrella if you plan to swim in the lagoon.

Lake Merritt Boating Center (Ages 3+)

(510) 238-2196; 568 Bellevue Avenue, Oakland, CA 94610
Gondola Rental: 866-SERVIZIO (866-737-8494)
(510) 663-6603 Oakland
(707) 257-8495 Napa
Boat rentals: <www.oaklandnet.com/parks/programs/boating_boatrates.asp>
Gondola tour: <www.gondolaservizio.com>

Description: In addition to the canoes and rowboats, there are authentic Venetian gondolas for romantic dates and birthday parties. Two separate boat rental concessions operate on this lake. One concession rents out the traditional rowboats, canoes, etc.; the other rents out the gondolas. Information on the gondolas is listed in "Follow-Up Activites" below.

Hours: *Boat rental* closing times reflect when the last boat can leave the dock. *Summer* (Memorial–Labor Day): Mon–Fri: 9am–6pm, Sat/Sun: 10am–6pm; *Fall* (September–October): Mon–Sun: 10:30am–5pm; *Winter* (November–February): Mon–Fri: 10:30am–3:30pm, Sat/Sun: 10: 30am–4pm; *Spring* (March–May): Mon–Fri: 10:30am–4pm, Sat/Sun: 10:30am–5pm.

Cost: Rent your own canoes, rowboats, kayaks, or pedalboats. All boat rentals require $10 deposit and a boat permit of $2/day. Canoes: $6/hr; pedalboats: $6/1/2 hr, $8/hr; rowboats: $6/hr; kayaks: $6/1/2 hr, $8/hr.

127

Bathrooms: Yes.

Facilities: Stroller friendly around the lake.

Food: No.

What to Bring: Picnic lunch, sunscreen, sunglasses, and rubber-soled comfortable shoes. Dress warmly in winter.

Follow-Up Activities: You can ride gondolas imported from Venice, Italy. Make reservations for the gondola rides Mon–Fri 10am–5pm. Open year round, seven days a week. Prices range from $45/couple and $10 per additional person for a 25-minute cruise around Lake Merritt. Other packages also available. Groups (12+ people): $14/person/½-hour cruise, $17/person/hour cruise.

San Pablo Reservoir (Ages 3+)

(510) 223-1661; 7301 San Pablo Dam Road, El Sobrante, CA 94803
<www.norcalfishing.com/sanpablo.html>

Description: This is a favorite lake for boating and fishing (well stocked). There is a child play area and plenty of picnic tables. There's also a bait and tackle shop on site, fish cleaning stations, and a handicap fishing dock.

Hours: Range 6am–9pm, depending on the month. Closed mid-November to mid-February. Open at least 6:30am–5:30pm, with extended hours to 9pm in June and July. Check Web site for specific times.

Cost: $6 park entry fee. Rowboats: $13/hour, $27/3–5 hours, $32/day, $35 deposit. Motorboats and other boats are also available.

Bathrooms: Yes.

Facilities: Stroller friendly at the park.

Food: San Pablo Grill serves cooked to order breakfast and lunch.

What to Bring: Sunscreen, sunglasses, shoes with good traction, and fishing gear if you want to fish also.

Shoreline Aquatic Center & Sailing Lake (Ages 3+)

Shoreline Lake in Shoreline Park

(650) 965-7474 Boathouse; (650) 965-1745 Café
3160 N. Shoreline Boulevard, Mountain View, CA 94043
<www.shorelinelake.com >

Description: This is a beautiful park. Although there are no expert naturalists to enrich your knowledge of the wetlands and wildlife, there is plenty to see and do here. *Rengstorff House* is a restored mansion that provides a time capsule of the history of the Santa Clara Valley in the 1880s

Hours: Open year-round, except during inclement weather. *Spring/ Summer* (April–October): 10am–6pm. *Fall/Winter* (November–March): 10:30am–5pm on weekdays and 10am–5:30pm on weekends. The best time to visit the lake area is during the morning if you go on weekends, as this is a popular destination and the marina parking lot and café get very crowded.

Cost: Free parking. Sailboats, paddleboats, rowboats, canoes, windsurfers, and kayaks are available for rent. Hourly rentals vary from $13/hour to $22/hour, depending on the equipment and the day of the week. Sailing and windsurfing classes are available for older children (9+) and adults.

Bathrooms: Yes.

Facilities: Day use lockers. Stroller friendly.

Food: Lakeside Café is located on the lake and directly next to the boat rental center. Lakeside Café has outdoor seating facing the lake. There are also quite a few restaurants located within the park.

What to Bring: Sunscreen, sunglasses, water shoes, and change of clothing and towels just in case you get a bit wet.

Follow-Up Activities: Consider visiting Baylands Nature Preserve at the end of Embarcadero Road East in Palo Alto, just a couple of exits north of Shoreline Blvd. off Hwy 101. This would be a nice activity for elementary school age children who enjoy learning about birds and the wetlands habitat. For more information on Baylands, look under the Nature Preserves section.

Stowe Lake, Golden Gate Park (Ages 3+)

(415) 752-0347; 50 Stowe Lake Drive, San Francisco, CA 94118
<www.surprise.com/whositfor/just_us/stowe_lake_boat_rental.cfm>

Description: Located in beautiful Golden Gate Park, this is a gorgeously landscaped and intimate boating lake, something you'd expect to see in old fashioned romantic movies. There are many areas to sit and view the beauty of this small lake. Many international visitors visit this lake, so you're likely to hear a variety of different languages spoken here.

Hours: Daily 10am–4pm.

Cost: Pedalboats: $17/hour, rowboats: $13/hour, $1 deposit. Cash only! Holds 4 passengers only, including small children. Must have someone 16 years old or older on the boat at all times.

Bathrooms: Yes.

Facilities: Stroller friendly.

Food: Snack bar.

What to Bring: Cash only for boat rental.

Follow-Up Activities: Consider visiting the Japanese Tea Garden, Strybing Arboretum, or the California Academy of Sciences since they're close by.

Vasona Lake County Park (All Ages)

(408) 356-2729; 333 Blossom Hill Road, Los Gatos, CA 95032
<www.parkhere.org/prkpages/vasona.htm>

Description: Vasona Lake rents paddleboats and canoes from early spring to early fall. Fishing is allowed. Vasona is directly adjacent to Oak Meadow Park.

Hours: 8am–sunset.

Cost: $4 parking fee. Boat rental fee: $6/first ½ hour, $10/first hour, $8/ each additional hour. For most current information, check the Web site: **www.parkhere.org/infofees.htm** or call.

Bathrooms: Yes, but good idea to bring towelettes.

Facilities: Stroller friendly.

Food: No. Picnic tables and barbecues.

What to Bring: Sunscreen, hats, photo ID for boat rental, and check-book or enough cash.

Follow-Up Activities: 1) The Billy Jones Wildcat Railroad, a miniature train, and the carousel are favorites at adjacent Oak Meadow Park in Los Gatos. The Billy Jones Wildcat Railroad Web site: **<www.bjwrr.com>**. Open daily during the summer but only on weekends the rest of the year. See the Mini-Trains Section for additional information. 2) Sailing classes are offered through the Los Gatos–Saratoga Parks and Recreation Dept. during the summer. Check the Local Parks and Recreation section for additional contact information. 3) The Youth Science Institute has great hands-on science classes for kids from preschool on up. Summer camps and afterschool science classes during the school year are popular. Class schedules are printed in the newsletter on the Web site: **<www.ysi-ca.org>**. See entry in Chapter 12—Science Education. In May, Sanborn YSI site has an annual Insect Fair. $3/adult, $1/child 12 and under. 4) During the Christmas holiday season, see the *Fantasy of Lights* drive-through lights display with music in Vasona Park. These are nightly from the end of November—December, from 6–10pm. *Admission Fees*: *Mon–Thur:* $9/vehicle with 9 or fewer people, *Fri–Sun:* $13/vehicle with 9 or fewer people, *Every Day:* $25/vehicle with 10–19 people, $35/vehicle with 20+ people. For additional information on the *Fantasy of Lights*, call the coordinator at (408) 355-2201 or visit the Web site: <**www.fantasyofligh ts.com**>.

Cruising the Bay

I've always loved seeing the landscape from different vantagepoints. The view of the skyline is different from the water. Take a boat ride and see the beautiful San Francisco skyline or the Monterey Bay coastline. There are cruise operators such as the Blue and Gold Fleet and the Red and White Fleet. Public ferries operating from departure points throughout the Bay Area run frequently and are very affordable. While ferries may not have tour narration, they provide a wonderful boating experience. If you go, don't forget your jacket, camera, sunglasses, sunscreen, and cash for food. Check Web sites for discount coupons, maps, and schedules, as these items get updated periodically.

Baywatch Cruises (All Ages)
Old Fisherman's Wharf, Monterey
(800) 200-2203; (831) 372-7150
90 Fisherman's Wharf #1, Monterey, CA 93940
<www.montereybaywatch.com>

Description: Cruises around the Monterey Bay Marine Sanctuary in a fully enclosed glass-bottom boat. Fully narrated tours last ~ 45minutes and focus on sea otters, spotted harbor seals, sea lions, birds, etc. Tours stay in the calm waters of the bay along Cannery Row.
Schedule: First trip departs at 10am. Hourly departures. Call for current schedule, rates, and reservations.
Cost: $14.95/adult, $7.95/child under 10. $2 discount coupon on the Web site.
Bathrooms: Yes, at dockside.

Facilities: Not stroller friendly. Baby carrier recommended.
Food: No. Restaurants are located nearby at the Monterey Fisherman's Wharf.

Blue and Gold Fleet (All Ages)

(415) 705-5555; Pier 41, Fisherman's Wharf, San Francisco, CA 94133
<www.blueandgoldfleet.com>

Description: This company provides bay cruises; tours to Alcatraz; and ferries to Sausalito, Tiburon, Alameda/Oakland, Vallejo, Angel Island, and Pacific Bell Park during baseball season. The San Francisco Bay Cruise is approximately 1 hour long. There are also land tours to the wine country, Muir Woods, San Francisco, Monterey/Carmel, and Marine World.
Schedule: See Web site for departure times.
Cost: San Francisco Bay Cruise: $11/child 5–11, $15/youth 12–17, and $19/adult. If you purchase tickets by phone or on-line, there's an additional convenience charge. You can also purchase tickets from the Box Office at Pier 41 Fisherman's Wharf, right next to Pier 39. Book through the Web site for special discounts or consider purchasing the City Pass <www.citypass.com/sanfrancisco> for the Bay Cruise tour if you're interested in other attractions in San Francisco within a 7-day period.
Bathrooms: Yes.
Facilities: Stroller friendly.
Food: Snack bars on the boat.

Red and White Fleet (All Ages)

(877) 855-5506; Pier 43-1/2, Fisherman's Wharf, San Francisco, CA 94133
<www.redandwhite.com>

Description: The San Francisco Bay Cruise is approximately 1 hour.
Schedule: See Web site for departure times.
Cost: San Francisco Bay Cruise costs $11/child 5–11, $15/youth 12–17, and $19/adult. Discount coupons on-line. In the past, special *Kids Sail Free on Bay Cruises* takes place in the spring. There are helicopter tours ($95–$210, depending on the tour).
Bathrooms: Yes.
Facilities: Stroller friendly.
Food: Yes.

Bay Area Ferries

Alameda and Oakland Ferry Service (All Ages)

(510) 522-3300; Alameda Dock: 2990 Main Street, Alameda, CA 94501; and
Oakland Dock: Jack London Square, Oakland, CA
<www.eastbayferry.com>

Description: This ferry goes between Alameda/Oakland and San
Francisco (Ferry Building and Pier 39), Angel Island, and Pacific Bell
Park.

Hours: Closed Thanksgiving, Christmas, and New Year's Day.
For schedules, check the Web site: <**www.eastbayferry.com/when/
when.html**>.

Cost: *Parking:* Free parking next to the Alameda terminal. Free Parking
in the 7-story garage at Washington Street and the Embarcadero, Jack
London Square at the Oakland terminal. Validate your parking ticket
onboard the ferry for free parking. *Fares:* Between Alameda/Oakland and
San Francisco: *One-way fare*: $5/adult, $2.25/junior (5–12), $3/senior
(65+ with ID), $3.75/active military personnel, $3/disabled person,
$1/between Alameda and Oakland, Free for children under 5 with an
adult. *Round-trip fares* are double the one-way fares. For the best value,
ticket books for frequent trips: $40/10-ticket book (5 round trips), $70/
20 ticket book (10 round trips), $130/40-ticket book (20 round trips).
Round-trip fares between Alameda/Oakland and Angel Island: $12/adult
(19+); $9/junior (13–18), seniors (62+), and disabled; $6/child (5–12);
free for children under 5. These fares include park admission.

Bathrooms: Wheelchair accessible bathrooms on the first deck.

Facilities: Stroller friendly. You can also bring bikes onboard.

Food: Concession with beverages and snacks.

What to Bring: Sunglasses, jacket, and camera.

Angel Island/Tiburon Ferry (All Ages)

(415) 435-2131; 21 Main Street, Tiburon, CA 94920
<www.angelislandferry.com>

Schedule: *Summer Schedule:* Mon–Fri departing Tiburon at 10am, 11am,
1pm, and 3pm. Sat/Sun hourly 10am–5pm. Mon–Fri departing Angel
Island at 10:20am, 11:20am, 1:20pm, and 3:30pm. Sat & Sun hourly
10:20am–5:20pm. *Winter Schedule:* Sat & Sun departing Tiburon hourly

10am–4pm. Departing Angel Island hourly 10:20am–4:20pm. Operates Mon–Fri only for groups or on request for 25+ passengers. *Sunset Cruises* from the end of May–mid-October on Fri & Sat evenings: 6:30–8pm. The sunset cruises usually are on the bigger ferryboat, but sometimes the smaller outdoor boat is used. Call for specific information prior to your trip if this is important to you.

Cost: Round-trip fare: $7/adult or senior, $6/child (5–11), $1/bike. Sunset cruises: $10/adult, $6/child 5–11, free/child under 5 per adult. $50 season passes available for unlimited number of cruises.

Bathrooms: Yes.

Facilities: Stroller friendly on the bigger ferryboat.

Food: No. Snacks available onboard for sunset cruises.

What to Bring: Jacket, camera, sunglasses and sunscreen, dinner picnic for sunset cruises.

Follow-Up Activities: 1) Special events: New Year's, Valentine's, May Fireworks, July 4 Fireworks, and October Fleet Week Blue Angels Cruises. Call for current information. 2) Historic cruises for school groups. 3) You can also charter the boats for birthday parties. 3) Summer camps on Angel Island through the Belvedere-Tiburon Recreation Department for children 6–13. Call the Belvedere-Tiburon Recreation Department at (415) 435-4355.

Golden Gate Ferry (All Ages)

(415) 455-2000 Marin County
(415) 923-2000 San Francisco
(707) 541-2000 Sonoma County
San Francisco Ferry Building Terminal at the foot of Market Street
San Francisco Pier 39 - Fisherman's Wharf (ferry docks at nearby Pier 39)
<www.goldengateferry.org>

Description: Golden Gate Ferry provides daily service between Larkspur or Sausalito (Marin County) and San Francisco, and between San Francisco and Pac Bell Park. Trips last 30 to 50 minutes, depending on the destination and the speed of the boat. Most trips take 30 minutes, except between San Francisco and Larkspur on the *Spaulding,* which takes 50 minutes.

Schedule: Check Web site or call for current schedule information. Holiday schedules are different from regular schedules. There is no service on Thanksgiving, Christmas, and New Year's Days.

Cost: *One-way fare—Larkspur:* Weekdays: $3.25/adult, $2.45/child

(6–12), $1.60/senior (65+), free/child 5 & under; Weekends/holidays: $5.60/adult, $4.20/child (6–12), $2.80/senior (65+). *Sausalito:* Daily: $5.60/adult, $2.80/senior (65+), $4.20/child (6–12), free for children 5 and under. *Family Fare* during weekends and holidays: youths 12 and under travel free with paying adult (limit 2 youths/full-fare adult).

Bathrooms: Yes.

Facilities: Stroller friendly.

Food: Snack bar.

What to Bring: Windbreaker or jacket, camera, sunglasses, sunscreen, and cash.

Directions: *Larkspur terminal* is located in Marin County, on East Sir Francis Drake Boulevard, just east of HWY 101. There are Park and Ride lots and street parking along Sir Francis Drake Blvd. You can also get $2 off the $4 parking rate at the Marin Airporter parking lot across from the terminal if you get a flyer with a dated coupon from the ferry ticket window. *Sausalito terminal* is located in downtown Sausalito, at Humbolt and Anchor streets.

Harbor Bay Ferry (All Ages)
(510) 769-5500; 1141 Harbor Bay Parkway, Alameda, CA 94501
<www.harborbayferry.com>; <www.transitinfo.org/harborbayferry>

Description: Provides commuter service between Alameda and San Francisco.

Hours: Runs only during early-morning and late-evening commuter hours.

Cost: *One-way Fare*: $5/person 12+ and under 62, $3/senior (62+), disabled, or military, $2.25/child (5–12), Free/child under 5. *Monthly Pass*: commuter book of tickets available. Free parking at the Harbor Bay ferry terminal. Purchase tickets once you board at the snack bar. There's a discount coupon in the Alameda phone book.

Bathrooms: Yes, on lower deck.

Facilities: Stroller friendly.

Food: Food and beverage service onboard, cash or check only.

What to Bring: Jacket, sunglasses, camera, and cash or check for food and parking.

Directions: Harbor Bay Isle Ferry Landing located at the end of Harbor Bay Parkway on Bay Farm Island (City of Alameda). Docks at the San Francisco Ferry Building by the Embarcadero.

Vallejo/Baylink Ferry (All Ages)

(707) 64-FERRY; (877) 64-FERRY
495 Mare Island Way, Vallejo, CA 94590
<www.baylinkferry.com>

Description: Ferry service between Vallejo Terminal and the San Francisco Ferry Building. Service to Marine World during the summer between May and Labor Day.

Schedule: Closed on Thanksgiving, Christmas, and New Year's Days. Check current schedule on the Web site.

Cost: $9/adult (13–64); $4.50/youth (6–12), seniors (65+), and disabled; free/child ages 0–5. Free parking across from the Vallejo Terminal on Mare Island Way. In the San Francisco Ferry Building Terminal, parking is available in the garage across from Pier 39 in San Francisco for a fee on an hourly basis.

Bathrooms: Wheelchair accessible restroom available.

Facilities: Stroller friendly.

Food: Snack bar.

What to Bring: Jacket, sunglasses, camera, and cash.

Whale-Watching

Whale-watching cruises depart from San Francisco, Santa Cruz, and Monterey Bay. See the whale-watching section in Chapter 1: Animal Kingdom—Marine Life for additional information.

Maritime Museums

Visit the maritime museums and see firsthand the submarine and gargantuan aircraft carrier. If you ever get the opportunity, it's well worth the trip to experience being in a submarine. Hawaii and many tourist destinations provide submarine tours. It's a wonderful firsthand experience of being underwater and seeing how colors change as the submarine submerges and less sunlight gets through to the deeper water. Although I had intellectually understood this from the Monterey Bay Aquarium's

Mysteries of the Deep exhibit, which has an interactive display that shows the effect of depth on color light, I truly didn't understand it until I experienced it myself. The experience made a tremendous difference because it was the event and the actual physical sensation of being in an underwater environment that helped me to really "get it."

San Francisco Maritime National Historic Park (All Ages)

This park is spread out between the Maritime Museum, the Library, the boats at Hyde Street Pier, and the *U.S.S. Pampanito*. It's within walking distance of both Pier 39 and Ghiradelli Square. The brand new visitor center opened in late August 2003 across from the entrance to Hyde Street Pier at the corner of Hyde and Jefferson Streets in San Francisco.
Hours: 9:30am–7pm daily in the summer (Memorial Day–October 1), 9:30am–5pm October 2–May 30.

Maritime Museum
(415) 561-7100; Beach Street and Polk Street, San Francisco, CA 94109
<www.maritime.org>

Description: The beautiful views of the San Francisco Bay and Alcatraz Island from the balcony of the museum are well worth the visit. There's also a sandy beach, Aquatic Park, just steps from the back of the museum. The museum has displays, videos, oral history recreations, interactive exhibits, and models. The Steamship Room provides an exhibit on the evolution from the wind to steam-powered technologies used in boats. Don't miss the demonstrations in the radio room that provide hands-on exhibits of the evolution of communications technology from signal flags to the radios and the use of Morse code.
Hours: 10am–5pm daily. Radio room demonstration on Sundays 1–3pm. Weekend tours start at 12:30pm.
Cost: Free.
Bathrooms: Yes.
Facilities: Stroller friendly only on the first floor. There are stairs to the 2nd and 3rd floors.
Food: Nearby restaurants across the way at Ghiradelli Square.
What to Bring: Jacket and camera.

Follow-Up Activities: 1) Beautiful beach, Aquatic Park, directly behind the museum. If you're in the mood for the beach, bring some beach gear. 2) Walking distance to Hyde Street Pier, Ghiradelli Square, and cable car terminus. 3) Many special events throughout the year include bird watching walks, historical talks, engineering talks about steam piston technology, concerts, and costumed Living History Days where you get to meet the captain and his wife and learn about life onboard ship. Check the calendar for specific programs: <www.maritime.org/calendar.htm>. 3) The Maritime Park Association also sponsors various educational programs such as the submarine school, gold rush prospecting, and boat building through group programs. Scout, YMCA, and school groups can register for these programs that are geared for the elementary grades 4 and up.

Hyde Street Pier

(415) 561-7100; (415) 556-6435 Sea Festival
Hyde Street at Jefferson Street, San Francisco, CA 94109
<www.nps.gov/safr/local/ship.html>

Description: A short distance from the Maritime Museum, there are 8 ships docked here, ranging from the full-rigged *Balclutha* to steam schooners, tugboats, and a ferry. This collection of ships is a nice sample of the ships in San Francisco Bay at the turn of the 19th century.
Hours: 9:30am–5pm regular hours. *Summer hours* (May 15–September 16): 9:30am–5:30pm. Last admission ½ hour before closing. Closed Christmas Day, New Year's Day, and Thanksgiving Day.
Cost: $5/adult; joint individual ticket to Hyde Street Pier and the submarine, *U.S.S. Pampanito*: $10; joint family ticket to Hyde Street Pier and *Pampanito*: $27.
Bathrooms: Yes.
Facilities: Limited stroller accessibility, good idea to bring baby in a baby carrier. Stroller accessible on the main decks of the boats, but then there are stairs to navigate.
Food: Nearby restaurants.
What to Bring: Jacket, sunglasses, cash, and camera.
Follow-Up Activities: Living History Days, Sea Music Festival/concerts, Gold Rush lectures, engine room tours, and more are available as special programs. Living History Days are scheduled on the second Saturday of each month from 10am–3pm. The engine room tours of the different vessels are on one Sunday a month. The Annual Sea Music Festival is on a

Saturday in the fall from 10am–5pm. The Sea Festival has hands-on kids' arts and crafts along with special performances for children. $5 donation suggested. Events calendar: <www.nps.gov/safr/local/calendar.html>. You can also ask to be put on the mailing list to receive the quarterly calendar.

Presidential Yacht Potomac (All Ages)
Jack London Square
(510) 627-1215 Voice Mail; (510) 627-1502 Recording
540 Water Street, Oakland, CA 94607
<www.usspotomac.org>

Description: This yacht is otherwise known as President F.D. Roosevelt's "floating White House" and has hosted many presidential events. It has been restored and provides public cruises on select days.

Hours: *Dockside Tours*: Wed. 10am–2pm, Sat/Sun: noon–4pm, with tickets sold 45 minutes before closing. Call (510) 627-1502 to confirm hours prior to your visit. *Two Hour History Tours* around SF Bay: August and September on Saturdays at 10am & 1:30pm.

Cost: *Two Hour Cruises*: $35/adult, $27/senior 60+, $25/person for groups of 20+, $15/youth 6–12 years old, free for children 5 and under. You can order tickets on-line or by calling 1-866-468-3399 or from <www.ticketweb.com>.

Bathrooms: Yes.

Facilities: Bring baby in baby carrier.

Food: Nearby restaurants in Jack London Square.

What to Bring: Jacket, sunglasses, cash, and camera.

S. S. Jeremiah O'Brien (Ages 3+)
(415) 544-0100; Pier 45 Fisherman's Wharf, San Francisco, CA
<www.geocities.com/jeremiahobrien/obrien.html>
<www.ssjeremiahobrien.org>

Description: This is an operational World War II cargo liberty ship.

Hours: Daily 9am–5pm. Closed major holidays. On the third weekend of each month, except May and December, the ship starts its engines to show off its engine and galley stove. Call to confirm dates, as it may be rescheduled due to holidays. Tours are available if reserved two weeks in advance.

Cost: $6/adult, $5/senior, $3/child under 14, free for military in uniform and for children under 6.
Bathrooms: Yes.
Facilities: Stroller friendly.
Food: Nearby.
What to Bring: Jacket, sunscreen, sunglasses, picnic lunch, and cash for parking and food.
Follow-Up Activities: 1) Birthday parties. 2) Cruises in May for Memorial Day require advanced reservations. Cost is $100/person. 3) You can also take a cruise during Fleet Week onboard the *S.S. Jeremiah O'Brien*. It costs $125 per person.

U.S.S. Pampanito (All Ages)
(415) 775-1943; Pier 45 Fisherman's Wharf, San Francisco, CA
<www.maritime.org/pamphome.htm >

Description: *The USS Pampanito* (SS-383) is a World War II Balao class fleet submarine.
Hours: *Mid-October–May:* Sun–Thur: 9am–6pm; *End of May–mid-October:* Thur–Tues: 9am–8pm, and Wed: 9am–6pm.
Cost: $8/adult, $4/child (6–12), free /child under 6 with an adult. $22/family (2 adults and up to 4 children). $27/joint family ticket to *Pampanito* and Hyde Street Pier.
Bathrooms: Public restrooms at the end of the pier.
Facilities: Not stroller friendly. Bring baby in baby carrier.
Food: Many restaurants nearby in Ghiradelli Square, Fisherman's Wharf, and Pier 39. Consider having lunch or dinner at the *Rainforest Café* just a few steps away, next to *Ripley's Believe It or Not!*
What to Bring: Camera, jacket, comfortable walking shoes, cash for food and parking.
Follow-Up Activities: Cable car terminus at Fisherman's Wharf, just a few steps away from the Maritime Museum, *USS Pampanito*, and the Hyde Street Pier.

U.S.S. Hornet Museum (Ages 5+)
(510) 521-8448; Pier 3, Alameda Point, Alameda, CA 94501
<www.uss-hornet.org>

Description: World War II era aircraft carrier known for its combat record and for its recovery of the Apollo 11 command module. Tours of many parts of the carrier are led by docents starting at 11am.

Hours: 10 am–5pm. Last entry at 4pm. Closed Tuesdays.

Cost: $12/adult, $7/senior, $8/child 5–18.

Bathrooms: Yes.

Facilities: Lots of stairs and ladders. Wheelchair accessible, but limited to the main flight deck. If you have a little baby/toddler, be prepared to put your little one in a baby carrier.

Food: No food available.

What to Bring: Camera, jacket, comfortable walking shoes, cash, picnic lunch and drinks.

Follow-Up Activities: 1) Independence Day celebration with music and children's activities. Celebration is from 4–7pm with fireworks viewing afterward. Call for special event prices. 2) *Western Aerospace Museum,* located at Oakland International Airport, North Field, is close by: 8268 Boeing Street, Building 621, Oakland, CA 94621. (510) 638-7100. For more information, refer to the Airplane Museum section in this chapter.

Trains

Both boys and girls seem to have a special love affair with trains. There are mini-trains in the zoos and parks, big steam trains, and commercial trains of CalTrain, Light-rail, and Amtrak. Take a leisurely ride, enjoy the scenery, and expose your child to the of sights and sounds of the city or the countryside. This section is divided into mini-trains, big trains, public trains, and railroad museums.

Mini-Trains at Parks & Zoos

Bianchi Railway Co. (All Ages)

Central Park, San Mateo

(650) 340-1520; El Camino Real & 5ᵗʰ Avenue, San Mateo, CA 94402

Hours: *Weekdays:* 10:30am–12:45pm, *Weekends:* 11am–3pm.

Cost: $1/ride.
Facilities: Stroller friendly.
Food: Snack stand with popcorn, snow cones, sodas, hot dogs, etc.
Stand Hours: 1–3pm on weekdays, and 11am–4pm on weekends. Closed Thursdays.
What to Bring: Picnic lunch, cash for the rides, sunscreen, and sunglasses.

Bonfante Gardens Theme Park (All Ages)
(408) 840-7100; 3050 Hecker Pass Highway, Gilroy, CA 95020
<www.bonfantegardens.com>

See full entry in Chapter 6: Transportation Favorites—Boats section.
Cost: Included with park admission.

Casa de Fruta (All Ages)
(831) 637-0051; (800) 543-1702 Mail Order
6680 Pacheco Pass Highway, Hollister CA 95023
<www.casadefruta.com>

Description: Has a miniature train and a zoo. See full entry in Chapter 1: Animal Kingdom—Farms section.
Hours: Call to confirm zoo and train operating schedule: 1-800-548-3813. Closed January and February. March–December, hours are generally 7am–9pm. Call ahead to confirm hours.
Cost: *Fun Pass:* $4.99/person includes a ride on the train, one admission to the zoo, and a bag of popcorn. *Two-Day Fun Pass:* $9.99/person with unlimited rides on the train and unlimited admission to the zoo during the two days. *Annual Pass:* $14.99/person with unlimited admission to the train and zoo, 10% discount at the motel and birthday party packages.
Bathrooms: Yes.
Facilities: Stroller friendly.
Food: Casa de Coffee restaurant (open 24 hours), a deli, and a fruit stand for snacks. Casa de Sweets has ice cream, coffees, and pies. Picnic grounds.
What to Bring: Sunscreen, sunglasses, camera, picnic lunch and drinks, and cash for train rides and food purchase.
Follow-Up Activities: For special events, check the Web site calendar. See full entry in Chapter 1: Animal Kingdom—Farms section.

Children's Fairyland (All Ages)

(510) 452-2259; 699 Bellevue Avenue, Oakland, CA 94610
<www.fairyland.org>

Cost: Included with park admission. See the full entry in Chapter 7: Arts & Performing Arts—Children's Theater section.

Grant Road Pumpkin Patch (All Ages)

Grant Road and Covington, Mountain View, CA 94040

Description: In October, for Halloween, there are a few animals and a pyramid of hay bales for kids to play with, a miniature train, and a pumpkin patch, of course.

Hours: Train open only during Halloween and Christmas seasons.

Cost: Free mini-train rides.

Happy Hollow Park and Zoo (All Ages)

(408) 277-3000; 1300 Senter Road, San Jose, CA 95112
<www.happyhollowparkandzoo.org>

See full entry in Chapter 1: Animal Kingdom—Zoos & Wildlife Museums section.

Hours: Train operates spring through summer 11am–4pm, depending on staffing. Call first to check since it varies day by day.

Cost: Train rides cost $1.75/person.

Directions: Train is located on the right field, outside of the main entrance.

Kennedy Park (All Ages)

(510) 670-7275; 19501 Hesperian Boulevard, Hayward, CA 94541
<www.haywardrec.org> or email: parkdept@haywardrec.org

Description: This park is home to the Triple Pines Ranch petting zoo, the miniature train, and a merry-go-round. It has pony rides and a bouncer, too. There's plenty of picnic areas, a playground, and tennis and horseshoe courts.

Hours: Open 11:30am–4:30pm on weekends, most holidays, and during school breaks.

Cost: Everyone must have a ticket, including infants and accompanying adults, on the merry-go-round, Triple Pines Ranch, and the train. Tickets sold at the snack bar. $1/ticket for the train, merry-go-round, bouncer, and petting zoo. The pony ride is $1.35/ride. *Discount* packages available for train, bouncer, merry-go-round, and Triple Pines Ranch:

Special Tickets $2.80 for 3–$1.00 tickets (single ticket)

Package A $20 for 25–$1.00 tickets (single ticket)

Package B $70 for 100–$1.00 tickets (separate tickets)

Bathrooms: Yes.

Facilities: Stroller friendly.

Food: Snack bar.

What to Bring: Sunscreen, sunglasses, picnic lunch, and cash for rides and food.

Lemos Farm (All Ages)

(650) 726-2342;

12320 San Mateo Road (Highway 92), Half Moon Bay, CA 94019

< www.hauntedbay.com/reviews/lemospastorinos.shtml>

Description: This farm has a petting zoo, pony rides, train, hayride, and jumper. In October, the haunted house, pumpkin patch, and hayrides are open for Halloween. In November and December, Christmas trees are available. Traffic can be extremely challenging during special events weekends such as the Pumpkin Festival Weekend.

Hours: Sat & Sun: 9am–5pm.

Cost: Admission is free, but rides cost extra. $4/pony ride, $2.50/train ride, $2.50/hayride, and the jumper costs $4/child. *Day pass*: $13/person for unlimited rides.

What to Bring: Sunscreen, sunglasses, cash, picnic lunch and drinks, and camera.

Follow-Up Activities: 1) Birthday parties offered. 2) Pastorino's Pumpkin Farm (650-726-6440, 8:30am–5:30pm daily) and Arata Pumpkin Farm (650-726-4359, 8am–6pm daily) are close by. Pastorino's has tractor and pony rides.

Oak Meadow Park/Vasona Park (All Ages)

Billy Jones Wildcat Railroad/ W.E. Mason Carousel

(408) 395-7433; Blossom Hill Road, Los Gatos, CA 95032

Train: <www.bjwrr.com>; Train and Carousel:

<www.los-gatos.ca.us/los_gatos/parks_and_rec/billy_jones_rr/bjwrr.html>

Map:< www.los-gatos.ca.us/los_gatos/gifs/oakmeado.html>

Description: This popular playground has a decommissioned airplane, an old-fashioned fire engine, an operating antique carousel, and a miniature train that loops between Oak Meadow and the adjacent Vasona Lake Park. Don't miss the turnaround at the end of the railroad. After your ride, go to the end of the train tracks and watch how the engine is manually turned around for another trip. During the winter, the ducks are in residence along the creek. Hidden spots along the creek provide wonderful opportunities to watch ducks in the winter months and sometimes ducklings in the early spring.

Hours: *Park Hours:* 10am–5pm. *Train Hours:* Spring (Starting March 15): Weekends 10:30am–4:30pm; Summer (Starting with summer vacation): Daily 10:30am–4:30pm; Fall (Starting after Labor Day): Weekends: 10:30am–4:30pm; Winter (Starting November 1): Weekends 11am–3pm.

Carousel Hours: Spring (starting March 15), Wed–Fri: 10:30am–3pm, Sat–Sun 10:30am–4:30pm; Summer (Starting with summer vacation): Daily 10:30am–4:30pm; Fall (After Labor Day): Wed–Fri: 10:30am–3pm, Sat–Sun 10:30am–4:30pm; Winter: (Starting November 1) Weekends: 11am–3pm.

Cost: $5/car parking fee during the summer. $1.50/ride for train or carousel. Free/child 2 & under. One-year passes available.

Bathrooms: Yes, located next to the carousel.

Food: On weekends, the kiosk next to the train station is open for snack foods such as icees, popsicles, popcorn, and hot dogs.

What to Bring: Cash for the carousel, miniature train, and snacks. Picnic lunch, sunscreen, and sunglasses.

Follow-Up Activities: 1) Paddleboat and canoe rentals are available at adjacent Vasona Lake Park during the summer. There's a pathway that leads to Vasona Lake Park via the footbridge next to the train station and carousel area. 2) The train has special events during Halloween and Christmas: *Haunted Forest* and *Phantom Express Train* (in the evening), *Holiday Train of Lights,* and Christmas *Fantasy of Lights* drive-through in the adjacent Vasona Lake Park. See Vasona Lake entry for more information on the *Fantasy of Lights.*

Oakland Zoo (All Ages)

(510) 632-9523; 9777 Golf Links Road, Oakland, CA 94605
<www.oaklandzoo.org>

Description: C.P. Huntington miniature train, a replica of the Civil War era train.
Hours: Daily 11am–4pm in the rides area (next to the main zoo entrance).
Cost: $1–$2 per ride.
See the full Oakland Zoo entry in Chapter 1: Animal Kingdom—Zoos & Wildlife Museums section.

Redwood Valley Railway (All Ages)
Tilden Regional Park

(510) 548-6100 Steam train; (510) 562-PARK Park info.
For *Mapquest.com* directions, enter:
Lomas Cantadas Rd & Grizzly Peak Boulevard, Orinda, CA 94563
Steam train: <www.redwoodvalleyrailway.com or www.ebparks.org/parks/tilden.htm>

Description: For a full description of the park, look in the Tilden Nature Study Area entry in Chapter 1: Animal Kingdom—Farms section.
Hours: *Winter* (September–May): Weekends and holidays: 11am–6pm. *Summer* (June 14–Labor Day): Weekends and holidays: 11am –6pm, Mon–Fri: noon–5pm. Closed Thanksgiving and Christmas Days.
Cost: No parking fee, $1.75/ride. $7/5-ride family ticket, free/child under 2.

San Francisco Zoo (All Ages)

(415) 753-7080; 1 Zoo Road, San Francisco, CA 94132
<www.sanfranciscozoo.org>

Cost: Little Puffer rides and Dentzel Carousel rides: $2/person (free for adult standing with the child on the carousel). See the full San Francisco Zoo entry in Chapter 1: Animal Kingdom—Zoos & Wildlife Museums section.

Uesugi Farms Pumpkin Patch (All Ages)

(408) 778-7225; (408) 842-1294 Office
14485 Monterey Highway, San Martin, CA 95037
Virtual photo tour: <www.sjsu.edu/faculty/satoru/LIB/ppatch1.htm>

Description: Learn how pumpkins grow from Uesugi Farms. An exhibit shows the development of the pumpkin from seed to seedling to plant to baby pumpkin to orange pumpkin. There's an accompanying educational video. The grounds are beautifully designed with scarecrows, a miniature train ride through a haunted tunnel, and a pumpkin vine tunnel for all to explore.

Hours: Open only in October. During the first week: 10am–6pm. Extended hours from 9am–9pm as it gets closer to Halloween. Call to confirm hours and costs.

Big Trains

Ardenwood Historic Farm Regional Park (All Ages)

(510) 796-0663; (510) 791-4196 Patterson House
34600 Ardenwood Boulevard, Fremont, CA 94555
<www.ebparks.org/parks/arden.htm>

Description: The horse-drawn train operates on special event days with costumed brakemen and drivers. The blacksmiths demonstrate how to shape iron and steel into boxcar parts. The carpenters make mortise and tenon joints to repair cars. Laborers lay track and the mechanics repair the brakes. See full entry in Chapter 1: Animal Kingdom—Farms section.

Hours: From April to mid-November, the horse-drawn train runs on Thur, Fri, & Sun 10am–4pm. Closed in the winter from mid-November through March.

Cost: Train ride is included with admission of $5/adult, $4/senior, $3/child, free/child 3 & under.

Follow-Up Activities: Historic Rail Fair over Labor Day weekend and Haunted Train are special events. Check the Ardenwood Historic Farm Regional Park calendar for events <www.fremont.gov/recreation/ardenwoodpark>.

Niles Canyon Railway & Museum (All Ages)
Pacific Locomotive Associations Museum
(925) 862-9063; (408) 249-2953 Reservations
Sunol Depot: 6 Kilkare Road, Sunol, CA 94586
<www.ncry.org>

Description: This was part of the first transcontinental railroad. There are steam and skunk trains.

Hours: 1st & 3rd Sundays of each month. Sunday operations 10am–4pm. Check Web site for departure times. Allow 1 hour for round trip. From December to March, departures start at 10:30am.

Cost: Donation request: $8/adult, $7/senior, $4/child 3+. Holiday trains (Holiday Train of Lights with Santa) $10/person (ages 3+). New Year's Train with lights, also $10/person (ages 3+).

Bathrooms: Portables by the parking lot only.

Facilities: Wheelchair accessible train. Baby carrier or umbrella stroller highly recommended.

Food: No food available onboard or at the depot. Some cafés and restaurants close by.

What to Bring: Sunscreen, sunglasses, picnic lunch, cash, and camera.

Follow-Up Activities: 1) Holiday Train of Lights (train is lit up with beautiful lights) with Santa is in December. Tends to sell out early, so make your reservations to avoid disappointment. *Auld Lang Syne Express* just after Christmas has the same lights on the train but no Santa. In the past, it ran from Fri–Sun, December 27–29 with 4:30pm and 7pm departures. These rides are $10 and may be purchased from Pacific Locomotive Association (or just "PLA") at 5943 Monzal Avenue, Oakland, CA 94611. Get the order form on-line and mail to above address, or call to order tickets (510) 658-8812. 2) Spend a few minutes in the museum to see the collection of old steam and diesel trains.

Railtown 1897 State Historic Park (All Ages)
(209) 984-3953; (916) 445-6645 Recording
5th & Reservoir Streets, Jamestown, CA
P.O. Box 1250, Jamestown, CA 95327
<www.californiastaterailroadmuseum.org>
<www.parks.ca.gov/default.asp?page_id=491>

Description: These steam and diesel trains have been featured in Hollywood productions such as "Little House on the Prairie," "High

Noon," and "Back to the Future." See the train engines used as movie props in the Roundhouse. For train aficionados only, the Roundhouse tour provides insight into the technology of steam engines, how to put new wheels on the train, how the turntable operates, and how replacement parts for the trains were made in the machine shop.

Hours: Railtown Depot Store & Center: Daily 9:30am–4:30pm. Closed Thanksgiving, Christmas, and New Year's Day. Steam trains: Hourly departures 11am–3pm on weekends April–October, which run a six mile loop for ~40 minutes. In November, trains run only on Saturdays. Roundhouse tours start at 10:10am and depart hourly, with the last tour departing at 3:10pm. Call ahead to confirm times and costs.

Cost: Free park admission. *Guided Roundhouse Tours*: $2/adult, $1/youth 6–12, free for children ages 5 & under. *Steam Train Rides*: $6/adult, $3/ youth (ages 6–12), free for children ages 5 & under.

Bathrooms: Yes, at the depot.

Facilities: Stroller friendly in the park, not on the train. You can leave the stroller with the cashier at the Depot Store.

Food: No. Picnic tables.

What to Bring: Picnic lunch, drinks, sunscreen, sunglasses, and camera.

Follow-Up Activities: 1) For special events such as Thomas the Train, check the Web site: <www.csrmf.org/doc.asp?id=390>. 2) Close to Columbia State Historic Park, a working historic town preserved from the 1850s Gold Rush Era. See Chapter 9: Historic Outings—Gold Rush section for more information.

Roaring Camp Railroads (All Ages)
(831) 335-4484; Graham Hill Road, Felton, CA 95018
<www.roaringcamp.com>

Description: Nestled in the Santa Cruz mountains and surrounded by redwoods, Roaring Camp Railroads provides a beautiful ride through the redwoods on a big steam train or a visit to Santa Cruz Beach Boardwalk by train.

Hours: 10am–5pm.

Cost: Steam trains through the redwoods: $15.50/adult, $10.50/child 3–12, free/child under 3 years old. Beach trains: Require 3 hours round trip. Beach trains go between Felton and Santa Cruz Beach Boardwalk ($17/adult, $13/child 3–12, free/child under 3 years old).

Bathrooms: Yes, at the depot.

Facilities: Stroller friendly in the park.

Food: Café on site. Picnic tables available.

What to Bring: Sunscreen, hat, and sunglasses. Picnic lunch and water bottles.

Follow-Up Activities: Lots of special events such as Day Out with Thomas the Train, Great Train Robbery reenactments, 1880s Harvest Fair in October (showcase old-fashioned crafts such as spinning, weaving, candle making, and pumpkin carving), and Pioneer Christmas in mid-December. In the summer, gold panning on certain weekends for an additional $5. You are guaranteed to find real gold in the dirt. Call in advance to see if it is being offered. School groups can arrange for these activities in advance. Check the Web site for event calendar.

Traintown (All Ages)

(707) 938-3912; (707) 996-2559

20264 Broadway - Hwy 12, Sonoma, CA 95476

<www.traintown.com>

Description: Besides the trains and the rides, there is a small petting zoo with llamas, sheep, goats, and ducks.

Hours: *June 1–Labor Day:* 10am–5pm; *September 1–May:* Fri–Sun: 10am–5pm. Not all rides open on Fridays. Trains run every ½ hour. Open major holidays except Thanksgiving and Christmas.

Cost: Train fare: $3.25/child or senior, $3.75/adult; rides on merry-go-round, ferris wheel, etc. are $1.25 – $1.75 per ticket. You can purchase a book of 8 tickets for $10.

Bathrooms: Yes, but no baby changing stations.

Facilities: Stroller friendly.

Food: Yes.

What to Bring: Sunscreen, sunglasses, picnic lunch, cash, and camera.

Public Trains

Depending on your location, it might be more accessible for you to ride the commuter trains and light-rails during noncommute times.

Cable Cars, San Francisco (Ages 4+)

(415) 673-6864; San Francisco, CA
<www.sfcablecar.com>

Description: This world-famous symbol of San Francisco is well worth a visit, even for locals who have never taken a trip. It's a wonderful experience. There are two lines: the Powell–Mason line and the Powell–Hyde line. The originating station for both lines is at Powell and Market streets. The Powell–Mason cable car line runs from Powell and Market to Bay Street at Fisherman's Wharf. The Powell–Hyde line goes to the Ghiradelli Square end of Fisherman's Wharf. For a route map: <www.sfcablecar.com/routes.html>. I recommend the age minimum to be at least four because care must be taken on the cable car; please use your best judgment. Note also that the extreme popularity of the cable cars, especially during tourist season and on weekends, can be very challenging, with very long lines. The best time to attempt this is in the early morning on weekends. You may also want to take the taxi to go back to the originating station due to crowds.

Hours: Runs daily with special weekend and holiday schedules. Check the Web site for schedule information for San Francisco light-rail, cable cars, trolley bus, and buses at: <www.sfcablecar.com/riders.html>.

Cost: $2/person one-way. Free for children under 4. You may also consider purchasing a day pass ($6/person), which allows you to ride on streetcars, buses, and cable cars.

Bathrooms: No.

Facilities: Not stroller friendly.

Food: No. Restaurants nearby at the termini: Fisherman's Wharf/Ghiradelli Square and Downtown San Francisco.

What to Bring: Jacket, sunglasses, camera, cash for fare (exact fare) and food.

Follow-Up Activities: 1) Cable Car Bell Ringing Competition event has the gripmen ring out melodies on the cable car bells. It was traditionally held on the 3rd Thursday in July. However, in 2002 and 2003, the competition was held in October. For current information, call in June to confirm. This event is held at Union Square at noon. Free to the public. For additional information, visit <www.sfmuni.com> or call. 2) Visit the cable car museum to better understand how the cable system works. See Cable Car Museum entry in the Train Museums section.

California Trolley & Railroad (Trolley Barn) (All Ages)

History Park, San Jose

(408) 287-2290; 1600 Senter Road, San Jose, CA 95112

<www.ctrc.org>

Description: Operational historic trolleys run on the weekends. The Trolley Barn houses a wonderful collection of antique trolleys and cars, definitely worth a visit for the train lover. Small model train on the side of the Trolley Barn. See full entry in Chapter 9: Historical Outings.

Hours: Thur–Mon: 9am–4pm. Closed Tues & Wed.

Light-Rail (MUNI Light-rail, San Francisco) (All Ages)

(415) 673-6864; San Francisco, CA

<www.sfmuni.com>

Description: There are 5 light-rail lines. The *N-Judah line* goes from the CalTrain Station on 4th & King to Ocean Beach via Judah Ave. The *J-Church line* goes from the Embarcadero via Church to Glen Park. *The L-Taraval line* goes from the Embarcadero and San Francisco Zoo. The *M-Ocean View line* goes from Embarcadero to Balboa Park via St Francis Circle, Stonestown, and San Francisco State University. The *K-Ingleside line* goes between Embarcadero and Balboa Park via Junipero Serra and Ocean and San Francisco City College. For a route map: <www.transitinfo.org/cgi-bin/muni/map/metro>.

Hours: For schedules, see Web site: <www.transitinfo.org/cgi-bin/muni/timetable#Light>.

Cost: $1/adult; 35cents/senior 65+, youth (5–17), or disabled person; free/child 4 & under.

Bathrooms: None onboard.

Facilities: Not all stations are stroller friendly; plan accordingly.

Food: No.

What to Bring: Exact fare required. Subway turnstiles require coins.

Light-Rail (VTA Light-rail, San Jose)

(408) 321-2300; San Jose, CA

San Jose: <www.vta.org/services/light_rail_services.html>

Description: The light-rail in Silicon Valley operates between downtown Mountain View through Sunnyvale and Santa Clara to the edge of Milpitas and south through downtown San Jose to Santa Teresa. Visit the map Web page <www.vta.org/schedules/SC_901_MAP.GIF> for more specific information on stations.

Hours: Operates 24 hours a day and seven days a week. See Web site for specific schedules: <www.vta.org/schedules/light_rail_schedules.html>.

Cost: Single ride tickets: $1.40/adult, 85cents/child 5–17, 45 cents/ senior or disabled person. Other fares available on the Web site: <www.vta.org/schedules/fares.html#Fares>.

Bathrooms: None onboard.

Facilities: Wheelchair accessible. Umbrella stroller highly recommended.

Food: Not onboard. Plan accordingly.

What to Bring: Exact fare. Drivers do not give change. Ticket vending machines do not provide change in nickels or dimes.

Follow-Up Activities: Historic Trolley Service runs April–September and during the Christmas season. The vehicles run 10:30am–5:30pm. These trolleys provide service between the San Jose Convention Center and the San Jose Civic Center. Historic trolleys do not have wheelchair access.

CalTrain
1(800) 660-4287
<www.caltrain.com>

Description: CalTrain services the San Francisco peninsula between San Francisco and Gilroy. 1) Consider taking a short trip from the Mountain View station to the San Jose Arena station; walk about 2 blocks to Arena Green with a carousel, playground, and concessions. The Arena Green Children's Carousel costs $1/ride. Hours vary seasonally, but it is open at least: Tues–Sun: 11am–4pm. During the summer it is also open on Mondays and has extended hours: 10am–7pm. For the most current information, call (408) 999-6817 for carousel operation information or see the Web site: <www.grpg.org/ArenaGreen.html>. For the Park Rangers at the Guadalupe River Park & Gardens Visitor Center: (408) 277-5904. The *Children's Carousel* is located at Autumn and Santa Clara Streets, directly across from the San Jose Arena on Autumn Street. 2) Alternatively you can take a short trip between the Mountain View station and Palo Alto California station. The Mountain View Evelyn Ave station is in downtown Mountain View, just a short block to Castro Street with its many restaurants and shops. The Palo Alto California station also has many restaurants and shops and a neighborhood park nearby. Bowden Park is located at 2380 High Street/Alma Street at Oregon Expressway, about two blocks away from the California Station.

Hours: For stations, schedules, and fares, visit the Web site.

Cost: Fares depend on distance. See Web site for more information. For example, between San Francisco 4th St and King station to Lawrence station in Sunnyvale, the one-way fare is $5.25 and the trains run approximately every ½ hour, with more frequent departures during the evening commute between 5 and 6pm.

Bathrooms: At some stations.

Facilities: Wheelchair accessible from most stations. Umbrella stroller or baby carrier is highly recommended.

Food: No, none onboard.

What to Bring: Picnic lunch, snacks, water bottles, cash for fare and food.

Follow-Up Activities: For those able and willing to walk a bit, CalTrain's San Francisco terminus is close to the Modern Art Museum and the Yerba Buena Gardens, about 6–7 city blocks from King and 4th Street, in the direction of Market Street.

BART (Bay Area Rapid Transit)

(510) 236-2278 Richmond/El Cerrito
(510) 465-2278 Oakland/Berkeley/Orinda
(415) 989-2278 San Francisco/Daly City
(650) 992-2278 South San Francisco/San Bruno/San Mateo
(925) 676-2278 Concord/Walnut Creek/Lafayette/Antioch/Pittsburgh/Livermore
(510) 441-2278 Hayward/San Leandro/Fremont/Union City/Dublin/Pleasanton
<www.bart.gov>

Description: BART is a public transportation system that extends from Downtown San Francisco to the East Bay and Fremont. Use the trip planner on the Web site to help you navigate the BART system and to find out how much fare you will need: <www.bart.gov/stations/tripPlanner/tripPlanner.asp>.

Hours: *Mon–Fri:* 4am–midnight, *Sat:* 6am–midnight, *Sun & Holidays:* 8am–midnight. For schedules of the BART trains at each station: <www.bart.gov/stations/schedules/lineSchedules.asp>.

Cost: Fares vary depending on distance. Here's an example of a one-way adult fare: From Fremont station in Fremont to the Downtown San Francisco Powell Street Station, the fare is $4.25. Children under 5 ride for free. You can purchase discounted tickets. Children 5 to 12 years old: $16 ticket costs only $4 (75% discount).

Bathrooms: At some stations.

Facilities: There are elevators available, but many stations require assistance of the station agent, who can be reached via the white courtesy phones. I'd recommend using a baby carrier or umbrella stroller that is light and can be easily folded up. Access to the station is most convenient on the escalators.

Food: No. Some stations may have street vendors outside.

What to Bring: Tickets can be purchased from ticket machines. These machines will accept cash: from coins up to $20 bills. Some stations have ticket machines that will accept credit cards. If you're planning on a long ride, consider bringing some reading materials or things for your little ones to do during the ride.

Follow-Up Activities: If you take BART to the Powell Street Station in downtown San Francisco, consider taking the cable car to Fisherman's Wharf or Ghiradelli Square or the Maritime Museum and Hyde Street Pier. See the Cable Car entry for more navigation details. This will be a long day, considering the lengths of the trips both on BART and on the cable car. I do not recommend this outing for younger children unless someone will meet you with the car at one of these destinations to drive home.

Train Museums

Golden Gate Live Steamers Club (All Ages)
Tilden Park, Grizzly Peak & Lomas Cantadas Road, Berkeley, CA 94708
<www.ggls.org>

Description: Located next to the Redwood Valley Railway, this club is one of the oldest steam train clubs in the country. The club members built the trains, which run on coal, diesel, propane, or even car batteries. For a full description of the park, look in the Tilden Nature Study Area entry in

Chapter 1: Animal Kingdom—Farms section.

Hours: Rides on passenger trains on Sundays noon–3pm, weather permitting.

Cost: Free.

Golden Gate Model Railroad Club (All Ages)
Located in the basement of the Randall Museum
(415) 346-3303; 199 Museum Way, San Francisco, CA 94114
<www.ggmrc.org>

Description: There's an HO scale model railroad layout with trains from 1938–1955 as well as modern trains. Thse model trains have freight and passenger cars. See the Randall Museum entry in Chapter 4: Science Museums.

Hours: Sat: 11am–4pm.

Cost: Free

Golden State Model Railroad Museum (All Ages)
(510) 234-4884; 900 Dornan Drive, Point Richmond, CA 94801
<www.gsmrm.org>

Description: This model railroad museum has N, HO, and O scale layouts of model trains on display. *Scale* refers to the proportion of the model size to the actual real size of trains. These model railroads display California scenery and use models of trains from many eras, from traditional steam engines to the most modern diesels.

Hours: *Weekends*: noon–5pm. Open on these holidays: President's Day, Memorial Day, July 4, and Labor Day. Closed January through March. Check the Web site for the "Schedule of Operations" for when the scale models will be running. Some days all three scale model layouts are operating, while on other days only two layouts are running.

Cost: Sundays and Holidays: $3/adult, $2/senior or child under 12, $7/family. Free admission on Saturdays, but model trains will not be operating.

Bathrooms: Yes.

Facilities: Stroller friendly.

Food: No.

What to Bring: Picnic lunch and cash for entry.

Golden Gate Railroad Museum (Ages 6+)
(415) 822-8728; Hunter's Point Naval Shipyard, San Francisco, CA
<www.ggrm.org>

Description: Authentic period trains from steam trains to passenger, freight, and commuter trains are included in this collection.
Hours: Weekends: 10am–5pm. Tours are available to groups Mon–Fri by appointment only.
Cost: $5/adult, $2/child or senior.
Bathrooms: Portables.
Facilities: Strollers OK, but not inside the railcars. Recommend baby carrier or backpack.
Food: No. Picnic area.
What to Bring: At the security gate, visitors must show valid driver's license, car registration, and proof of vehicle insurance. All visitors, except small children, must show picture ID.
Follow-Up Activities: 1) Spring Train Festival in early May, 11am–4pm, held in conjunction with the open studios of Hunter's Point Artists. For more information about the artist studios: <**www.zpub.com/sf/thepoint**>. 2) Birthday parties: You can rent a train and drive it alongside the engineer. Visit the Web site and call Dee at (408) 943-0515 for details and reservations.

San Francisco Cable Car Museum (Ages 5+)
(415) 474-1887; 1201 Mason Street, San Francisco, CA 94108
<**www.cablecarmuseum.com**>

Description: This museum shows how the cable system works. A video show of the San Francisco cable car system plays every 17 minutes. Best of all, the underground cable system can be viewed during its operation here at the museum.
Hours: *April–September:* Daily 10am–6pm, *October –March*: Daily 10am–5pm. Closed Thanksgiving, Christmas, and New Year's Day.
Cost: Free admission.
Bathrooms: Yes.
Facilities: Stroller friendly.
Food: No.
What to Bring: Jacket and cash for parking.
Follow-Up Activities: The Web site shows how cable cars work in the

"Anatomy of How a Cable Car Works" section. There are also pictures of historic cable cars, and a cable car timeline for additional insights. You may also want to visit <www.sfcablecar.com>

South Bay Historical Railroad Society (All Ages)

(408) 243-3969; 1005 Railroad Avenue, Santa Clara, CA 95050
<www.sbhrs.org>

Description: This museum is dedicated to the preservation and renovation of the historic Santa Clara Depot. The museum is a complex of historic buildings that gave this organization life. Besides operational scale model railroads on display, there are railroad artifacts, railroad signaling equipment, and right-of-way maps. There's also a library with a collection of railroading books and videos. Perhaps the best part of this museum is its proximity to the Union Pacific Santa Clara freight yard, where both freight and commuter trains can be seen and heard.
Hours: *Tues:* 6–9pm. *Sat:* 10am–3pm.
Cost: Free.
Bathrooms: Yes.
Facilities: Stroller friendly.
Food: No, restaurants across the street.
Follow-Up Activities: 1) Open House & Model Railroad Show first weekend in April and first weekend in November on both Sat & Sun: 10am–5pm. $3.50/adult, $1/child (6–17), $8/family. **2)** *Great American Train Shows:* All shows are 11am–5pm, $7/adult and free/child 12 and under. Discount coupon available on-line. Visit the Web site: <www.gats.com> for current information and show schedule. In general, the Train Show schedule is:

- March   Cal Expo, Sacramento; and Cow Palace, Daly City.
- May   Marin Center, San Rafael.
- December   Marin Center, San Rafael.

These shows tour the U.S. with the largest model railroad displays.

Tiburon Railroad–Ferry Depot Museum (All Ages)

(415) 435-1853; 1920 Paradise Drive, Tiburon, CA 94920
<www.weblink.com/landmarks/train XE "train" _ferry.html>

Description: This is a small museum with model train displays and historical exhibits of the old Tiburon trains.

Hours: Open April to October. Wed & Sun: 1–4pm.
Cost: Free. Donation appreciated.
Bathrooms: No, public restroom ½ block away.
Facilities: Stroller friendly.
Food: No, nearby restaurants.
What to Bring: Cash for parking, picnic lunch, sunscreen, and sunglasses.
Follow-Up Activities: Close to the Bay Area Discovery Museum in Sausalito and the Tiburon/Angel Island Ferry. See entries in Chapter 4: Science Museums and in Chapter 6: Transportation Favorites.

Western Railway Museum (All Ages)
(707) 374-2978; 5848 State Highway 12, Suisun, CA 94585
<www.wrm.org>

Description: This museum has 50 historic railcars on display as well as train rides on operational streetcars and interurban electric trains. The rides are unlimited with admission.
Hours: *Year-round:* Sat & Sun: 10:30am–5pm. *Summer extended days* (Memorial Day to Labor Day): Wed–Sun: 10:30am–5pm.
Cost: $7/adult, $6/senior 65+, $4/child.
Bathrooms: Yes.
Facilities: Stroller friendly.
Food: Café with hot dogs, ice cream, drinks, and snacks.
What to Bring: Cash, sunscreen, sunglasses, and camera.
Follow-Up Activities: Santa Trains run on the weekends in December prior to Christmas.

California State Railroad Museum (All Ages)
Out of Area
(916) 445-7387 Business Office; (916) 323-9280 Museum Front Desk
(916) 445-6645 Recording; 111 "I" Street, Sacramento, CA 95814
<www.Railtown1897.org>

Description: Located in Old Sacramento, this is considered to be one of the finest railroad museums in North America. The museum is housed in a complex of historic buildings with restored, authentic trains on display, as well as an operating steam train visitors can ride. There are changing exhibits such as the *Toy Trains on Parade* with a million-dollar toy train collection. Don't miss the *Evidence of a Dream* video documenting the importance of the railroad to California's growth and development. Docent-led tours follow the video. Tours last 30–40 minutes. Group tours can be scheduled in advance. For families, self-guided tours are available, with docents stationed throughout the museum to share their knowledge and answer questions.

Hours: Daily 10am–5pm. *Train rides*: Every weekend April–September. Depart hourly (11am–5pm) from the Central Pacific Railroad Freight Depot/Public Market in Old Sacramento, just two blocks south of the Railroad Museum on Front Street. *Evidence of a Dream* video shown hourly, on the hour. The video lasts approximately 20 minutes.

Cost: *Museum Admission:* $3/adult, free/youth or child 16 and under. *Train Tickets:* $6/adult, $3/ child 6–12, free/child 5 and under.

Bathrooms: Yes.

Facilities: Stroller friendly, except on certain exhibits due to stairs and in narrow openings on passenger trains.

Food: Silver Palace restaurant located in the Central Pacific Railroad Passenger Station, one block from the main entrance of the museum. Other restaurants are nearby.

What to Bring: Sunscreen, sunglasses, camera, and cash for food and parking.

Follow-Up Activities: 1) Visit Old Sacramento where this museum is located. This state park harkens back to the days of the Gold Rush. For additional information, see the Old Sacramento entry in Chapter 9: Historical Outings—Gold Rush section. 2) For special events such as *Day Out with Thomas* in June, *Gold Rush Days* on Labor Day weekend, *Spookomotive* Halloween trains, and *Santa's Yuletide Express* in December, check the Web site. 3) For school field trips, call for free tours by reserving with Reserve America at (866) 240-4655. 4) For more railroad and Gold Rush history, look up information from the California State Railroad Museum Web site: <www.csrmf.org/doc.asp?id=15>.

Directions: Public garage parking is located on either end of Old Sacramento, and metered parking is also available.

Airplanes

Mankind has been fascinated with flight: from the days of Greek myths and the story of Icharus and Daedulus, to the Renaissance and Leonardo da Vinci's models, to the first planes invented by the Wright Brothers, to today's supersonic jets and space shuttle. Of course, flight has to be experienced by taking a ride. Before taking the first trip with your little one, consider visiting the airport just to familiarize your child with the hustle and bustle. There are three international airports and numerous municipal airports in the Bay Area. Visit the aviation museums for the history of flight and historic aircraft. Best of all, attend an air show to see these wonderful machines in action.

For an answer to "How do Planes Fly?" visit the following Web sites:

<www.aero.hq.nasa.gov/edu>

<www.allstar.fiu.edu/aero/fltmidfly.htm>

Airports

Oakland International Airport

(510) 577-4000; 1 Airport Drive, Oakland, CA 94621

<www.flyoakland.com>

Bathrooms: Yes.

Facilities: Stroller friendly.

Food: Yes.

What to Bring: Cash for parking and cart.

Follow-Up Activities: Western Aerospace Museum and the *U.S.S. Hornet* are nearby.

San Jose International Airport (SJC)

(408) 501-7600 Admin.; 1732 N. First Street, Ste 600, San Jose, CA 95112
<www.sjc.org>

For Internet Mapping:

> Terminal A: 2077 Airport Boulevard, San Jose, CA 95110
> Terminal C: 1661 Airport Boulevard, San Jose, CA 95110
> Kidport, an aviation-themed play area, is located in the Main
> Lobby by the Information Booth.

San Francisco International Airport (SFO)

(650) 821-8211; South San Francisco, CA 94128
<www.flysfo.com>

Hours: Tours available, require advanced booking. Usually conducted Mon–Thur: 10:45am–12:45pm. Call the tour manager at (650) 821-5120.
Bathrooms: Yes.
Facilities: Stroller friendly.
Food: Yes.
What to Bring: Cash for parking and cart.
Follow-Up Activities: San Francisco Airport Museum is located within the terminal.

Watsonville Airport (Ages 8+)

(831) 728-6075; 100 Aviation Way, Watsonville, CA 95076
<www.watsonvilleairport.com>

Description: This small municipal airport has some wonderful events for plane enthusiasts. 1) On the first Saturday of each month, there's an *Antique & Classic Aircraft exhibit* on the ramp, in front of the terminal building. 2) May–November, on the first Saturday of each month 10am–3pm, the Experimental Aircraft Association Chapter 119 sponsors the Young Eagles Flight Rally and gives *free airplane rides* to youths ages 8–17. There's a short pre-flight class explaining the theory of flight, a safety inspection of an aircraft, then a 20 minutes flight around the Watsonville–Santa Cruz area. The release forms require parental approval and must be signed by parents. 3) *Watsonville Fly-In & Air Show* on Memorial Day Weekend every year. 4) There's also an *Airport Open House* in the fall. Visit the Web site for events schedule.

Cost: Free, except for the Fly-In & Air Show. See Air Shows section for more details.

Bathrooms: Yes.

Facilities: Stroller friendly.

Food: Yes.

What to Bring: Cash for food.

Air Shows

Air Expo at Moffett Field (All Ages)

(650) 568-7866; NASA Ames Research Center, Mountain View, CA
<http://airshownetwork.com/home.html>

Description: Air show display of historic and futuristic aircraft with aerobatics and a demonstration by the Navy's F/A 18 Hornet. There are combat rescue simulations and interactive displays, as well as the historic aircraft displays. In the past, educational booths for kids and even a moon rock were on display.

Schedule: Mid-September weekend: 9am–5pm.

Cost: $15/adult, $10/child (4–12), free/child 3 & under. $10 parking. For additional information, call (800) 367-5833 or purchase tickets via the Web site.

What to Bring: Sunscreen, sunglasses, camera, and cash for parking and food.

California International Air Show (All Ages)

Salinas Municipal Airport

1-888-845-SHOW

30 Mortensen Avenue, Salinas, CA 93905 (off of Highway 101)
<www.ca-airshow.com>; <www.salinasairshow.com>

Description: This weekend-long air show features U.S. Air Force *Thunderbirds*, the Stealth fighter, antique aircraft, and aerobatics. The Friday evening show has a fireworks display.

Schedule: Mid-October weekend starting at 9am. Flying events start at 11am. Visit Web site for most current information.

Cost: For tickets, call (800) 225-2277 or visit Web site at www.tickets.com.
Bathrooms: Yes.
Facilities: Stroller friendly.
Food: Yes.
What to Bring: Sunscreen, sunglasses, camera, and cash for parking and food.

Fleet Week in San Francisco (All Ages)

Pier 39, Beach Street & The Embarcadero, San Francisco, CA 94133
<www.military.com/Content/MoreContent1?file=main>
<www.airshownetwork.com>
<www.fishermanswharf.org/Events.htm>

Description: Fleet Week includes air shows and the *Parade of Ships* sponsored by the Navy.

Schedule: The event takes place usually on an October weekend at the San Francisco waterfront from the Ferry Building, along Fisherman's Wharf and on the Marina Green. The schedule of events usually includes a *Practice Air Show* on Friday afternoon at the Municipal Pier/San Francisco waterfront. *Parade of Ships* usually is on Saturday morning from 11am–noon, with the best view at the Marina Green. *Air Shows* (415) 487-6453 on both days noon –5pm, with the *Blue Angels* flying at 3pm. Pier 39 (415) 705-5500, Ghiradelli Square, Marina Green, The Cannery (415) 771-3112, and Muni Pier all have entertainment scheduled on both Sat & Sun.

Cost: Free along the waterfront, but premium seating can be purchased through the Air Show Network at the Web site above. Entertainment listed above is free except for food and parking. For discount coupons to businesses and attractions at Fisherman's Wharf, visit Fisherman's Wharf's Web site and look under "Discount Coupons."

Bathrooms: Yes.
Facilities: Stroller friendly.
Food: Yes.
What to Bring: Sunscreen, sunglasses, camera, cash for parking and food, and a jacket (San Francisco can be foggy and cold, even in the summer).

Pacific Coast Dream Machines (All Ages)
Half Moon Bay Airport
(650) 726-2328; HWY 1, 5 miles North of Hwy 92, Half Moon Bay, CA
<www.miramarevents.com>

Description: Display of 2000 driving, flying and working machines including classic cars, army tanks, antique motorcycles, military aircraft, Model-T cars, steam tractors and other farm equipment, race cars, and show planes. Helicopter and biplane rides are available. Live music and food booths.
Schedule: Last Sunday in April: 10am–4pm.
Cost: $15/adult, $5/senior 65+ or youth 5–17, free/child 4 & under. Parking included with admission. Tickets available at the gate only.
Bathrooms: Yes.
Facilities: Stroller friendly.
Food: Yes.
What to Bring: Sunscreen, sunglasses, camera, cash for parking and food, and jacket. The coast can be foggy and cold, even in the summer.

PortFest at Jack London Square
(510) 645-5968; Jack London Square, Oakland, CA 94607
<www.jacklondonsquare.com>

Description: The Annual PortFest is a "don't miss" event for boat and airplane enthusiasts. It includes an air show, free harbor boat tours, and a huge boat exhibit. There are even whale boat races and live music, dance, and stories.
Schedule: Saturday in early June: 11am–6pm.
Cost: Free to the event. $5 parking.
Bathrooms: Yes.
Facilities: Stroller friendly.
Food: Yes.
What to Bring: Sunscreen, sunglasses, hat, camera, comfortable walking shoes, and cash for parking and food.

Vertical Challenge Helicopter Air Show (All Ages)
Sponsored by the Hiller Aviation Museum
(650) 654-0200; 601 Skyway Road, San Carlos, CA 94070
<www.hiller.org>

Description: Besides performing flying feats, the air show exhibits the full range and use of helicopters, from military to lifesaving functions. Attractions include: helicopter rides; Otto the Clown helicopters; ShowCopters demonstrating formation maneuvers and the helicopter's versatility; search and rescue helicopter demonstrations; and firefighting, police, and emergency helicopters. There is also a pyrotechnics show from Canada.

Schedule: Event occurs in late June, with ticket sales starting June 1 at the Hiller Aviation Museum, 9am–5pm. Two air shows: 11:30 am morning air show and a different air show at 2pm in the afternoon.

Cost: $15/adult, $10/youth (8–17) or senior 65+, $10/child 5–7, free/child under 4.

Bathrooms: Yes.

Facilities: Stroller friendly.

Food: Yes.

What to Bring: Sunscreen, sunglasses, camera, and cash for food.

Watsonville Fly-In & Air Show
(831) 728-6075; 100 Aviation Way, Watsonville, CA 95076
<www.watsonvilleflyin.org>

Description: See daredevils stunts and aerobatics, military fly-bys, and military aircraft displays. Get a close-up view of antique aircraft, helicopters, military planes, and home-made aircraft, too. There are fireworks for the Friday night performance.

Schedule: Every Memorial Day Weekend.

Cost: Check Web site for ticket information.

Bathrooms: Yes.

Facilities: Stroller friendly.

Food: Yes.

What to Bring: Sunscreen, sunglasses, camera, and cash for food and parking.

Aviation Museums

Hiller Aviation Museum (Ages 4+)
(650) 654-0200; 601 Skyway Road, San Carlos, CA 94070
<www.hiller.org>

Description: The museum chronicles one hundred years of flight, with vintage aircraft, airplane models, prototypes of future aircraft, and pictures. The Restoration Shop shows restoration projects in progress. Docent-led tours and school field trips are available with advanced reservations. Don't miss the virtual exhibits on the Web showing different aircraft through the years, including the *Flying Platform*.
Hours: Daily 10am–5pm.
Cost: $8/adult, $5/senior 65+ or youth (8–17), free/child under 8. Get a $1 discount coupon from the Web site.
Bathrooms: Yes.
Facilities: Stroller friendly.
Food: Restaurants next door.
What to Bring: Picnic lunch or cash for food.
Follow-Up Activities: 1) Offers a *Young Eagles* program for children 8–17 to fly over San Francisco Bay for free on the third Saturday of each month from 11am–1pm at the San Carlos Airport. A legal guardian must sign the registration form. The flights are in a registered airplane flown by a licensed pilot. For more details: <www.hiller.org/education/young-eagles/young-eagles.html>. 2) Many special events offered by the museum, including the air show in June. Visit the Web site for current events schedule. 3) Summer camp available for children 10–15 years old. 4) A wonderful list of aviation resources for the Bay Area, including educational programs for young people, is on their Web site: <www.hiller.org/education/parent-resource.html>.

U.S.S. Hornet Museum (Ages 5+)
(510) 521-8448
Pier 3, Alameda Point, Alameda, CA 94501 (Atlantic Avenue and the Bay)
<www.uss-hornet.org>

Description: WW II-era aircraft carrier known for its combat record and for recovery of the Apollo 11 command module. Current displays include only a few planes, but aircraft from the 1940s through the 1960s, including dive bombers and torpedo planes, will be added as restoration work on the vessel continues. Visiting this aircraft carrier is truly an "event" or an "experience" because the humongous ships parked at the dock require your presence to appreciate their awesome size. Just driving onto the dock and seeing the ships looming above is an awesome experience. It's also a bit of a thrill to get to the boat as you go up the catwalk onto the main deck. Tours take you to all parts of the boat, from flight simulators and navigation to the top deck where the planes lift off and land. My then 5-year-old daughter said, "This is cool!" Overnight parties for scouts, school groups, corporate events, and birthday parties are available.

Hours: Wed–Mon: 10am–5pm. Closed Tues. *Tours* start at 11am. Last admission is at 4pm.

Cost: $12/adult, $9/senior, and $8/child 5–18.

Bathrooms: Yes.

Facilities: Wheelchair accessible through the elevator in the back of the boat, but access is limited. Stairs and ladders throughout the boat. Strollers not recommended.

Food: No.

What to Bring: Jacket, camera, and cash.

Follow-Up Activities: Western Aerospace Museum at the Oakland Airport is close by.

Western Aerospace Museum (Ages 6+)
Oakland International Airport, North Field
(510) 638-7100; 8268 Boeing Street, Bldg. 621, Oakland, CA 94621
<www.aerospace.org>
<www.cyberair.com/museums/usa/ca/wam.html>

Description: This collection has 15 historically significant planes including a flying boat (extra $2 for a tour), a plane similar to Amelia Earhart's, and a former NASA vertical-take off Harrier jet. There are many model airplanes and some large model ships as well as a few planes that youngsters can board and experience with adult supervision.

Hours: Wed–Sun: 10 am–4pm. Closed Monday and Tuesday.

Cost: $4/adult or senior, $2/child 6–12.

Bathrooms: Yes.

Facilities: Stroller friendly.

Food: No, area with tables and soft drinks. Deli's nearby also.

What to Bring: Picnic lunch.
Follow-Up Activities: *U.S.S. Hornet* is close by.

Wings of History Air Museum (Ages 5 +)
(408) 683-2290; Mailing address: PO Box 495, San Martin, CA 95046
12777 Murphy Avenue, San Martin, CA 95046;
<www.wingsofhistory.org>

Description: Many gliders and an exact replica of the 1903 Wright Flyer built by the Wright brothers are on display.
Hours: Tues & Thur: 10am–3pm, Sat & Sun: 11am–4pm.
Cost: Free. Requested donation of $5/adult, $3/child.
Bathrooms: Yes.
Facilities: Stroller friendly.
Food: No. Picnic lunch OK. Restaurants are nearby in Morgan Hill.
What to Bring: Picnic lunch. Sunscreen, sunglasses, camera and cash for food if you're planning to visit the Cinco de Mayo event.
Follow-Up Activities: 1) Cinco de Mayo event at the South County Airport in San Martin is from sunrise to sunset and includes hot air balloons, display of vintage model airplanes, antique cars and model Ts, steam and diesel trains, bi-plane rides, and Young Eagles free rides program for kids 8–17. Food is available during the special event. 2) Check Web site events schedule for other special events.

Cars

From the first wagons and carriages to today's cars and trucks, automotive history has evolved. Want to see how cars are made? The New United Motor Manufacturing plant in Fremont, a joint venture between Toyota and General Motors, will show you. For a selection of vintage cars, visit the Blackhawk Museum in Danville or attend the classic car shows. Your child is fascinated with fire trucks? Visit the Fire Truck Museum in San Francisco, or take a tour of San Francisco in an antique red fire truck. Need for speed? Visit Malibu Grand Prix for a taste of racecar driving or the Mazda Raceway Laguna Seca in Monterey.

Blackhawk Museum (All Ages)

(925) 736-2277; 3700 Blackhawk Plaza Circle, Danville, CA 94506
<www.blackhawkauto.org>

Description: Located in Blackhawk Plaza with its beautiful water fountain and waterfall (home to resident ducks), shopping and restaurants are plentiful. For automotive history and classic vintage cars, visit this automotive museum. Beyond the cars, the museum collection includes natural history exhibits of spiders and snakes. Don't miss the Spider Lab and the Children's Discovery Room. Affiliation with the Smithsonian Institute provides another source for high-quality changing exhibits.

Hours: Wed–Sun: 10am–5pm. Open most holidays except Thanksgiving, Christmas, and New Year's Day. *Docent-led tours* are available on weekends at 2pm. Tours last approximately one hour and are included with paid admission.

Cost: $8/adult, $5/student with ID or senior 65+, free/child 6 and under accompanied by adult.

Bathrooms: Yes.

Facilities: Stroller friendly.

Food: No, but restaurants in the plaza. You can also bring a picnic lunch and picnic on the lawn.

What to Bring: Cash for food.

Follow-Up Activities: 1) Tours for groups and school field trips are available. 2) Car shows and car events throughout the year. Ask to be placed on the mailing list for current information.

Bonfante Gardens Family Theme Park has a ride featuring

antique 1920s and 1950s vintage cars.

Children's Discovery Museum in San Jose has a real

ambulance and an old-fashioned fire truck on display for children to sit in and explore.

Hillsborough Concourse (All Ages)

Classic Car Show and Carnival at Crocker Middle School

2600 Ralston Avenue, Hillsborough, CA 94010

Description: Sponsored by the parents of Hillsborough public schools, this event is a fundraiser to generate money for the schools. The carnival includes entertainment and food for the whole family. See map on the Web site.
Schedule: First Sunday in May. Confirm on Web site.
Cost: $10/adult, $5/youth 5–15, free/child 5 & under.

History Park, San Jose at Kelly Park has a few antique automobiles on display at the Trolley Barn.

Malibu Grand Prix and Malibu Castle (See height requirements)

(650) 366-6463; 340 Blomquist Street, Redwood City, CA 94063
<www.malibugrandprix.com/redwood>

Description: This entertainment complex includes miniature golf, batting cages, an arcade, and a mini-racing track with smaller scale "race" cars. The driving course accommodates go-carts, one-seater cars, and two-seater cars.
Hours: *Summer:* Mon–Sun: 10am–midnight. *Winter:* Sun–Thur: 10am–10pm, Fri–Sat: 10am–midnight. The *minimum height requirements* are 3'6" for car passenger, 4'8" for go-cart rider, and 5' for Grand Prix driver with a valid driver's license.
Cost: License: $3.50 + tax. *One-seater & go-carts*: $3.50/lap, $14.95/5 laps, $18.95/7 laps, $24.95/11 laps. *Two-seaters*: Add $1 for each of the above prices for the one-seater.
Bathrooms: Yes.
Facilities: Strollers not recommended.
Food: Yes.
What to Bring: Plenty of cash, sunscreen, and sunglasses.

Jack London Square (All Ages)

(510) 645-5968; Jack London Square, Oakland, CA 94607
<www.jacklondonsquare.com>

Description: Jack London Square has many events throughout the year, including the *MG Car Show* in early May, the Renaissance School Art Show, and the annual PortFest in early June. The *Annual PortFest* is an event for boat and airplane enthusiasts. There is also a *July 4th* celebration with fireworks and a free concert, *dragon boat races* in August, an *annual art show* of Bay Area artists, a *boat show* in September, and more. See the Web site for details.

NUMMI (Min. Age: 10)
(New United Motor Manufacturing)
(510) 498-5649; 45500 Fremont Boulevard, Fremont, CA 94538
<www.nummi.com>

See Chapter 7: How Things Work—Site Tours section.

Oak Meadow Park in Los Gatos has an antique fire truck
on the playground. See Chapter 6: Transportation Favorites—Trains section.

Palo Alto Concours D'Elegance, Classic Car Show (All Ages)
Stanford University
(650) 961-5444; Stanford University, Stanford, CA 94305
<www.paconcours.com>

Description: Sponsored by the Palo Alto Lions Club for charity, this car show includes exhibits of race cars, vintage cars, cars from private collections, military cars, hot rods, and a working miniature engine by the Bay Area Engine Modelers on display. Food and drinks are available at the show. See the map on the Web site.
Schedule: Late June Sunday, 8:30am–3pm.
Cost: $20/adult, free/child 16 and under.

San Francisco Fire Department Museum (All Ages)
(415) 563-4630; 655 Presidio Avenue, San Francisco, CA 94115
(between Bush & Pine)
<www.sffiremuseum.org>

Description: The San Francisco Fire Department Museum has displays of antique fire vehicles previously used by the fire department, including horse-drawn steamers, hand pumps, trucks from the 1800s, a fire bell, a fire alarm, and the fire department's history and memorabilia.
Hours: Thur–Sun: 1–4pm.
Cost: Free.

Bathrooms: No. Fire deptartment next door has one, but not always available.

Facilities: Stroller friendly.

Food: No, nearby.

Follow-Up Activities: 1) Antique fireboats are docked at Pier 22 1/2 at Embarcadero and Harrison Streets. For pictures and information of the fireboats, visit: <www.sffiremuseum.org/fireboat.html>. 2) Visit the Web site to learn about the great fires of San Francisco, including the 1906 earthquake and fire.

San Francisco Fire Department Open Houses (Ages 5+)

You can visit fire stations throughout the city on Open House days. For detailed dates and stations closest to you, visit the Web site: <www.ci.sf.ca.us/fire/events/openhouse.htm>. or <www.ci.sf.ca.us/fire/events.htm>. For additional information, contact the San Francisco Fire Department Community Affairs Dept: (415) 558-3422.

San Francisco Fire Engine Tours (All Ages)
At The Cannery, Fisherman's Wharf

(415) 333-7077; 2801 Leavenworth Street, San Francisco, CA 94133
<www.fireenginetours.com>; <www.thecannery.com>

Description: Ride a shiny red fire engine for a 75-minute tour of the Presidio, Fort Point, Sausalito, Fort Baker, and over the Golden Gate Bridge.

Schedule: Tours leave daily at 1pm, except on Tues. On certain days, there are additional tours at 11am, 3pm, & 5pm. Tours depart from The Cannery, located at Courtyard Level, Beach Street and Columbus. Advanced reservations are required.

Cost: $30/adult, $25/teen, $15/child 12 & under for the first 2 children, and $20/additional child (more than 2 children).

Bathrooms: None onboard. Bathrooms located at The Cannery.

Facilities: Some strollers can fit into the truck to be stowed. It's best to leave the stroller in the car in the parking garage across the street.

Food: No, nearby restaurants.

What to Bring: Cash for parking.

Follow-Up Activities: Birthday party and charters offered.

San Jose Fire Department (Min. Age: 5)
Office of Public Education
(408) 277-2878; 255 S. Montgomery Street, San Jose, CA 95110
<www.sjfd.com>
<www.sjfd.com/PubEd/index_pubed.htm>

Description: The San Jose Fire Department does not have Open Houses like San Francisco. However, you may ring a bell at any fire station and ask to speak with the chief on duty if you have a group of five or less. Depending on their duties, you may be able to get a station tour. However, their first priority must be to fight fires, and your visit may be interrupted. Only children 5 and older may visit. *Do not bring strollers and children under 5 years old*; the fire stations are not childproof and may be dangerous for children under 5. For larger groups or school groups, contact the office of public education to arrange for tours and presentations.

Towe Auto Museum in Old Sacramento has vintage cars on display. See entry in the Chapter 9: Historical Outings—Gold Rush section under Old Sacramento.

Chapter 7
How Things Work

Many companies and organizations provide tours of their facilities to show the public how they make their products. These tours are usually free or are very affordable. They provide the company with free publicity and the public with knowledge of the processes involved in making the products we see and use every day. Help your child learn about how things work.

Site Tours

Basic Brown Bear Factory (Ages 3+)
(800) 554-1910; (415) 626-0781
444 DeHaro Street, San Francisco, CA 94107
<www.basicbrownbear.com>
For a mini Virtual Tour: <www.basicbrownbear.com/tour.htm>

Description: Learn how the teddy bear got its name, the process of making a teddy bear from designing to cutting to stuffing and cleaning. Each child can make his own bear.
Hours: Open 10am–5pm. Drop-in tours daily at 1pm. An extra tour at 11am is available on Saturdays. Reservations required for groups with 8 people or more.
Cost: Free tour, but to stuff your own bear, $12 for the smallest bear. Prices vary depending on the size of bear and clothing purchased.
Bathrooms: Yes.
Facilities: Stroller friendly.
Food: No, nearby restaurants.
Follow-Up Activities: Birthday parties offered. Group tours available.

Dreyer's Grand Ice Cream (Min. Age: 6)

Do not bring any child less than 6 years old!
(510) 471-6622; 1250 Whipple Road, Union City, CA 94587
<www.fabuloustravel.com/gourmet/tours/dryers.html>

Description: Take this tour to learn how ice cream is made. Don't forget to bring a jacket and wear comfortable walking shoes. You'll be touring through a cold freezer.

Hours: 8am–5pm. *Tours:* Mon–Fri: 9:15 am, 11:15 am, and 2pm by appointment only. Closed on federal holidays. Call 4–6 weeks in advance to make reservations.

Cost: $2 per person. Cash or checks only.

What to Bring: Jacket, cash, or checkbook.

Money Exhibit (Ages 6+)

Lobby of Federal Reserve Bank, San Francisco

(415) 974-3252; 101 Market Street, San Francisco, CA 94105
<www.frbsf.org/currency/index.html>
<www.federalreserveeducation.org> For High School & College level info.

Description: Tours of the bank is expected to restart in Spring 2004 due to reconstruction. Call for reservations: (415) 974-3252. For visiting information: **www.frbsf.org/federalreserve/visit/index.html**. For more on-line money facts, history, and information, visit the Web site: **www.frbsf.org/ federalreserve/money/index.html**. For educational exhibits on-line produced by the U.S. Treasury: **www.treas.gov/education**. Take a virtual tour of the main Treasury Building in Washington D.C. The Web site for kids, **www.treas.gov/kids**, has links to the U.S. Mint, Bureau of Engraving and Printing, and more. For U.S. Mint history: **http://usmint.gov/about_the_ mint/mint_history** or **http://us-mint.org**.

Fortune Cookie Factory (All Ages)

(510) 832-5552; 261 12th Street, Oakland, CA 94607

Description: See how fortune cookies are made.

Hours: Mon–Fri: 10am–3pm for groups of less than 10 people. Self tour. Guided tour only for groups of 10 people or more; call for reservations.

Cost: $1/person. You also get a bag of cookies.

Bathrooms: Yes.

Facilities: Stroller friendly.
Food: Restaurant next door.

Golden Gate Fortune Cookie Company (All Ages)
(415) 781-3956; 56 Ross Alley, San Francisco, CA 94108

Description: See how fortune cookies are made.
Hours: 9am–8:30pm.
Cost: Free tour with a free sample. $3/bag of cookies.
Bathroom: Yes.
Facility: Stroller friendly.
Food: No. Nearby restaurants.

Jelly Belly Factory Tour (All Ages)
(800) 522-3267; One Jelly Bean Lane, Fairfield, CA 94533
<www.jellybean.com>

Description: Walking tour shows the candy making process. Tour lasts ~40 minutes. Besides jelly beans, the factory also makes Gummi candy, chocolates, and taffy. There's an exhibition kitchen where hand-dipped chocolates are made in front of visitors. Free samples. Virtual tour on Web site.
Hours: Visitor Center and tours open daily 9am–5pm. Tours run every 15 minutes; reservations are not required. Closed Thanksgiving, Christmas, New Year's, and Easter Sunday. Call to verify dates and hours prior to departure. On weekends, only videos show the candy making process since the workers have the weekend off. For additional tour information: 800-953-5592.
Cost: Free.
Bathrooms: Yes.
Facility: Stroller friendly.
Food: Jelly Belly Café. Open 11am–3pm.

Le Boulanger Bread Factory
(408) 774-9000; 305 N Mathilda Road, Sunnyvale, CA

Reservations required. Most recent available is 4 to 5 years out.

Levi Strauss Visitor Center
(415) 501-6000; 1155 Battery Street, San Francisco, CA 94111

Description: Although the factory tours have been discontinued, there is a Visitor Center on Battery Street. See exhibits of jeans styles, video booths running a video on old advertisements, and a video on how jeans were made.
Hours: Daily 10am–5pm.
Cost: Free.
Bathrooms: Yes.
Facilities: Stroller friendly.
Food: No.
Follow-Up Activities: Company history on-line: <www.levistrauss.com/about/history>.

Marin French Cheese Company (All Ages)
(800) 292-6001; (707) 762-6001
7500 Red Hill Road, Petaluma, CA 94952
<www.marinfrenchcheese.com>

Description: See how Camembert and Brie cheeses are made in this factory tour. The Web site has a collection of recipes using these cheeses.
Hours: 8:30am–5pm. *Tours:* Wed—Thur at10 am, 11am, and 12pm. Call ahead for confirmation. Reservations required for groups of 10 or more.
Cost: Free.
Bathroom: Yes.
Facilities: Strollers can be left at the store. Baby carrier recommended.
Food: Deli and gift store.
What to Bring: Picnic lunch and drinks. Don't forget the sunscreen and sunglasses during the summer.

Mee Mee Bakery (Ages 5+)
(415) 362-3204; 1328 Stockton Street, San Francisco, CA

Description: This bakery makes the Shangri-La brand of Chinese fortune cookies as well as other Chinese baked goods. Custom cookie orders are $15/100 cookies.
Hours: Daily 10am–3pm. Call for a tour appointment.

Cost: Free.
Bathrooms: No.
Facilities: Not stroller friendly.
Food: No.
What to Bring: Cash for parking.

Monterey Bay Chocolates (All Ages)

(800) 648-9938; (831) 899-7963
1291 Fremont Boulevard, Seaside, CA 93955
<http://montereybaychocolates.com>

Description: See how chocolates are made—over 100 types of chocolates.
Hours: Mon–Fri: 10am–3pm. Free tours every 15 minutes. Free samples of the chocolates at a chocolate bar, set up like a salad bar. Virtual tour available on-line at: <**www.endorphin.com/places/mont_bay_choc_400.html**>.
Cost: Free.
Bathrooms: Not open to the public
Facilities: Stroller friendly
Food: No, restaurants across the street
What to Bring: Picnic lunch and drinks

Mrs. Grossman's Stickers (All Ages)

(800) 429-4549; (707) 763-1700
3810 Cypress Drive, Petaluma CA 94954
<www.mrsgrossmans.com>

Description: Take a tour and learn how stickers are made. The Visitor Center has an exhibit of all the stickers ever made by Mrs. Grossman's. Sticker art classes available. Check Web site for the calendar of events.
Hours: *Store:* 9:30am–5:30pm. *Tours:* Mon–Fri: 9:30am, 11am, 1pm, and 2:30pm. Reservations are required.
Cost: Free.
Bathrooms: Yes.
Facilities: Strollers OK in the store, but not on the tour.
Food: Vending machines with snacks only. Dining room and picnic tables outside.
What to Bring: Picnic lunch and drinks.

NASA Ames Research Center (Ages 5+)
Visitor Center
(650) 604-6274; Moffett Field, Mountain View, CA 94035

<www.arc.nasa.gov/about_ames/visitors_center.html>

<http://amesnews.arc.nasa.gov/assets/Images/lgmap.gif> Map

Description: The visitor center shows the research and technology of this world renown organization. Tours are available both to groups and individuals. Call for the next available tour. Tours require a minimum age of ten or 4th grade and up. It is a two-hour, two-mile, outdoor walk starting at 9:30am. Groups need to be 15 to 20 people.

Cost: Free.

Hours: Mon–Fri: 8am–4:30pm. Closed federal holidays. Tours are on weekdays only at 9:30am. Call to see when the next tour is available.

Bathrooms: Yes.

Facilities: Stroller friendly.

Food: No. Downtown Mountain View is relatively nearby with plenty of restaurants.

What to Bring: Sunscreen, sunglasses, comfortable walking shoes, a jacket during cool weather, food and drinks.

Follow-Up Activities: A wonderful Web site for kids explains how things fly, from a balloon to aerobatic planes: **www.aero.hq.nasa.gov/edu.** Webcast lectures discuss robotic technology (archived online) and its use in research and exploration. The Web site is <**http://robotics.nasa.gov**>. For tours: <**www.arc.nasa.gov/about_ames/tours.html**> or call (650) 604-6497. Tours are available for children 9 years or older, or for classes in grades 4 and up. Tours for families and individuals require at least two week advanced reservation, while tours for school groups require reservations three to six months in advance. There are resources for educators geared for different age groups, from K–12 grades. Don't miss the Ames Aerospace Encounter, geared for 4th—6th grade classes; it brings math, science, and technology to life with interactive programs.

NUMMI (Min. Age: 10+)
(New United Motor Manufacturing)
(510) 498-5649; 45500 Fremont Boulevard, Fremont, CA

<www.nummi.com >

Description: You can take a tour and follow the car manufacturing process. It is appropriate only for children ages 10 and up. For younger children, visit the Web site for an on-line tour to learn about the process.

Hours: Free tours offered Tues – Fri: 10am and 1pm. Reservations required (510) 770-4008 or book on-line.

Cost: Free.

Follow-Up Activities: For a virtual tour, <www.nummi.com/web_tour.html>.

Oakdale Cheese & Specialties (Ages 5+)

(209) 848-3139; 10040 Hwy 120, Oakdale, CA 95361
<www.oakdalecheese.com>

Description: Learn how cheese is made with the tour and educational video. This site also features a petting zoo and picnic area. Besides making Gouda cheese, brownies, and cheesecake are made. Bakery and gift shop.

Hours: Daily 9am–6pm.

Cost: Free tours. Groups over 10 require advanced reservations.
Company requests 50 cents per child for groups with children to provide feed for the animals.

Bathrooms: Yes.

Facilities: Stroller friendly.

Food: French bread and cheese are available for purchase.

What to Bring: Picnic lunch and drinks.

Practicum Kids (Ages 6–9)

(510) 744-0843
<www.practicumkids.com>

Classes at Fremont, Union City, and Newark community centers show kids how things work in local businesses and factories.

Scharffen Berger Chocolate Maker (Min. Age: 10)

(510) 981-4050; (800) 930-4528 Retail orders
914 Heinz Avenue, Berkeley, CA 94710
<www.scharffenberger.com>

Description: Tours show visitors how chocolates are made. Tours last approximately 1 hour.

Hours: 10am–5pm. Mon–Sun: 10:30am, 2:30pm, and 3:30pm tours. Call (510) 981-4066 for tour reservations. Reservations can also be made on the Web site. While walk-ins are welcome, due to space availability, reservations have first priority.

Cost: Free.

Stanford Linear Accelerator Tour (Recommended Age: 11)

(650) 926-2204; 2575 Sand Hill Road, Menlo Park, CA 94025
<www2.slac.stanford.edu/vvc>

Description: Visitor Center has displays on the forefront of particle physics programs of the laboratory. Children under 11 may come with parents, but it is recommended that children be older due to the complexity of the information presented. The Web site has information and a virtual tour on the linear accelerator and how it works; the particle detectors and how they work; and how electron beams and synchrotron x-ray technologies are used in medical, biological, and industrial applications. For a virtual tour: <www.slac.stanford.edu/grp/pao/tour.html#special>.

Hours: Mon–Fri: 8am–5pm. *Tour Schedule:* Tours conducted several times a week for the public, generally at 10am and 1pm. Tours last approximately two hours. Advanced reservations required. Groups can call to select the best times available; some evening tours.

Cost: Free.

Bathrooms: Yes.

Facilities: Wheelchair accessible.

Food: Available at the cafeteria next to the Auditorium. Reservations must be made in advance.

What to Bring: Cameras OK. Don't forget the film.

Uesugi Farms Pumpkin Patch (All Ages)

(408) 778-7225; (408) 842-1294 Office
14485 Monterey Highway, San Martin, CA 95037
Virtual photo tour: <www.sjsu.edu/faculty/satoru/LIB/ppatch1.htm>

Description: Learn how pumpkins grow. An exhibit shows the development of the pumpkin from seed to seedling to plant to baby pumpkin to orange pumpkin. There's an accompanying educational video. The grounds are beautifully decorated with scarecrows. There's a miniature train ride through a haunted tunnel and a pumpkin vine covered walk-through tunnel for all to explore.

Hours: Open only in October. During the first week: 10am–6pm. Extended hours from 9am–9pm as it gets closer to Halloween. Call to confirm hours and costs.

Bathrooms: Portables only.

Facilities: Stroller friendly.

Food: No.

What to Bring: Sunscreen, sunglasses, picnic lunch, and cash.

U.S. Geological Survey (Recommended Age: 8+)
Western Region Center, Menlo Park

(650) 853-8300 Operator;(650) 329-4390 Recording; (650) 329-5392 Speaker and Tour requests; 1-888-ASK-USGS
345 Middlefield Road, Menlo Park, CA 94025
<http://openhouse.wr.usgs.gov>
<http://online.wr.usgs.gov/calendar>
<http://online.wr.usgs.gov/kiosk/mptour.html>

Description: 1) *Tours* of the facility are available to groups of 10–20. Larger groups can be accommodated by splitting into separate tour groups. Chaperone ratio of 8–10 children per adult is requested. Tours last approximately 1 hour. The first 30 minutes are spent on earthquakes, followed by 30 minutes at the Information Center with explanations on how to read topographic maps and the products in the Info Center. The tour can be extended with a self-guided tour that directs the visitor to a collection of rocks (including the second largest rock found in Antartica) and globes, as well as the library. For tour reservations, call the tour co-ordinator. 2) The *Open House* provides a very rare opportunity to see the inner workings of the USGS, to talk to the scientists, and to see the latest research and exhibits. It occurs only every three years, due to lack of funding. There's food and live music at this event. There are exhibits and hands-on activities for kids, including free gold panning. Activities include touring the USGS laboratories, learning how maps are made, watching educational videos, and learning about science and nature. You can learn to identify rocks, experience the rock hardness scale with different types of rocks, and see which rock can float. There are also exhibits on earthquakes where children 11 and under can ride a simulated earthquake and experience the earth scope to learn how it detects earthquakes. See exhibits on volcanoes and landslides, as well as the ecosystem of the mudflats and the San Francisco Bay.

Hours: The next Open House will be in 2006. The event is usually held in early or mid-May. It's open to the public on Sat–Sun 10am–4pm. Schools have a special preview day on the Friday prior, 9am–3pm, by invitation only. Call to ask about the Schools Preview Day at (650) 329-4477.

Cost: Free.

Bathrooms: Yes.

Facilities: Stroller friendly.

Food: Snack bars and concessions at the Open House event only.

What to Bring: Sunscreen, sunglasses, camera, and cash for food and souvenirs.

Follow-Up Activities: 1) *Ask-a-Geologist* by e-mail: <ask-a-geologist@usgs.gov> 2) The Web site, The Learning Web at <www.usgs.gov\education>, has lots of information on a huge range of science topics for students, teachers, and explorers.

Whole Foods (All Ages)

<www.wholefoods.com>

(408) 371-5000	1690 S. Bascom Avenue, Campbell, CA 95008
(408) 257-7000	20830 Stevens Creek Boulevard, Cupertino, CA 95014
(408) 358-4434	15980 Los Gatos Boulevard, Los Gatos, CA 95032
(415) 381-1200	414 Miller Avenue, Mill Valley, CA 94941
(415) 451-6333	340 Third Street, San Rafael, CA 94901
(415) 674-0500	1765 California Street, San Francisco, CA 94109
(510) 649-1333	3000 Telegraph Avenue, Berkeley, CA 94705
(650) 358-6900	1010 Park Place, San Mateo, CA 94403
(650) 326-8676	774 Emerson Street, Palo Alto, CA 94301
(831) 333-1600	800 Del Monte Center, Monterey, CA 93940
(925) 355-9000	100 Sunset Drive, San Ramon, CA 94583
(925) 274.9700	1333 E. Newell, Walnut Creek, CA 94596

Description: This grocery store chain specializes in providing organic and environmentally friendly products whenever possible. Tours are catered to the specific group. There is no minimum number of participants, but the maximum is 20 per group. For young children in kindergarten or preschool, adult chaperons of one adult for every three kids are requested. The tours cover the various departments of the store, and how organic methods are used to produce the products. For example, in the fish department they discuss how fish can be farm raised; in the dairy department, they discuss how butter is made; and in the meat department, they talk about what makes an organic chicken different from a "regular" chicken. At the end of the tour, they provide goody bags with stickers, crayons, and a booklet for the children.

Hours: At the Los Gatos location, tours can be booked on Tues or Thur at 11am. Call to confirm with the store located closest to you. Ask to speak with the Marketing Coordinator and make an advance reservation.

Cost: Free.

Bathrooms: Yes.

Facilities: Stroller friendly.

Food: Yes.

For factory tours outside of the Bay Area:

<www.howstuffworks.com/factory-tour.htm>

Virtual Tours

Cargill Salt

(888) 385-7258; Minneapolis, MN

<www.cargillsalt.com>

Description: Learn about salt's history and how it is made from Cargill Salt's Web site. Click on the "About Salt" icon. Visit the Salt Institute's Web site to learn even more about salt: <www.saltinstitute.org>.

Hershey's Visitors Center

(209) 848-8126; 120 South Sierra, Oakdale, CA

<www.hersheys.com/oakdale>

Description: There is no longer a factory tour at this location. However, see a virtual tour of chocolate making on their Web site: <www.hersheys.com/tour/index.shtml>.

Jelly Belly

(800) 522-3267; One Jelly Bean Lane, Fairfield, CA 94533
<www.jellybean.com>

Description: Virtual tour on Web site.

Wiebe Family Farms

(888) 441-5117; 5351 Avenue, 424, Reedley, CA 93654
<http://wiebefamilyfarms.com/index.htm>

Hours: Mon–Sat: 9am to 4pm.
Cost: Tour: $8/person.
For a virtual tour of peach and nectarine packing:
<http://wiebefamilyfarms.com/virtual.htm>.

Chapter 8
Art & Performing Arts

Art

"I am enough of an artist to draw freely upon my imagination. Imagination is more important than knowledge. Knowledge is limited. Imagination encircles the world."
—Albert Einstein (1875–1955)

"Every child is an artist. The problem is how to remain an artist once he grows up."
—Pablo Picasso (1881 – 1973)

"Creativity is allowing yourself to make mistakes. Art is knowing which ones to keep."
—Scott Adams, *The Dilbert Principle*

Bay Area Children's Discovery Museum in Sausalito, Habitot Children's Museum in Berkeley, and the Randall Museum in San Francisco have drop-in art areas for children. See respective entries in Chapter 4: Science Museums for detailed information.

Ceramics & Drop-In Art Outings

The following are studios where you can create one-time art projects.

Brush Strokes Studio (Ages 7+)
(510) 528-1360; 745 Page Street, Berkeley, CA 94710
<www.brushstrokestudio.com>

Description: Paint your own pottery. Birthday parties, art camps through-out the year, afterschool classes for kids 7–12.
Hours: *Weekdays:* 11am–8pm. Closed on Tuesday. *Weekends:* 11am–6pm.
Cost: $5.50/hour per person, prorated after the 1ˢᵗ hour. *Wednesdays:* Flat rate: $10/person, $5/child under 12. *Parties:* $10/person for a 2-hour party, $15/person for a 3-hour party. Ceramic pieces range from $3 to $40 per item.

Color Me Mine
> *Belmont:*
> (650) 595-8439; 1003 Alameda de Las Pulgas, Belmont, CA 94002
> **Hours:** Sun–Thur: 11am–7pm, Fri and Sat: 11am – 9pm.
>
> *Menlo Park:*
> (650) 328-4486; 602 Santa Cruz Avenue, Menlo Park, CA 94025
> <www.colormeminemenlopark.com>
> **Hours:** Mon–Sat: 11am–9pm, Sun: 11am–6pm.
>
> *San Francisco:*
> (415) 474-7076; 2030 Union Street, San Francisco, CA 94123
> <www.colormemine-sf.com>
> **Hours:** Sun: 11am–7pm, Mon–Sat: 11am–9pm.
>
> *Walnut Creek:*
> (925) 280-2888; 1950 Mt. Diablo Boulevard, Walnut Creek, CA 94596
> <www.walnutcreek.colormemine.com>
> **Hours:** Mon–Sat: 11am–9pm, Sun: 11am–5pm.

Description: This franchise "paint your own" pottery studio has locations throughout the Bay Area. Birthday parties and classes for all.

Habitot Children's Museum (Ages 1–4)

(510) 647-1111; 2065 Kittredge Street, Berkeley, CA 94704

<www.habitot.org>

Description: This is a very small museum. There are separate play areas dedicated to various types of play: a little fire engine structure and a train playtable, a little market and kitchen area, and a pretend play dress up area. There is a drop-in art studio with a ceramic clay play table, a water play area, and a book nook for quiet time and reading.

Hours: Mon & Wed: 9:30am–1pm, Tues & Fri: 9:30am–5pm, Thur: 9:30am–7pm, Sat: 10am–5pm, Sun: 11am–5pm only from after Labor Day to just before Memorial Day. Closed New Year's Day, Easter, July 4, Labor Day, Thanksgiving Day, and Christmas.

Cost: $6/child, $5/adult, 10% discount to the disabled and seniors.

Bathrooms: Yes.

Facilities: Stroller friendly once inside the building, but getting inside the building is a bit tricky. There's a side door that allows easier access to the museum. Call prior to your visit to get directions on stroller navigation.

Food: No, but restaurants nearby in the same building.

What to Bring: Extra cash for parking. Parking structure is across the street.

Follow-Up Activities: 1) Carpentry, art, music, dance, and literacy classes, as well as camps for the very young child. 2) Birthday parties.

Petroglyph (Ages 4+)

<www.petroglyph.com/studios.htm>

Los Gatos:
(408) 395-6278; 37 N. Santa Cruz Avenue, Los Gatos, CA 95030
Hours: Mon–Thur: 10am–9pm, Fri & Sat: 10am–10pm, Sun: 10am–7pm.

Willow Glen:
(408) 971-4278   1140 Lincoln Avenue, San Jose, CA 95125
Hours: Mon–Thur: 10am–9pm, Fri & Sat: 10am–10pm, Sun: 10am–7pm.

Santa Cruz:
(831) 458-4278   125 Walnut Avenue, Santa Cruz, CA 95060
Hours: Mon–Thur: 10am–8pm, Fri & Sat: 10am–10pm, Sun: 10am–7pm.

Description: This is a ceramic studio where you can paint your own ceramic. You first purchase a pre-made piece of pottery, then paint the piece (paint is provided). The studio fires the piece and you come back to pick it up in 24 hours. Takes a bit of time and patience, but it's lots of fun.
Cost: $9.75/adult, $7/child under 12 flat rate, plus cost of the ceramic piece you want to paint.
Bathrooms: Yes.
Facilities: Stroller friendly. Kid friendly. Even has a TV to occupy little ones while you work.
Food: Nearby restaurants.

Charles M. Schulz Museum (Ages 3+)
(707) 579-4452; 2301 Hardies Lane, Santa Rosa, CA 95403
<www.schulzmuseum.org>

Description: This museum is dedicated to the art of *Peanuts* comic strip creator, Charles Schulz. There's a *Snoopy* labyrinth, a drop-in art studio for art activities and cartooning, and video shows noon–4pm.
Hours: Weekdays: noon–5:30pm, Sat & Sun: 10am–5:30pm. Closed Tuesdays, New Year's, July 4, Thanksgiving, Christmas Eve, and Christmas Day.
Cost: $8/adult, $5/youth or senior, free/child under 4.
Bathrooms: Yes.
Facilities: Stroller friendly.
Food: No. Food available across the street next to the Empire Ice Arena.

Museum of Children's Art (MOCHA) (Ages 18 months+)
(510) 465-8770; 538 Ninth Street, Oakland, CA 94607
<www.mocha.org>

Description: Small museum with an art scavenger hunt. Friendly staff. Appropriate for the preschooler. Drop-in art studios for children over 18 months old.
Hours: *Gallery:* 10am–5pm. The *Little Studio* (downstairs): Tues–Sun: 11am–2pm. *Big Studio* (upstairs): Tues–Fri: 3:30–5pm.
Cost: *Gallery*: free. *Little Studio* for children 18 months—6 year-old: $3/child. *Big Studio*: $3/child.
Bathrooms: Yes.

Facilities: Stroller friendly.

Food: Restaurants next door.

What to Bring: Wear clothes that can get messy from art activities.

Follow-Up Activities: 1) Weekend workshops: Sat & Sun: 1–4pm on a variety of themes including music makers, puppet play, kinetic art (mobiles, pinwheels, etc), adorable adornment (friendship bracelets, hair accessories), color my world (painting and color mixing techniques), and mosaics. 2) Birthday parties. 3) Classes. 4) Art camps.

Paint Brush Diplomacy
Formerly the International Children's Art Museum
(650) 326-3561

<www.paintbrushdiplomacy.org>

Description: Bringing art from children all over the world, this former museum's collection is awaiting a new home, pending fundraising efforts. Currently exhibits at the San Mateo County Historical Museum located at 777 Hamilton Avenue, Redwood City, CA through fall 2003. The collection includes 25 years of children's art from all over the world. Contact Louise Valeur at <**pdiplomacy@sbcglobal.net**> for information on future exhibits.

Museums

For the older child (elementary school age) who is mature enough to appreciate the finer museums, there are some great museums to visit in the local area. Some of the museums have developed activity books for children to help involve them in the art collections. Ask at the information desk at the beginning of your visit.

Asian Art Museum, Civic Center Plaza (Ages 4+)
(415) 581-3500; 200 Larkin Street, San Francisco, CA 94102

<www.asianart.org>

Description: The brand new facility is a rehabilitation and reuse of the old San Francisco Main Library. This museum's permanent collection of

Asian art spans the centuries and includes countries such as Japan, China, India, Iran, and Korea.

Hours: Closed Mondays. Tues–Sun: 10am–5pm. Open until 9pm every Thursday.

Cost: $10/adult, $7/senior, $6/youth 12–17, free/child under 12. Thur after 5pm: $5/person and free/child under 12. *Free on the first Tuesday of each month.*

Bathrooms: Yes.

Facilities: Stroller friendly.

Food: Yes.

What to Bring: Jacket and cash for food and parking.

Follow-Up Activities: Check the calendar for family days and events. First Saturday of each month 1–4pm, drop-in art with self-guided gallery activity, first come first served. The *Asia Alive* program with story telling and cultural entertainment is daily noon–4pm for all ages. Sign up at the Information Desk to participate. Learn about selected art objects with related stories retold—first Saturday and every Sunday at 1pm.

Berkeley Art Museum and Pacific Film Archive (Ages 8+)

(510) 642-0808 Main; 2626 Bancroft Way, Berkeley, CA 94704
(510) 548-4366 Café; 2621 Durant Avenue, Berkeley, CA 94704
(510) 642-5249 Film; 2575 Bancroft Way, Berkeley, CA 94704
<www.bampfa.berkeley.edu>

Description: The Berkeley Art Museum provides exhibits on contemporary and avant garde art, as well as historical and international art, including Asian art. There are changing exhibits throughout the year. The Pacific Film Archive has over 6000 films and videos on archive, including international, silent, animation, and classic films. The theater shows some of these films. See the Web site for a schedule of performances.

Hours: Wed–Sun: 11am–7pm.

Cost: $8/adult; $5/youth 12–17, senior 65+, or disabled person, or non-UC student; free/child under 12 or UC students, faculty and staff, members. *Free first Thursday of each month.*

Bathrooms: Yes.

Facilities: Stroller friendly.

Food: Yes.

What to Bring: Cash for food and parking.

Follow-Up Activities: Guided tours are generally on Thursdays at 12:15pm and 5:30pm, and Sundays at 2pm. Check the calendar for current schedule. School groups can take self-guided tours with advanced reservations by calling (510) 642-5188.

Cantor Arts Center (Ages 4+)
Stanford University
(650) 723-4177; 328 Lomita Drive, Stanford, CA 94305 (Cross St: Museum Way)
<www.stanford.edu/dept/ccva>

Description: This art museum is located in the beautiful Stanford University campus environment. It has a wonderful selection for such a small museum with exhibits on African artifacts, Egyptian artifacts, Asian ceramics and painting, European and American painting, as well as modern abstract sculptures and paintings. Probably the best part of this museum is the wonderful collection of Rodin bronze sculptures both in the outdoor garden and the indoor gallery. To see a more extensive collection of Rodin sculpture, you'd probably have to visit the Rodin Museum in Paris, France.

Hours: Wed–Sun: 11am–5pm, Thur: 11am–8pm. Closed Monday, Tuesday, & holidays. *Family tours* on the 2nd Saturday of each month at 3pm. *General tours* on Wednesdays at noon and on the weekends at 1pm. Group tours available Wed–Sun: 11am–3pm. School groups have Tuesdays available in addition. Advanced registration required for group tours.

Cost: Free admission. Parking fee required on weekdays until 4pm. Free parking after 4pm on weekdays and all day on weekends.

Bathrooms: Yes.

Facilities: Stroller and wheelchair friendly. However, the stroller access is located by the café entrance on the side of the building next to the outdoor Rodin sculpture garden.

Food: Café features organic food and drinks. Little ones may find the fare a bit too "gourmet" for their tastes. Bring a bag lunch for your child if your child likes select foods.

What to Bring: Bring quarters and dollar bills for parking, as needed.

Follow-Up Activities: 1)The beautiful Stanford Memorial Chapel facing the main quad of the horseshoe entrance is within walking distance. Stanford University offers tours of its beautiful campus, including an art tour. 2) Offers art classes and camps for children. For information on art classes, see Chapter 12: Science & Arts Education—Art Education.

California Palace of the Legion of Honor (Ages 3+)
Lincoln Park
(415) 863-3330; 100 34th Avenue, San Francisco, CA 94122
<www.thinker.org/legion>

Description: This is a gorgeous museum. Enrich your visit by planning to attend the special tours/art classes for kids. On Saturday mornings, (10:30am–noon), special tours and art classes for children 3½–6 years old are offered. These tours are included with museum admission. No preregistration is required, but class sizes are limited. At the same time, tours and classes are offered to children 7 to 12 years old, on the same bases.

Hours: Closed Monday. Tues–Sun: 9:30am–5pm. On Saturdays, 10:30 am–noon, there are special tours for children ages 3½ to 12 years old.

Cost: $12/adult, $10/senior 65+, $9/youth 12–17, $4/child 5–11, free/child under 5. *Tuesdays are free for everyone.* Some special exhibits have additional charges.

Bathrooms: Yes.

Facilities: Stroller friendly.

Food: Café.

What to Bring: Cash for food.

Follow-Up Activities: 1) Art classes for children require advanced registration. Call the Education Department at (415) 682-2483 for specific classes and schedules. 2) Children's Theater at the Florence Gould Theater, Legion of Honor. For additional information, call (415) 387-7089 or (415) 750-3640

Cartoon Art Museum (Ages 4+)
(415) CAR-TOON (227-8666)
655 Mission Street, San Francisco, CA 94105
<www.cartoonart.org>

Description: Exhibits on the history of cartoon art and its evolution from animation, comic strips, comic books, editorial cartoons, magazine cartoons, and underground cartoons.

Hours: Closed Monday. Tues–Sun: 11am–5pm. "Pay what you wish" day is on the first Tuesday of each month. Closed New Year's Day, Easter, July 4, Thanksgiving, and Christmas.

Cost: $6/adult, $4/student or seniors, $2/child 6 & over, free/child 5 & under.

Bathrooms: Yes.

Facilities: Stroller friendly.

Food: No, but restaurants close by.

What to Bring: Cash for parking and food.

De Young Museum (Ages 3+)

Reopening in 2005.

Interim de Young Museum

(415) 863-3330; (415) 750-7636 Info

245-A South Spruce Avenue, South San Francisco, CA 94080

<www.thinker.org>

De Young Art Center: 2501 Irving Street (at 26th Avenue), San Francisco, CA. For more information, call (415) 682-2485 or e-mail: wfang@famsf.org. The Art Center is where educational programs are conducted during the reconstruction of the De Young Museum. 1) On Saturday mornings at 10:30am, there are drop-in art workshops for families with children 3½–12 years old. These workshops are open to members only. 2) On Saturday afternoons 2–3:30pm, there are free drop-in programs for families with children 3½–12 years old. Programs are conducted by artist-teachers and preregistration is not required. Call (415) 682-2483 between Wednesday and Sunday to for schedule information.

Oakland Museum of California (Ages 4+)

(510) 238-2200; 1000 Oak Street, Oakland, CA 94607

<www.museumca.org>

Description: This museum has permanent exhibits on the history of California, the natural sciences of California, and a collection of California art including sculptures, paintings, photographs, prints, and decorative arts. For prehistoric beast lovers, the museum is currently working on a mastodon (ice age animal resembling an elephant) exhibit. Watch the work in progress, with the making of casts, on the virtual exhibit on-line.

Hours: Wed–Sat: 10am–5pm. Sun: 12–5pm. Closed Mondays and

Tuesdays. First Friday of each month: opens at 9am. Closed on New Year's Day, July 4, Thanksgiving Day, and Christmas Day.

Cost: $6/adult, $4/senior 65+ or student w/ ID, free/child under 6 years old. *Free second Sunday of each month.*

Bathrooms: Yes.

Facilities: Stroller friendly.

Food: Café– great food!

What to Bring: Cash for food.

Follow-Up Activities: For family events, visit the calendar of events page: <www.museumca.org/cal-public/calendar.cgi> then select "Kids and Family Events" for a listing. Past exhibits included *Biological Illustrations for Families* to learn drawing techniques using nests, eggs, etc; *Gold Rush Family Day* to hear the stories, take tours, do hands-on activities, including gold panning; and *Songs for my Father* with a series of performances and hands-on activities to celebrate Father's Day.

San Francisco Museum of Modern Art (Ages 4+)
(415) 357-4000; 151 Third Street, San Francisco, CA 94103
<www.sfmoma.org>

Description: Collections include modern art paintings and sculptures, architecture and design, media arts, and photography.

Hours: Closed Wed. *Thur–Tues:* 11am–6pm. *Summer* (Memorial Day–Labor Day): 10am–6pm. Open late Thursdays until 9pm. The Museum is closed on Thanksgiving, Christmas, and New Year's Day.

Cost: $10/adult, $7/senior, $6/students w/ ID, free/child under 12. *Free the first Tuesday of each month. ½ price every Thursday evening 6–9pm.*

Bathrooms: Yes.

Facilities: Stroller friendly.

Food: Café.

What to Bring: Cash for food and parking.

Follow-Up Activities: Check the calendar for family days and events.

San Jose Museum of Art (Ages 4+)
(408) 271-6840; 110 South Market Street, San Jose, CA 95113
<www.sjmusart.org>

Description: This museum focuses on contemporary art, including ceramics sculpture, abstract and realist painting, and new media art. They also have changing exhibits.

Hours: Tues–Sun: 11am–5pm, Fri: 11am–10pm.
Closed Mondays, Thanksgiving, Christmas, and New Year's Day.
Cost: Free.
Bathrooms: Yes.
Facilities: Stroller friendly.
Food: Café.
What to Bring: Cash for food and parking.
Follow-Up Activities: Kids Art Sunday is on the last Sunday of the month. These art classes/workshops are free.

Santa Cruz Museum of Art & History (MAH) (Ages 3+)
McPherson Center
(831) 429-1964

705 Front Street, Santa Cruz, CA 95060 (Corner of Front and Cooper Streets)
<www.santacruzmah.org>

Description: The Museum of Art & History focuses on contemporary art and the history of Santa Cruz County. A permanent exhibit, *Where the Redwoods Meet the Sea,* provides a glimpse into the lives and culture of the Ohlone Indians who lived in the area before the Spanish came to California. Family Free Days, *Creativity in Motion,* has games, art activities, and history. Call the Education Dept. at (831) 429-1964 ext. 20 for information on the next Family Free Day.
Hours: Tues–Sun: 11am–5pm. Thur: 11am–7pm. Closed on Mondays.
Cost: $4/adult; $2/students (18+), senior (62+); free for members, students under 18, and children. *Free admission on the first Friday of each month.* Family Free Days are on the first Saturday of each month.
Bathrooms: Yes.
Facilities: Stroller friendly.
What to Bring: Picnic lunch.
Follow-Up Activities: School tours must sign up during two periods: mid-August to mid-October or December through January. Call the receptionist at (831) 429-1964 ext. 10 to schedule the tour.

Triton Museum of Art (Ages 4+)

(408) 247-3754; (408) 247-9340
1505 Warburton Avenue, Santa Clara, CA 95050
<www.tritonmuseum.org>

Description: Exhibits works by California artists. Art tours given by docents can be arranged in advance for both contemporary art and Native American art. Call (408) 247-9352 for reservations for art tours.
Hours: Mon–Sun: 11am–5pm, Thursdays open until 9pm.
Cost: Free.
Bathrooms: Yes.
Facilities: Stroller friendly.
Food: No.
What to Bring: Picnic lunch.
Follow-Up Activities: 1) Provides classes for children and adults. 2) Family Art Days include art activities, live performances, and hands-on guided tours. 3) Summer art camps for children – see their calendar for most recent events.

Galleries

Art galleries are wonderful to visit. Best of all, they feature contemporary artists, the visits are free, and you can learn about the art and the artists firsthand from the galleries! There are three specific galleries I'd like to suggest for outings: the Rodrigue Studio, featuring the Blue Dog Gallery; the Lynn Lupetti Gallery; and the Peter Max Gallery. The Rodrigue Studio and the Lynn Lupetti Gallery are very close to each other and provide an easy entrée into the world of art galleries because the art is so fun and approachable. Both of these galleries are wonderful for children. They are located by the Carmel Public Library and within a short walk of Carmel Beach at the bottom of Ocean Ave. For a more complete listing of galleries in the Carmel/Monterey area, visit this Web site: <**www.monterey-carmel.com/galleries.htm**>. The Peter Max Gallery is in San Jose, in the newly opened Santana Row shopping center across from Valley Fair.

Carmel Art Association (Ages 3+)

(831) 624-6176; PO Box 2271, Carmel, CA 93921
<www.carmelart.org>

Description: This gallery features a collection of art from local artists.
Hours: 10am–5pm daily.
Cost: Free.
Bathrooms: Yes.
Facilities: Stroller friendly.
Food: Nearby restaurants.

Lynn Lupetti Gallery (Ages 3+)

(831) 624-0622; PO Box 5776, Carmel, CA 93921
6th between Dolores & Lincoln, Carmel, CA

Description: Lynn Lupetti paints magical and imaginary landscapes with children and animals.
Hours: 10am–5pm, daily.
Cost: Free.
Bathrooms: Public restrooms located diagonally across the street at the Public Library.
Facilities: Stroller friendly.
Food: Nearby restaurants.

Rodrigue Studio (Ages 3+)
Blue Dog Gallery

(831) 626-4444; P.O. Box 8-3214, Carmel, CA 93921
On 6th Ave between Lincoln & Dolores
<www.bluedogart.com>

Description: Famous for his Blue Dog paintings of his dog in various poses with brightly colored landscapes. The dog is usually painted blue in the paintings, hence the name.
Hours: 10am–6pm daily.
Cost: Free.
Bathrooms: Public restrooms located diagonally across the street at the Public Library.
Facilities: Stroller friendly.
Food: Nearby restaurants.
Follow-Up Activities: *Why is Blue Dog Blue?* written by the artist,

George Rodrigue, and Bruce Goldstone is a fun, colorful children's book explaining why the dog is blue.

Peter Max Gallery (Ages 3+)

(408) 615-1590; 334 Santana Row, Suite 1035, San Jose, CA 95128
<www.petermax.com>
Description: Peter Max's colorful and enticing paintings will delight your child. It is approachable for even the very young child.
Hours: Mon–Sat: noon–9pm; Sun: noon–6pm.
Cost: Free.
Bathrooms: Public restrooms in the Santana Row shopping center.
Facilities: Stroller friendly.
Food: Nearby restaurants in Santana Row shopping center.
Follow-Up Activities: The Winchester Mystery House is very close by. It is located next to the intersection of Winchester Blvd and Interstate 280.

Music

"Music is a moral law.
It gives a soul to the universe,
wings to the imagination,
a charm to sadness,
and life to everything."
—Plato

Music is the universal language that speaks to our souls. We are all inherently musical. We can all appreciate and understand music. Help your children develop their innate musical appreciation by finding concerts or musical performances that they can relate to and understand. It's hard to separate music from other performing arts since music is such an inherent part of musicals, dance, etc. There are many touring shows such as *The Wiggles, Dragon Tales, Annie, Sound of Music, Disney on Broadway,* and *Disney on Ice* that are very approachable for children. Please refer to the

Theater Performances section for more outing ideas. In this section, I will focus on purely musical performances.

The holidays are a great time to introduce musical performances by attending traditional family concerts such as *Peter and the Wolf* and ballets like the *Nutcracker*. For very young children, the *Nutcracker* or musicals may be more suitable because the activity of the performers and visual spectacle will better engage their attention. For information on *Nutcracker* performances, see the Ballet Performances section later in this chapter.

In this section, you will find symphonies and orchestras that cater to families, free concerts, local youth symphonies or orchestras, and a music museum—the Beethoven Museum.

Family Concerts

Cal Performances (Ages 4+)
Zellerbach Hall, UC Berkeley
(510) 642-9988; 101 Zellerbach Hall # 4800, Berkeley, CA, 94720
<www.calperfs.berkeley.edu>

Description: Family Fare Series provides half-price tickets for children 16 and under. Search under "Family Fare" once you're at the Cal Performances Web site for event schedule and prices.

Deck the Halls, (Ages 4+)
San Francisco Symphony, Davies Symphony Hall, San Francisco
(415) 864-6000; (800) 696-9689
201 Van Ness Avenue, San Francisco, CA 94102
<www.sfsymphony.org>

Description: This is a family oriented concert with Christmas carols. The post-show party includes arts and crafts and refreshments. See San Francisco Symphony below.
Schedule: Early December only 2 performances.
Cost: $27 per person. Check Web site for most current information.
Follow-Up Activities: There is a "Weekday Concert for School Groups" program with the Children's Concerts series targeted for K-grade 3 and

the Youth Concerts series for grades 4-9 during weekday mornings in April. Cost is only $3.50/person. For each series, there is a docent training workshop for parents, educators, and volunteers.

Fremont Symphony Orchestra (Ages 5+)
Ohlone College, Fremont
(510) 794-1659; P.O. Box 104 Fremont, CA 94537
43600 Mission Boulevard, Fremont, CA 94539
<www.fremontsymphony.org>

Description: The performances are held at Jackson Theater at the Gary Soren Smith Center for the Fine and Performing Arts, Ohlone College. Family Concert series for ages 5+ on Sunday afternoons. Check the Web site for current schedule.

Le Petit Trianon (Ages 5+)
(408) 995-5400; 72 North Fifth Street, San Jose, CA 95112
<www.trianontheatre.com>

Mountain View Center for the Performing Arts (Ages 3+)
(650) 903-6000; (650) 903-6565 Admin. Office
500 Castro Street, Mountain View, CA 94039
<www.ci.mtnview.ca.us/mvcpa/mainmenu.html>

Description: Provides wonderful family entertainment including plays, musicals, concerts, etc. Parking available in basement underneath the Performing Arts Center. Follow signs to the "Civic Hall" parking.

Music for Minors (Concerts for kids) (All Ages)
(650) 941-9130; 97 Hillview, Los Altos, CA 94022
<www.mfm.org>

Family Concert Series.

Music at Kohl Mansion (Ages 3+)
(650) 343-8463; 2750 Adeline Drive, Burlingame, CA 94010
<www.musicatkohlmansion.org>

Description: Provides daytime Children's Concerts and two evening

Family Concerts—an introduction to chamber music for children and their families. The Pocket Opera group presents introductions to opera for young children. The prices are refreshingly affordable.

Palo Alto Children's Concert Series (All Ages)
Palo Alto Art Center Auditorium
(650) 329-2527; 1313 Newell Road, Palo Alto, CA 94303
<www.city.palo-alto.ca.us/artsculture/music.html>

Schedule: Concert schedule on the Web site, or call Suzanne Warren for additional information.
Cost: $6/adult and $4/child or senior. Tickets available only at the door.

Peter and the Wolf (Ages 4+)
San Francisco Symphony, Davies Symphony Hall
(415) 864-6000; (800) 696-9689
201 Van Ness Avenue, San Francisco, CA 94102
<www.sfsymphony.org>

Description: This is a holiday favorite and a wonderful way to introduce young children to the symphony. After Prokofiev's *Peter and the Wolf,* there's a performance of Christmas carols and a sing-along. Before you come to the symphony, it's a good idea to read the story of *Peter and the Wolf* together and watch the video. This helps prepare your child and enriches his first symphonic experience. I recommend a 30-minute ballet video, *The Royal Ballet School in Prokofiev's Peter and the Wolf,* with choreography by Matthew Hart and Narrator Anthony Dowell. Distributed by BBC and RM Arts. The picture book, *Peter and the Wolf,* by Russian artist Vladimir Vagin retells the story (Scholastic Press). Plan on arriving at least 30 minutes early to allow time for parking and getting seated. Traffic to downtown San Francisco can be quite challenging, so allow enough time for getting there without being stressed.
Schedule: Only 2 performances in early December. Visit the Web site or call for specific times and dates.
Cost: Varies, depending on seating.
Bathrooms: Yes.
Food: Snacks only. There is a California Pizza Kitchen (415) 436-9380 at 524 Van Ness Avenue and McAllister Street within a short walk of

Davies Symphony Hall. Nearby are also a few fast food places, including McDonald's.

What to Bring: Opera glasses or binoculars, and cash for parking and food. Dress warmly, as San Francisco can be windy and foggy.

Follow-Up Activities: 1) *Carnival of the Animals* by Camille Saint-Saens is a fun and humorous musical piece that will captivate your child. Composed as a musical joke, it quickly became so popular that it is now considered his masterpiece. The children's book of the same title by Barrie Carson Turner and Sue Williams provides a guide to understanding the composition. The book comes with a CD. The book introduces the instruments, and provides explanations and illustrations for each track on the CD. 2) The San Francisco Symphony has a wonderful music Web site for kids: <www.sfskids.org>. It introduces kids to musical instruments. There is a music lab to help kids learn about rhythm, pitch, tempo, and dynamics. It even has a *Performalator* to let you play tunes like *Twinkle Twinkle Little Star* and a *Composerizer* to assemble your own tune using preset measures of music. 3) The children's concert series for grades kindergarten and up is on weekdays. 4) Lecture series for parents on music education.

Villa Montalvo (Ages 2+)

(408) 961-5800; 15400 Montalvo Road, Saratoga, CA 95071
<www.villamontalvo.org>

Description: Features family theater with wonderful performances of puppet shows, fairy tales, plays, musicals, and concerts.

Free Concerts

Ghiradelli Square, Golden Gate Park, and Yerba Buena Gardens in San Francisco and Jack London Square in Oakland have regularly scheduled events, throughout the year that include musical performances. For event information, visit the San Francisco Convention and Visitor's Bureau Web site, <www.sfvisitor.org/calendar>, and Jack London Square's Web site, <www.jacklondonsquare.com/eventsframe.html>.

Don't forget to check with your cities and local public libraries because they provide free public concerts usually during the summer, as special holiday events or as part of arts and wine festivals. The free summer concerts are usually sponsored by the city and usually take place at the civic center plazas or city parks. Parks and Recreation Department catalog usually announces free concerts.

Community Concerts (East Bay)
<www.communityconcerts.com>

Provides a list of concerts in the East Bay, including free concerts.

Community School of Music & Arts (Ages 3+)
(650) 961-0342; 220 View Street, Mountain View, CA 94041
<www.arts4all.org>

Description: Provides free family events performed at the Mountain View Center for the Performing Arts. Offers art and music lessons. Check the Web site or Mountain View Center for the Performing Arts's Web site for current schedule.

Memorial Park Amphitheater (Ages 4+)
(408) 777-3120; Memorial Park, Cupertino, CA 95014

Description: Located at the corner of Mary Ave and Stevens Creek Boulevard, across from De Anza College. Summer performances on Thursdays 6–8pm. No concerts July 4, due to the fireworks on De Anza College grounds.

Linden Tree Children's Recordings and Books (All Ages)
(650) 949-3390; 1-800-949-3313
170 State Street, Los Altos, CA 94022
<http://lindentree.booksense.com/NASApp/store/IndexJsp>

Description: *Family Concert Series:* During the summers, Linden Tree offers free concerts titled *Wednesdays in the Courtyard* on Wednesdays at 10am. Contact the Linden Tree for its concert schedule. Admission is donation of a new book for literacy programs. Special events are often advertised in *Bay Area Parent* magazine and *San Jose Mercury News*.

Mountain View Center for the Performing Arts (Ages 3+)

(650) 903-6000; 500 Castro Street, Mountain View, CA 94039
<www.ci.mtnview.ca.us/mvcpa/mvcpa.html>

Description: Free family performing arts series, "*Sunday Family Series,*" through the Community School of Music & Arts on a first come first served basis. The performances are on Sunday afternoons at 2:30pm and 4:30pm. Check the Web site <www.arts4all.org> for current schedule.

Music at Noon Series (Ages 3+)
Center of Performing Arts Recital Hall, Santa Clara University

(408) 554-4429; (408) 554-4015
Franklin and Lafayette Streets, Santa Clara, CA 95050
<www.scu.edu/cpa>

Schedule: Music at Noon Series is held on Wednesdays at noon. Visit Web site for calendar, map, and directions.

San Francisco Conservatory of Music (Ages 5+)

(415) 564-8086; 1201 Ortega Street, San Francisco, CA 94122
<www.sfcm.edu>

Description: Provides free concerts and low-cost events. Check Web site for concert and events schedule.

San Francisco Youth Arts Festival (All Ages)
Yerba Buena Gardens

(415) 759-2916; 221 4th Street, San Francisco, CA 94103
For administrative purposes contact Youth Arts Program:
(415) 750-8630; 20 Cook Street, San Francisco, CA 94118
<www.sfyouthartsfestival.org>

Description: In mid-May, the nine-day-long Youth Arts Festival features music and art exhibits, performances, workshops, and demonstrations along with kids' entertainment, including jugglers and face painting. See Web site for event times and details.

Sigmund Stern Grove Festival (All Ages)

(415) 252-6252; 19th Avenue & Sloat, San Francisco, CA
Mail: 44 Page Street, Ste. 600, San Francisco, CA 94102

<www.sterngrove.org>

Description: High-quality performances in the past have featured the San Francisco Symphony, San Francisco Ballet, and San Francisco Opera, as well as the Russian National Orchestra. A brand new *The Wolf and Peter* by Jean-Pascal Beintus premiered in the 2002 season. *The Wolf and Peter* is a "sequel" to Prokofiev's *Peter and the Wolf.*
Schedule: Sunday afternoons at 2pm, June through August. Check the Web site for current schedule. You can request to be on the mailing list to get information for next season's events.

Tassajara Symphony Orchestra (All Ages)

(925) 820-2494; 696 San Ramon Valley Blvd. #104, Danville, CA 94526
<www.tassajarasymphony.org>

Description: *Free Kids' Concerts.* Visit the Web site and click on the "Kids" tab. Free concerts include a talk and demonstrations.

Tapestry in Talent (All Ages)

(408) 494 3590; Admin: 255 North Market Street, Suite 124, San Jose, CA 95110
<www.tapestryintalent.org>

Description: This annual event held on the streets of downtown San Jose has attracted houndreds of thousands of visitors. This festival celebrates the visual and performing arts, with a special section, Creativity Zone, devoted to interactive kids' art activities. There are hundreds of artists showcasing their work, and music performers entertaining visitors on multiple stages. This fund-raiser provides seed money to neighborhood schools and the community for arts education.
Schedule: Annually over the 3-day Labor Day weekend, 10am-6pm.
Cost: Free; visit <www.sjdowntownparking.com> for parkimg information.
Bathrooms: Yes.
Facilities: Stroller friendly.
Food: International food booths.
What to Bring: Sunglasses; sunscreen; cash for food, drinks, souvenirs, and shopping.

Yerba Buena Gardens Festival (All Ages)
At Esplanade of Yerba Buena Gardens
(415) 543-1718 Arts & Events
Mission Street, San Francisco, CA, 94103 (between 3rd & 4th St.)
<www.ybae.org>

Description: Events include music, art, dance, theater, puppet shows, festivals, children's programs, and special events. The music variety is comprehensive, including jazz, classical, opera, and international music. The San Francisco Symphony and the San Francisco Opera perform here. Dance includes ballet performances by the Smuin Ballet and the San Francisco Ballet School. Festival and concerts highlight Italian, Filipino, Native American, and African American cultures. Picnic style lawn seating is available. There are plenty of restaurants nearby, but picnics are allowed and encouraged. Picnic blankets can be no larger than 8' x 8'.
Schedule: Annual festival from May through October with hundreds of performances, events, and festivals, all free. See the Web site for details on individual events, dates, and times.

Youth Symphonies & Local Musical Groups

For older children who are able to sit through more challenging musical pieces, there are many local youth orchestras, community symphonies, and musical groups that provide lower cost concerts to the community.

Bay Area Music Links for Classical Music
<http://kzsu.stanford.edu/~romain/mixed_links.html>

Provides links from this Web site to the Web sites of Bay Area community musical groups.

California Youth Symphony
(650) 325-6666; 441 California Avenue #5, Palo Alto, CA 94306

El Camino Youth Symphony
(650) 327-2611; 2439 Birch Street, Suite 3, Palo Alto, CA 94306
<www.ecys.org>

International Russian Music Piano Competition
1177 Branham Lane, Suite 200, San Jose, CA 95118
Email: russianmusiccomp@yahoo.com
<www.russianmusiccompetition.com>

Description: Annual piano competition featuring musicians from ages 6 to 18. The winners' concert is held in late May. The final event, held on a Saturday, features Russian opera, folk music, art songs, dancing, and the winner of the annual competition. Performances take place at Le Petit Trianon in San Jose (72 North 5th Street, San Jose, CA). To purchase tickets or to get more information, write to the e-mail address.

Oakland Youth Orchestra
Alice Arts Center
(510) 832-7710; 1428 Alice Street, #202M, Oakland, CA 94612
<www.oyo.org>

Peninsula Youth Orchestra
(650) 325-7967; 1219 Ralston Avenue, Belmont, CA 94002
<www.peninsulasymphony.org>

Palo Alto Chamber Orchestra
(650) 856-3848; 4000 Middlefield Road, #M-1, Palo Alto, CA 94303
<www.paco66.org>

Ragazzi Boys Chorus
(650) 342-8785; 20 N. San Mateo Drive, Suite 9, San Mateo, CA 94401
<www.ragazzi.org>

This Bay Area Boys Choir also trains boys to sing. Visit the Web site for concert schedule: <www.ragazzi.org/concerts.htm>.

San Francisco Symphony Youth Orchestra (Ages 12+)
Davies Symphony Hall
(415) 864-6000; 201 Van Ness Avenue, San Francisco, CA 94102
<www.sfsymphony.org>

San Jose Symphony Youth Orchestra
(408) 287-7383; 100 N. Almaden Avenue, San Jose, CA 95110
<www.webcom.com>

Santa Cruz Chamber Players
(831) 425-3149; P.O. Box 4174, Santa Cruz, CA 95063-4174
<www.scchamberplayers.org>

Steinway Society of the Bay Area
Le Petit Trianon
(408) 246-4200; 72 North 5th Street, San Jose, CA 95112
<www.steinwaythebayarea.com>

Music Museum

Ira F. Brilliant Center for Beethoven Studies & Museum (Ages 13+)
San Jose State University (Modular A Bldg.)
(408) 924-4590; One Washington Square, San Jose, CA 95192
<www.sjsu.edu/depts/beethoven>

Description: This center is devoted to the life and works of Ludwig van Beethoven. It has the largest collection of Beethoven materials outside of Europe. It has sponsored exhibits, concerts, and piano competitions. To get the most out of this center, plan ahead and attend the lectures and concerts.

Hours: Mon–Fri: 1–5pm and by appointment. Confirm prior to visit by calling or visiting the Web site. Closed most federal holidays.

Cost: Free admission. Tickets to concerts and other events vary.

Follow-Up Activities: Most concerts are performed at the Concert Hall at San Jose State University. The annual Young Pianists' Beethoven Competition is in mid-May. These competitions are open to the public and are inexpensive. Check Web site for events schedule and cost: <www.sjsu.edu/depts/beethoven/events/events.html>.

Ballet Performances

The *Nutcracker,* usually performed during the holiday season, is another wonderful way to introduce young children to dance, music, and musical theater. The *Nutcracker* is probably the easiest ballet for children to appreciate with its toys, toy soldiers, and battle of the Nutcracker against the Mouse King. Other ballets that are harder to find, but with equally beautiful music and still approachable for children, are *Sleeping Beauty, Swan Lake,* and *Giselle.* Prior to attending the ballet, read the corresponding stories from children's picture books to help prepare your child to understand the ballet and the music. These ballets have toured the Bay Area recently at the San Francisco Ballet and at CalPerformances in U.C. Berkeley. Ballet performances can be expensive, but they're worth it. If you get the rare opportunity to watch world class ballet by the Bolshoi and the Kirov ballet companies, don't miss it!

These ballets are fairly long, usually approximately 2½ to three hours, with intermission approximately halfway through the ballet. Consider the attention span and interest of your child in deciding whether to attend. My daughter loved the *Nutcracker* and *Sleeping Beauty;* she was hooked. Although it was a bit of a challenge to keep a four-year-old from wriggling during the last hour of the performance, she was so enthralled with *Sleeping Beauty* that she requested *Swan Lake* and *Giselle.* It probably helped that she'd seen Disney's *Sleeping Beauty* multiple times and loved to sing with it. The *Barbie in the Nutcracker* and *Barbie of Swan Lake* videos can also be used to introduce your child to these ballets.

For the most current Bay Area dance performance events in ballet and modern dance, visit this Web site: <**www.baydance.com**>.

Nutcracker Ballet at the San Francisco Ballet (Ages 4+)
At War Memorial Opera House

(415) 865-2000; 455 Franklin Street, San Francisco, CA 94102
Performs at: 301 Van Ness Avenue, San Francisco, CA
<www.sfballet.org>

Description: A holiday favorite and a great way to introduce children to ballet and the fine arts. This ballet is about a little girl, Clara, who receives a Nutcracker from her uncle, who is believed to be a magician. When the Mouse King attacks the Nutcracker, Clara comes to the Nutcracker's rescue. They are whisked away to a magical land where they are entertained by dancers from around the world. The music is engaging and the costumes are sumptuous. To help prepare your child, read the *Nutcracker* story prior to attending the performance. The SF Ballet Web site has the *Nutcracker* story and history of the ballet. The *Barbie in the Nutcracker* video is a great way to introduce children to the story, even though it is a different version of the traditional *Nutcracker* story. If you're new to ballet, check out San Francisco Ballet's "Frequently Asked Questions" section on its Web site. Detailed directions and map are also in the "First Time at SF Ballet" section under the "Performances" tab of their Web site.

Schedule: December. New "Family Nights" include character appearances before the performance and free cookies and milk during intermission.

Tickets: Prices vary depending on date/times and seating. Price ranges from $12 to $130 per seat. Sugar Plum Party: $20/person.

Bathrooms: Yes.

Food: Snacks only. The Opera Café located at the very bottom level of the Opera House is open for meals for certain performances. California Pizza Kitchen is located within walking distance at 524 Van Ness Ave (McAllister Street is the cross street). The phone number is (415) 436-9380.

What to Bring: Opera glasses (or you can rent them there), cash for parking and snacks, and a camera if you're attending the Sugar Plum Party following the performance.

Follow-Up Activities: If you really want to splurge, there's a Sugar Plum Party for children ages 4–11 immediately following select matinees that allows children to meet their favorite *Nutcracker* characters. Featured are cookies and treats and sometimes arts and crafts like making ornaments.

Other Nutcracker Performances

Ballet San Jose at Center for the Performing Arts (Ages 3+)

(408) 288-2800; 255 Almaden Boulevard, San Jose, CA 95113
<www.balletsanjose.org>

Schedule: In the 2nd half of December with Sat & Sun performances at 1:30pm and 7:30pm. In addition to the Nutcracker, there is a children's ballet performance series. See Web site for current performances.

Cost: Price per ticket ranges from $42 to $129, depending on age, seating, and performance times. Convenience fee charged for on-line orders. Tickets go on sale in mid-September.

Berkeley City Ballet (Ages 3+)

(510) 841-8913; 1800 Dwight Way, Berkeley, CA 94703
<www.berkeleycityballet.org>

Berkeley Ballet (Ages 3+)
Julia Morgan Center for the Arts

(510) 845-8542; 2640 College Avenue, Berkeley, CA 94703
<www.juliamorgan.org>

California Ballet (Ages 3+)
At the Dean Lesher Regional Center for the Arts

(925) 943-7469; 1601 Civic Drive, Walnut Creek, CA 94596
<www.dlrca.org>

Contra Costa Ballet Centre (Ages 3+)
At the Dean Lesher Regional Center for the Arts

(925) 943-SHOW (7469); 1601 Civic Drive, Walnut Creek, CA 94596

Oakland Ballet (Ages 4+)

(510) 286-8914; 1428 Alice Street, Oakland, CA 94612
<www.oaklandballet.org>; <www.paramounttheatre.com/ballet.html>

Description: Nutcracker performed at the Paramount Theater in the 2nd half of December. Purchase tickets from ticketmaster.com or from the Paramount Theater at: (510)465-6400. Paramount Theater is located at 2025 Broadway, Oakland, CA.

The Pacific Theater Ballet (Ages 3+)
Mountain View Center for the Performing Arts

(650) 903-6000; 500 Castro Street, Mountain View, CA 94039
<www.mvcpa.com>

Schedule: Early December.

Peninsula Ballet Theatre (Ages 3+)
San Mateo Performing Arts

(650) 340-9448; 600 North Delaware Street, San Mateo, CA 94401

Peninsula Youth Ballet (Ages 3+)
San Mateo Performing Arts

(650) 631-3767; 600 North Delaware Street, San Mateo, CA 94401
<www.pyb.org>

San Jose Dance Theater (Ages 3+)
San Jose Center for the Performing Arts

(408) 286-9905; 255 Almaden Boulevard, San Jose, CA 95113
<www.sjdt.org>

Schedule: Early December with matinee and evening performances.
Cost: Ranges from $14 to $40, depending on seats.
Description: Danced by children with adult guest dancers. Candy Kingdom and backstage tours also available for an additional cost.

Santa Clara Ballet (Ages 3+)
Performs at Santa Clara Convention Center

(408) 748-7000; 5001 Great America Parkway, Santa Clara, CA 95054
<www.geocities.com/vienna/strasse/7530/Nutcracker XE "Nutcracker" .htm>

Schedule: In mid-December with both matinee and evening performances.

Cost: Preferred Admission: $25/person, General Admission: $25/adult, $20/student or senior, $15.50/child. You can purchase tickets on-line at <www.santaclaraballet.tix.com>, by calling the Santa Clara Ballet Box Office: (408) 881-0879, or by mail from the Santa Clara Ballet Association, 3086 El Camino Real, Santa Clara, CA 95051.

Santa Cruz Civic Auditorium (Ages 3+)
(831) 420-5260; 307 Church Street, Santa Cruz, CA 95060
<www.santacruzcivic.com>

Smuin Ballets (Ages 3+)
(415) 978.2787; Email: info@smuinballets.com
<www.smuinballets.com/Performances.htm>

Description: Performances held at various venues in the Bay Area. Check the Web site for performance schedule, location, and ticket information.

Western Ballet (Ages 3+)
The Mountain View Ballet Company and School
(650) 968-4455; 2028 Old Middlefield Way, Mountain View, CA 94043
<www.westernballet.org>

Description: The dancers are from the Western Ballet School. The choreography and performance are wonderful. Like the San Francisco Ballet, the Western Ballet also has a follow-up tea party, "The Land of the Sweets Party," which provides an opportunity to meet some of the dancers and have some cookies and treats.

Schedule: In mid-December with matinee and evening performances.

Cost: $22.50/adult, $18.50/child. Land of the Sweets Party: $7/person. To purchase tickets, contact the Mountain View Center for the Performing Arts at (650) 903-6000 or on-line: <www.mvcpa.com>.

What to Bring: Camera, if you're planning to attend the party.

Children's Theater

Theater helps bring favorite stories to life and inspires the imagination. There is a huge selection of companies and venues that provide family theater. There are Broadway tours that are appropriate for children. Many performing arts centers have special family programs. A huge number of community groups provide children's theater, sometimes by children for children. There are also puppet shows and plays at Children's Fairyland, Happy Hollow Park & Zoo, and Children's Discovery Museum in San Jose as well as the Bay Area Children's Museum in Sausalito.

Develop your child's love of reading and explore the world through stories. Reading with your child develops listening skills, increases attention span and concentration, broadens vocabulary, and nurtures the imagination.

American Musical Theatre of San Jose
The Center for the Performing Arts
(408) 453-7108; 255 Almaden Boulevard, San Jose, CA 95113
<www.amtsj.org>

Bay Area Storytelling Festival
Kennedy Grove Regional Recreation Area, El Sobrante, CA
<www.bayareastorytelling.org>

For mapping on the Internet Web sites, use 7000 San Pablo Dam Road, El Sobrante, CA. In mid-May, this two-day weekend festival brings story-tellers from around the state and country. The genres include fables, fairy tales, and many other types of stories.

Best of Broadway
(415) 551-2000; (415) 551-2050
<www.bestofbroadway-sf.com>
For a current list of shows: www.bestofbroadway-sf.com/goldengate.html

Description: Brings the "Best of Broadway" series to San Francisco. Many Broadway musicals are appropriate for children, including Disney's *Beauty and the Beast* and *Lion King, Annie, My Fair Lady, The Sound of Music,* and *Peter Pan.*

Venues:

    Orpheum Theater: 1192 Market Street, San Francisco, CA 94102

    Golden Gate Theater: 1 Taylor Street, San Francisco, CA 94102

    Curran Theater: 445 Geary Street, San Francisco, CA 94102

Broadway by the Bay
San Mateo Performing Arts Center
(650) 579-5568 ext. 1; 600 North Delaware Avenue, San Mateo, CA 94401

<www.broadwaybythebay.com>

Description: Past performances included *Singing in the Rain, Sound of Music,* and *West Side Story.* Season tickets for all 3 shows: $45–$66/adult, $45/youth (6–18). Single ticket prices: $15–$18/youth (6–18), $15–$27/ adult. Price varies by seating section.

Bus Barn Stage Company
Los Altos Youth Theater
(650) 941-0551; 97 Hillview Avenue, Los Altos, CA 94022

<www.busbarn.org>

California Shakespeare Festival/California Shakespeare Theatre Midsummer Stage (Ages 7–18)
(510) 548-3422 x105; (510) 548-9666 Box Office

701 Heinz Avenue, Berkeley CA 94710

<www.calshakes.org>

Description: Performance is at the Bruns Amphitheater in the hills between Berkeley and Orinda, off Highway 24. Student matinees and outreach programs for East Bay schools and year-round classes for youths, teens, and adults are offered.

Center for the Arts Theater
(415) 978-ARTS; BASS Ticket Centers: (415) 776-1999 or (510) 762-BASS

Corner of Howard and 3rd Street, San Francisco, CA 94105

Children's Discovery Museum (All Ages)
(408) 298-5437; 180 Woz Way, San Jose, CA 95110
<www.cdm.org>

Description: Features plays related to the current exhibit. Plays are $1 per person plus general admission. Check the Web site for the calendar.

Children's Fairyland (Ages 2–10)
(510) 452-2259; 699 Bellevue Avenue, Oakland, CA 94610
<www.fairyland.org>

Description: Bring your toddler's nursery rhymes to life by visiting Children's Fairyland in Oakland and enrich your child's reading experience. This is a great little park where the rides and exhibits are built around nursery rhymes, fables, and stories. Don't miss the "Magic Key," which can be rented for $2, to hear stories at the exhibits. The Puppet Shows are "must see." Live shows are performed by kids through the Children's Fairyland Theater. See the Web site for current schedules. The park also has a small carousel and a mini-train.

Hours: *Spring* (April 3–June 16): Wed–Sun: 10am–4pm. *Summer* (June 17–August 25): weekdays: 10am–4pm, weekends: 10am–5pm. *Fall* (August 26–October 31): Wed–Sun and holidays: 10am–4pm. *Winter* (November 2–March 31): weekends and holidays: 10am–4pm.

Cost: $6/person includes unlimited rides. Free/child under one.

Bathrooms: Yes.

Facilities: Stroller friendly.

Food: Yes. You can also bring your own picnic lunch, but no glass bottles.

What to Bring: Your favorite nursery rhyme book to make the stories come alive.

Follow-Up Activities: 1) In late October, costume parades and costumed fairy tale characters celebrate Halloween at Fairyland's "Jack O'Lantern Jamboree." Hours are 11am–7pm. Admission is $7/person, all ages. Check the Web site or call for current dates/times. **2)** If your 8- to 10-year-old likes to perform, Fairyland has a free one-year Children's Theater training program. Summer Performing Arts Day Camp is also available for ages 5–11.

Children's Musical Theater, San Jose
(408) 288-5437; 1401 Parkmoor Avenue, San Jose, CA 95126
<www.cmtsj.org>

Performs at the Montgomery Theater at Market and San Carlos streets in downtown San Jose and the Sobrato CET Theater at 701 Vine Street in downtown San Jose. Visit Web site for maps and directions. These shows are performed by youngster ages 6-18.

City Lights Theater Company of San Jose
(408) 295-4200; 529 S. Second Street, San Jose, CA 95112
<www.cltc.org>

Coastal Repertory Theatre
(650) 726-0998; (650) 569-3266 Single Tickets; (650) 726-9208 Season Tickets
1167 Main Street, Half Moon Bay, CA 94019
<www.coastalrep.com>

Description:Performances as well as drama classes for kids ages 4 through 18 are offered. Performs at Mel Mello Center for the Performing Arts, 1167 Main Street, Half Moon Bay, CA 94019.

Disney on Broadway
<www.disneyonbroadway.com>

Beauty and the Beast, The Lion King, Aida and other musicals tour throughout the United States. Visit the Web site for the most current information.

Disney on Ice (All Ages)
<www.disneyonice.com>

To check for most current Disney stories translated into ice skating performances, visit the official Web site.

Douglas Morrisson Theatre (All Ages)

(510) 881-6777; 22331 North Third Street, Hayward, CA 94541
<http://hard.dst.ca.us/index.html> then "Signature Facilities" then "Morrisson Theater"

Description: Plays, musicals, and concerts.
Hours: Mon–Fri: 10am–1pm for information. *Show times*: Thur, Fri, & Sat: 8pm, Sun: 2pm.
Cost: *Musicals:* $20/adult, $13/junior (under 18), $17/senior (over 50).
Plays: $17/adult, $12/junior (under 18), $15/senior (over 50).
Concerts: $10/adult, $5/junior (under 18), $8/senior (over 50).
Season subscription packages are also available.
Follow-Up Activities: All the stage costumes are available for rental. Rental Prices range from $55 to $70. Special discounts available for group rentals. Costume Rental Department is open Mon–Fri: 10am–4pm by appointment only. Call (510) 881-6760 for an appointment.

Dublin Theatre Company (All Ages)

(925) 551-5DTC (5382); Box Office: (925) 551-0200
6620 Dublin Boulevard, Dublin, CA 94568
<www.dublintheatre.com>

Happy Hollow Park & Zoo (All Ages)

(408) 277-3000; 1300 Senter Road, San Jose, CA 95112
<www.happyhollowparkandzoo.org>

Puppet show is included with park admission. Summer camp.

Hillbarn Theatre & Conservatory

(650) 349-6411; 1285 E. Hillsdale Boulevard, Foster City, CA 94404
<www.hillbarntheatre.org>

Julia Morgan Center for the Arts

(510) 845-8542; Box Office: (925) 798-1300
2640 College Avenue, Berkeley, CA 94704
<www.juliamorgan.org>
<www.juliamorgan.org/kal.shtml>

There are two places for event information on the Web site. One is under "Theater Events" and the other is under "Kaleidoscope" and "Performances." The Sunday matinee series is at 2pm under the Kaleidoscope section. The matinee series costs $10/adult, $5/child per show.

Kids on Broadway
(831) 425-3455; P.O. Box 3461, Santa Cruz, CA 95063
<www.kidsonbroadway.org>

Performs at Louden Nelson Community Center, located at 301 Center Street, Santa Cruz, CA 95060.

Lyric Theatre of San Jose
(408) 986-9090; 430 Martin Avenue, Santa Clara, CA 95050
<www.lyrictheater.org>

Performs at various venues.

Menlo Players Guild
(650) 322-3261; PO Box 301, Menlo Park, CA 94026
<www.menloplayersguild.com>

Performs Shakespeare and other pieces. Shakespeare Festival is cosponsored with the Festival Theatre Ensemble. The festival is in June at Burgess Park. Check the Web site at <www.festivaltheatreensemble.org> for current information on the festival. The Menlo Players Guild performs at various venues on the peninsula.

Mountain View Center for the Performing Arts
Tickets: (650) 903-6000; Administration: (650) 903-6565
500 Castro Street, Mountain View, CA 94039
<www.mvcpa.com>

This performing arts center features many local theater and dance companies, as well as visiting troupes. Visit the Web site for the calendar of events and to purchase tickets.

Peninsula Youth Theatre
(650) 988-8798; 2500 Old Middlefield Way, Mountain View, CA 94043
<www.pytnet.org>
Quality Children's Theater. Performs at the Mountain View

221

Center for the Performing Arts. During the summer from late June to mid-August, free Children's Theater in the Park series perform on Fridays at 6:30pm. Performances at the outdoor Parkstage next to Pioneer Park. Each production is 45 minutes. You may bring a picnic dinner and blanket.

Theatre Works
Admin. (650) 463-1950; Tickets: (650) 463-1960 (11am– 5pm)
<www.theatreworks.org>
Performs at the Mountain View Center for the Performing Arts and Lucie Stern Theatre in Palo Alto.

Palo Alto Players
(650) 329-0891; 1305 Middlefield Road, Palo Alto, CA 94301
<www.paplayers.org>
Performs at the Lucie Stern Theatre in Palo Alto.

Pleasanton Playhouse
Studio Theatre: (925) 462-2121; 1048 Serpentine, #307, Pleasanton, CA 94566
Amador Theatre: (925) 484-4486; 1155 Santa Rita Road, Pleasanton, CA
<http://pleasantonplayhouse.com>

San Jose Repertory Theater
(408) 367-7255; 101 Paseo de San Antonio, San Jose, CA 95113
<www.sjrep.com>

Santa Clara Players
(408) 248-7993; 1900 Don Avenue, Santa Clara, CA 95050
<www.scplayers.org>
Performs at the Triton Museum of Art's Hall Pavilion.

Saratoga Civic Theater
(408) 868-1249; 13777 Fruitvale Avenue, Saratoga, CA 95070

Features both the Saratoga Drama Group and the West Valley Light Opera on a rotating basis.

Saratoga Drama Group
Located at the Saratoga Civic Theater
Box Office: (408) 882-5099; (408) 741-9508
P.O. Box 182, Saratoga, CA 95071
<www.saratogadramagroup.com>

West Valley Light Opera
(408) 268-3777; P.O. Box 779, Los Gatos, CA 95031
<www.wvlo.org>

Festival Theatre Ensemble
(408) 996-0635; 708 Blossom Hill Road, #121, Los Gatos, CA 95032
<www.festivaltheatreensemble.org>
Performs plays by Shakespeare. Some shows are at the Saratoga Civic
Theater. Shakespeare in the Park series through the Town of Los
Gatos performs at Oak Meadow Park in July in the evenings. Tickets
are $15/adult, $10/child 18 & under or senior 60+. Coproduces the
Burgess Shakespeare Festival with the Menlo Players Guild at Burgess
Park in Menlo Park. See Web site for details. The company also offers
school site performances. Call for more information.

Shady Shakespeare Company
(408) 298-0649; 483 N 15th Street, San Jose, CA 95112
<www.shadyshakes.org>

Free Shakespeare in the Park
<www.sfshakes.org/park/index.html>

1) Free performances held at various venues throughout the Bay Area.
In the past, performed in Pleasanton, Cupertino, Oakland, and San
Francisco. Performances are in the summer, from July to early October.
Visit Web site for dates, locations, maps, and directions. 2) Sponsors
the Bay Area Shakespeare Camps for children ages 7–18 to learn acting and perform Shakespeare's works. These summer camps are located
throughout the Bay Area: San Francisco, Oakland, Cupertino, Los Altos,
Pleasanton, Pacifica, Berkeley, Danville, Walnut Creek, San Jose, etc. For
more information on the camps, call (800) 978-PLAY or (415) 422-
2222.

Shakespeare Santa Cruz
UCSC Theater Arts Center & Festival Grove
UCSC Ticket Office: (831) 459-2159

Performing Arts Center, 1156 High Street, Santa Cruz, CA 95064

<http://shakespearesantacruz.org/>

Season: July & August. Tickets go on sale starting in May.

Stage One Theatre
(510) 791-0287; 39375 Cedar Boulevard, Newark, CA

<www.stage1theatre.org>

Shows performed at Newark Memorial High School.

Sunnyvale Community Center Theatre
(408) 733-6611; 550 E. Remington Drive, Sunnyvale, CA 94087

Both the California Theater Center and Sunnyvale Community Players use the Sunnyvale Community Center Theatre.

California Theater Center
(408) 245-2978; P.O. Box 2007, Sunnyvale, CA 94087

E-Mail: boxoffice@ctcinc.org

<www.ctcinc.org>

Sunnyvale Community Players
(408) 733-6611; P.O. Box 60399, Sunnyvale, CA 94088

<www.sunnyvaleplayers.org>

Tabard Theatre (Ages 4–18)
(408) 979-0231; 5663 Chambertin Drive, San Jose, CA 95118

<www.tabardtheater.org>

Performs at South Valley Christian Church: 590 Shawnee Lane, San Jose, CA 95123. For advanced ticket purchase, call (408) 679-2330. Drama classes are offered for kids 4 to 18 years old. Visit the Web site for details: <www.tabardtheater.org/workshop.html>.

U.C. Santa Cruz Theater Arts MainStage
Theater Arts Center
(831) 459-2159; (831) 459-3552; 1156 High Street, Santa Cruz CA 95064

E-mail: tickets@cats.ucsc.edu

<www.events.ucsc.edu/tickets>
<www.events.ucsc.edu/artslecs/Calendar.html>

Box Office Hours: Tues–Fri: noon– 6pm, Sat: 10 am–4pm. Closed
Sun & Mon. Ticket office opens one hour prior to performance time for
event sales to ½ hour after start time of performance.

Villa Montalvo
(408) 961-5800; 15400 Montalvo Road, Saratoga, CA 95070
<www.villamontalvo.org>
Features Family Theater showcasing puppet shows, fairy tales, and musicals in an intimate theater with beautiful surroundings.

Young Performers Theatre (Ages 3+)
Fort Mason Center
(415) 346-5550; Building C, Room 300, San Francisco, CA 94123
<www.ypt.org>

Kids' shows and classes for kids 3 and older. Birthday parties.
$8/adult and $5/child.

Ticketmaster's Web Site With Upcoming Events for Families:
<www.ticketmaster.com/section/family?tm_link=tm_home_a_family>
Or www.ticketmaster.com.

Once you're at the site, select the "Family" icon across the top bar, and
then select the location to N. California/N. Nevada to see a list of up-
coming events. These events include children's TV shows that tour such
as *The Wiggles*, *Dragon Tales*, and *Barney*. It also sell tickets to *Disney on
Ice*, *Champions on Ice*, etc.

Web Site Links for Theaters in California
<www.curtainrising.com/usa/usa_ca_pz.html>

Web Sites for Additional Events in the Bay Area
A selection of events and happenings in the San Francisco Bay area
<www.scaruffi.com/travel/sfoevent.html>

Children's Events

Our public libraries and children's bookstores are wonderful resources. Local libraries and bookstores have story times and other events geared toward families. These include sing-along concerts; arts and crafts; lectures; and special events such as puppet shows, magic shows, and plays. Even the Nutcracker ballet and the Dickens Christmas Fair have performed at these venues during the holiday season. Check your local library and bookstores for events schedule as these change frequently.

Library Events

In addition to special family events, many libraries have summer reading programs to encourage reading and literacy. These summer reading programs have reward programs such as discounts and free merchandise to a large selection of attractions and merchants. Ask your local library for details.

Bay Area Library Web Site Links
<www.bayarealibraries.com/libraries.htm>

Alameda County Public Libraries
Fremont Main Library
(510) 745-1400;
(510) 745-1421 Children's Services
(510) 745-1444 Reference Desk
(510) 505-7001 Business Library
2400 Stevenson Boulevard, Fremont, CA 94538
<www.aclibrary.org> For additional information and branch locations
<www.aclibrary.org/kidsplace> Great kids' Web site.

Berkeley Public Library
(510) 981-6100; 2090 Kittredge, Berkeley, CA 94704
<www.infopeople.org/bpl/kids>
<www.infopeople.org/bpl> Kids' page.

City of Mountain View Public Library
(650) 903-6337; 585 Franklin Street, Mountain View, CA 94041
<http://library.ci.mtnview.ca.us/>
Children's services: <http://www.ci.mtnview.ca.us/citydepts/lib/cs/cs.htm>

City of Palo Alto Children's Library
(650) 329-2134; 1276 Harriet Street, Palo Alto, CA 94303
<www.city.palo-alto.ca.us/palo/city/library/about/children.html>

Contra Costa County Library
(800) 984-INFO within Contra Costa County only
(925) 646-6434 outside of Contra Costa County
<www.ccclib.org or www.contra-costa.lib.ca.us>
<www.contra-costa.lib.ca.us/libinfo/branch.html> for branch locations
Links for kids' sites:<www.ccclib.org/youth/kidsites.html>

Los Gatos Public Library
(408) 354-6891; 110 East Main Street, Los Gatos, CA 95030
<www.library.town.los-gatos.ca.us>
<www.library.town.los-gatos.ca.us/kidsaftprog.html> for kids' afternoon programs
including ventriloquists and plays.

Oakland Public Library
Main Library
(510) 238-3134; 125 14th Street, Oakland, CA 94612
<www.oaklandlibrary.org>
<www.oaklandlibrary.org/links/kids> Kids' page.

Palo Alto City Libraries
Main Library
(650) 329-2436; 1213 Newell Road, Palo Alto, CA 94303
<www.city.palo-alto.ca.us/palo/city/library>
<www.city.palo-alto.ca.us/palo/city/library/kids-teens>

Peninsula Library System
Covers S. San Francisco and Daly City to Redwood City and Woodside
<www.plsinfo.org>
<www.plsinfo.org/reads/for_kids/kids_place> Kids' page.

San Francisco Public Library
Main Branch
(415) 557-4400; 100 Larkin Street, San Francisco, CA 94102
<http://sfpl.lib.ca.us/> Listing of branch library locations.

San Jose Public Library
Dr. Martin Luther King Jr. Main Library
(408) 277-4846; 180 W. San Carlos Street, San Jose, CA 95113
<www.sjpl.lib.ca.us>
<www.sjpl.lib.ca.us/Kids> Great kids' page!

Santa Clara City Library
Central Library (Temporary)
(408) 615-2900; 3345 Lochinvar Avenue, Santa Clara, CA 95051
<www.library.ci.santa-clara.ca.us/kids/kids-page.html>

Has a great Web site with the "Kidspace" that provides suggested reading lists for children; an event calendar with story times, special shows, and craft projects; homework Web site links featuring missions, government pages, countries, history, science, math, etc.

Santa Clara County Libraries
Includes Alum Rock, Campbell, Cupertino, Los Altos, Saratoga, Milpitas, Morgan Hill, and Gilroy libraries.
<www.santaclaracountylib.org> with links to each of these libraries.
<www.santaclaracountylib.org/kids/kidssites.html> Links to Kids' sites.

Sunnyvale Public Library
(408) 730.7300; 665 W. Olive Avenue, Sunnyvale, CA 94086
<www.ci.sunnyvale.ca.us/library>

Store Events

Barnes and Noble
<www.bn.com>

Once you've entered the Web site, type in "Store Locator" and click on the "Go" button, in the "Search" field. The "Stores & Events" page should come up. Then type in your zip code and click on the "Search" button. This should bring up the stores closest to you. Then you can click on "Events" of the store(s) you're interested in to find out detailed information on the events. Different stores have different events. Some stores have much more family oriented programs, so don't be discouraged if you look at the first one and there's not much there.

Borders Books
<www.bordersstores.com>

Once you've entered the Web site, select the "Store Locator" icon, enter your zip code, then select (click on) the store(s) closest to you. This will bring up store specific events, address, hours, and map. Different stores have different events. Some stores have much more family oriented programs, so don't be discouraged if you look at the first one and there's not much there.

Linden Tree Children's Recordings and Books
(650) 949-3390; (800) 949-3313
170 State Street, Los Altos, CA 94022
<http://lindentree.booksense.com/NASApp/store/IndexJsp>

Family Concert Series, free sing-alongs for children.
Admission: a new book to donate.

The Wooden Horse
(408) 356-8821; 798 Blossom Hill Road, Los Gatos, CA 95032
<www.woodenhorsetoys.com>

Special event in late April for the National TV Turn Off Week with week-long activities including storytime, arts and crafts, Earth Day celebration, and play day. "Sleepover parties" and play days throughout the year. Check the Web site for special events.

Chapter 9
Historical Outings

H istorical outings show us what life was like in the old days. This section includes history parks and outings to learn about California history, including Native Americans, Spanish Missions, and the Gold Rush.

LearnCalifornia.org is a Web site resource that provides information on California's history including California Indians, Missions, the Gold Rush era, and railroad history. The Web site is <www.learncalifornia.org.

History Parks & Museums

Ardenwood Historic Farm (All Ages)
(510) 796-0663; 34600 Ardenwood Boulevard, Fremont, CA 94555
<www.ebparks.org/parks/arden.htm>

Description: Ardenwood is the site of many historical and cultural events. See the full entry for Ardenwood Historic Farm in the Animal Kingdom: Farms section.

* *Johnny Appleseed Day* is in early March.
* *Gathering of the Scottish Clan.* Tartan Day celebration with the Scottish folk. Enjoy highland children's games, bagpipes, dancing, traditional Scottish food, and reenactments with Mary, Queen of Scots, and her Court.
* *Annual Civil War Reenactments* are on Memorial Day.
* *Celtic Festival* is in early June. Enjoy Celtic dance and Welsh and Irish music along with historic enactments and children's activities.
* *Fire Truck Day and Antique Engine Show* are in mid-June.
* *July 4th: Old Fashioned Independence Day Celebration.*

- *Victorian Christmas* during the holiday season.

Hours/Cost: See the Web site's event calendar for current event details and costs.

California Historical Society
(415) 357-1848; 678 Mission Street, San Francisco, CA 94105
<www.californiahistoricalsociety.org>

Description: The museum provides information on the 300 years of California history. Photography and fine arts collections show the history of California from the pre-Gold Rush era to the early decades of the 1900s.

Hours: Tues–Sat: 11am–5pm. Public tours on Saturdays at 2pm, included with admission. Closed Mondays.

Cost: $3/adult, $1/student or senior over 62, free/child under 5. *Free on the first Tuesday of every month.*

Bathrooms: Yes.

Facilities: Stroller friendly.

Food: No. Nearby restaurants.

What to Bring: Cash for admission, food, and parking.

Follow-Up Activities: 1) There is a lecture series on the first Tuesday of each month 5:30–7pm. 2) Virtual exhibit of California's history spanning 300 years: <www.californiahistoricalsociety.org/exhibits/online.html>.

History Park, San Jose (All Ages)
(408) 287-2290; 1650 Senter Road, San Jose, CA 95112
<www.historysanjose.org/plan-sjhm.html>

Description: This park has historic buildings and exhibits that showcase an old-fashioned small town, with an operational trolley, antique cars, and trolleys from San Jose's bygone days at the Trolley Barn; a working print shop; an old-fashioned ice cream parlor; and an old firehouse. The old firehouse is open during the guided tour and on special event days. *The Hellenistic Heritage Institute/Museum* and the *Portuguese Museum* are also housed here at the park. There is an old Chinese temple and community center, *Ng Shing Gung*, the last of the six San Jose China Towns from the 1880s. For more information on the San Jose China Town: <www.chcp.org/Ng_Shing_Gung.html>.

Hours: Closed Mondays. *Weekends:* noon–5pm, *Tues–Fri:* noon–5pm, grounds open, most buildings closed. *Museum Store:* Tues–Fri: 11am–4pm, Sat & Sun: noon–4pm. *Guided tours* begin at 12:30pm, 1pm, 2pm, and 2:30pm. Don't miss the print shop demonstrations on the first and second weekends of each month. Trolleys run every weekend.

Cost: $5 parking fee. Tour tickets are available in the Museum Store. Tues–Fri: Free. Sat & Sun.: $6/adult, $5/senior, $4/child (ages 6–17), free/child (5 and under). Admission includes galleries.

Bathrooms: Yes.

Facilities: Stroller friendly.

Food: *O'Brien's Ice Cream & Café:* Tues–Fri: 11am–3pm, Sat & Sun: noon–4pm.

What to Bring: Cash for parking and tickets, sunscreen, sunglasses, camera, and picnic lunch.

Follow-Up Activities: 1) Happy Hollow Park & Zoo and the Japanese Friendship Garden are both within Kelly Park. 2) On the Cinco de Mayo event weekend, the Portuguese Museum sponsors a Portuguese Heritage Festival with parades, cooking demonstrations, arts and crafts for kids, and music and dancing to celebrate their heritage. 3) Around Memorial Day weekend in late May, History Park sponsors a Multicultural Festival with parades, print shop demonstrations, ethnic foods, music, etc. 4) School programs on historic topics such as the Gold Rush, Victorian school, Ohlone Indians and environmental programs, history of Santa Clara Valley and its transformation from an agricultural to a technologically driven society.

Hyde Street Pier (Ages 3+)

(415) 561-7100; Hyde Street at Jefferson Street, San Francisco, CA 94109
<www.maritime.org/calendar.htm>

Description: 1) Hyde Street Pier hosts a costumed living history event called *A Day in the Life: 1901.* Meet a costumed captain and his wife, cook, and chief engineer. Learn what life was like aboard ship around the turn of the 20th century. This event takes place every 2nd Saturday of the month: 10am–3pm. 2) Sea Music Festival for kids is held on the 3rd Saturday of the month: 3–3:45pm. 3) Family life onboard ship event, "Pet Goat and a Chart House of Her Own" is held on one Saturday a month: 3–4pm. 4) Chantey Sings are on the 1st Saturday of each month: 8pm–

midnight. The kid-appropriate tunes are sung 8pm–10pm. The bawdy tunes are not performed until after the 10pm break. Call (415) 556-6435 for reservations to the Chantey Sings. Call to confirm specific dates. See Hyde Street Pier entry in Chapter 6: Transportation Favorites —Boats.

National Steinbeck Center (Ages 5+)

(831) 796-3833; One Main Street, Salinas, CA 93901
<www.steinbeck.org>

Description: Situated in Old Town Salinas, the Steinbeck Center serves to educate the public about the life, times, and works of John Steinbeck, author of *East of Eden, Cannery Row, Of Mice and Men, The Grapes of Wrath,* and more. The center provides not only interactive exhibits to bring Steinbeck's experiences to life, but also serves as a cultural and artistic venue for lectures, films, art exhibits, and community activities.

Hours: 10am–5pm, 7 days a week. Closed on Thanksgiving, Christmas, New Year's Day, and Easter.

Cost: $9.95/adult; $7.95/senior 62+, student with ID, or Military with ID; $6.95/youth 13–17; $5.95/child 6–12; free/child 5 and under.

Bathrooms: Yes.

Facilities: Stroller friendly.

Food: Café open 11am–3pm for lunch.

What to Bring: Sunglasses and cash for food.

Follow-Up Activities: 1) Special events such as Kids Art Festival, Day of the Dead, and the Annual Steinbeck Festival in early August feature tours, films, lectures, and more. Call (831) 796–3833 for additional information or look under *Event Calendar* on the Web site. 2) School and group tours available on a first come first served basis. 1 month advanced reservations required. During the summer, walking tours visit locales frequented by John Steinbeck.

Roaring Camp Railroads

hosts many living history events. See Chapter 6: Transportation Favorites—Big Trains section for the full entry. Here's a sample list of living history events.

- Memorial Day: Civil War Reenactment.
- Labor Day: Summer Gathering of Mountain Men and Great Train Robberies.
- October: 1880s Harvest Fair (wool spinning, weaving, and candle

making).

- November: Annual Mountain Man Rendezvous (encampments of the 1840s trappers and traders, and demonstration of wilderness skills).

Rosicrucian Egyptian Museum (Ages 5+)
(408) 947-3635; 1342 Naglee Avenue, San Jose, CA 95191
<www.egyptianmuseum.org>

Description: Learn about Egyptian culture and the Egyptians' view of afterlife. You can walk through a collection of Egyptian artifacts and a replica of a noble's tomb.
Hours: Tues–Fri: 10am–5pm, Sat–Sun: 11am–6pm, closed Mondays. Last admission ½ hour prior to closing.
Cost: $9/adult, $7/senior or student w/ID, $5/child (5–10), free/child under 5. $1 discount available for AAA, KQED, or military members.
Bathrooms: Yes.
Facilities: Not stroller friendly.
Food: No. No picnicking allowed on the property or in the park.

Wax Museum, Fisherman's Wharf (Ages 5+)
(800) 439-4305; (415) 202-0416
145 Jefferson Street, San Francisco, CA 94133
(between Mason and Taylor Streets)
<www.waxmuseum.com>

Description: This wax museum has a large collection of famous and historically significant people, including King Tut and Cleopatra, U.S. presidents, famous scientists, movie stars, religious and world leaders, and artists and writers. It's a big variety, from the famous to the infamous.
Hours: Weekdays: 10am–9pm, Weekends: 9am–9pm. Special holiday hours. Call to confirm hours. Box office closes 1 hour prior to closing time.
Cost: $12.95/adult, $6.95/child, $10.95/senior 55+. $3 discount coupon on Web site.
Bathrooms: Yes.
Facilities: Stroller friendly.
Food: Nearby restaurants at Fisherman's Wharf, and Rainforest Café is next door.

What to Bring: Cash for parking, food, etc. Don't forget your jacket and sunglasses.

Follow-Up Activities: Educational programs available. To learn how wax figures are made, visit the Web site for a brief description.

Wilder Ranch State Park (All Ages)

(831) 423-9703; (831) 426-0505; 1401 Old Coast Road, Santa Cruz, CA 95060
(Off of Hwy 1, 2 miles North of Santa Cruz)
<www.santacruzstateparks.org/parks/wilder/index.php>

Description: This park showcases a dairy ranch from the 1900s. It has a small farm with a few animals and restored ranch buildings including a working blacksmith shop and a wood shop with water-powered tools. Don't miss the demonstration of this ingenious wood shop with its water wheel and pulley system that powered a drill, a grinder, and even an electric generator! You can tour the Victorian house where the Wilder family lived and see the exhibits at the visitor center. Guided tours about the ranch and living history demonstrations help us envision what life was like in the old days. The docents dress in period costume. In the spring, around late April/May, both the cliff and barn swallows come back to nest every year. It's a sight to watch them build their nests. A Nature Preserve is on the property, but closed to the public. However, there's an overlook from the Old Cove Landing trail for bird watching.

Hours: 8am–sunset. *Visitor Center:* Fri–Sun, 10am–4pm during the winter months. *Saturdays:* Ranch tours led by knowledgeable docents. *The third Saturday of each month* features a Living History Demonstration with costumed docents.

Cost: $5 parking fee.

Bathrooms: Yes, by the parking lot.

Facilities: Stroller friendly. Small bookstore in the visitor center.

Food: No, except for the July 4th celebration.

What to Bring: Cash for parking and binoculars for bird watching. If you visit during the July 4th old-fashioned Independence Day celebration, don't forget to bring your picnic gear, picnic lunch, sunscreen, sunglasses, hat, umbrella for shade, camera, and cash for food/ice cream/drinks.

Follow-Up Activities: 1) Ranger Explorers (6- to 10-year-olds) program in the summer through the Santa Cruz State Parks. Call 831-335-1743 for additional information. There is also a Jr. Ranger program for younger children. 2) Very close to both Natural Bridges and to the UCSC Seymour Marine Labs site. 3) Special event days:

- July 4th celebration is the biggest event on the ranch. Don't miss this event; the ranch is in full operation with demonstrations, hourly tours, old-fashioned games, music, and food.
- Harvest Festival in the fall.
- Victorian Holiday celebration in December.

Check the Web site for additional information: **<www.santacruzstate parks.org/education/events_list.php>**.

Woodside Store (Ages 4+)

(650) 851-7615; 3300 Tripp Road, Woodside, CA 94062;
(Cross St.: Kings Mountain Rd)

<www.eparks.net/Parks/Woodside>

Description: This is a museum set up as a general store filled with the goods that blacksmiths, wagon makers, lumbermen, or teamsters might have needed in the 1880s. There's also a recreated blacksmith shop.

Hours: Tues & Thur: 10am–4pm, Sat & Sun: noon–4pm. Closed other days and holidays.

Cost: Free.

Bathrooms: Yes.

Facilities: Stroller friendly.

Food: Snacks only. Food is available from concessions only on Woodside Days. Small souvenirs, books, and snacks available at the store regularly.

What to Bring: Sunscreen, sunglasses, camera, and picnic lunch.

Follow-Up Activities: On Woodside Days (once a year on the first Sunday of May), see demonstrations of horseshoeing and blacksmithing.

California History

Native American Indians

The California Indian Museum and Cultural Center
(707) 579-3004; 5250 Aero Drive, Santa Rosa, CA 95403
<http://cimcc.indian.com>
This museum is in its developmental stages. Although it is not yet open to the public, a lecture series on Saturday afternoons is free to the public. See Web site for current schedule.

Casa de Fruta hosts pow-wows in May. See the Casa de Fruta entry in Chapter 1: Animal Kingdom—Farms section.

Coyote Hills Regional Park Visitor Center (Ages 4+)
(510) 795-9385; 8000 Patterson Ranch Road, Fremont, CA 94555
<www.ebparks.org/parks/coyote.htm>
Description: This regional park preserves the Ohlone Indian shellmound sites and the rich wetlands surrounding the Fremont Bay. The visitor center has exhibits on the Ohlone way of life, a tule reed boat made using native American methods by the park staff and volunteers, and the park's wildlife and natural history. There are open houses and tours of the main shellmound site with a reconstructed tule house, shade shelter, dance circle, and sweat lodge.
Hours: *Park:* April–October: 8 am–8pm, October–April: 8 am–6pm.
Interpretive Center: Tues– Sun: 9:30 am–5pm. Closed on Thanksgiving, Christmas, and New Year's Day. *Butterfly & Hummingbird Garden:* Open on the second Saturday of each month.
Cost: $4 parking. Program fees vary, some free.
Bathrooms: Yes.
Facilities: Stroller friendly.
Food: No. Picnic tables available.

What to Bring: Binoculars, camera, picnic lunch, and cash for parking. Wear comfortable walking shoes.

Follow-Up Activities: Naturalist programs on weekends include wildflower walks in April, Ohlone Indian crafts such as basket weaving and arrowhead making, and shellmound workdays to learn how to build mats to thatch houses. Call or visit Web site for specific details on programs: <www.ebparks.org/events/byloc/coyote.htm>.

Miwok Park/Marin Museum of the American Indian (Ages 4+)
(415) 897-4064; Miwok Park, 2200 Novato Boulevard, Novato, CA 94947
<www.marinindian.com>

Description: Learn about the history and culture of Native Americans.
Hours: Closed Mondays and Holidays. Tues–Fri: 10am–3pm, Sat & Sun: noon–4pm.
Cost: $5/adult, free/child under 12.
Bathrooms: Yes.
Facilities: Stroller friendly.
Food: No.
What to Bring: Picnic lunch.
Follow-Up Activities: 1) Summer camp program for children ages 6–10. 2) Annual Trade Feast Celebration is held in mid-September. The Trade Feast or Annual Dance is held for American Indians to get together to exchange supplies, foods, tools, songs, stories, and dances. 3) Visit the Web site for other special events for families.

Kule Loklo: a Replica Coast Miwok Village (Ages 2+)
Point Reyes National Seashore
(415) 663-1092; Bear Valley Visitor's Center: (415) 464-5100
<www.mapom.com/kuleloklo.htm>

Description: Kule Loklo is a short walk from the Bear Valley Visitor's Center at the Point Reyes National Seashore. It is a replica of the Coast Miwok Village. Visit the village and learn about Miwok Indian skills, history, and culture.
Hours: Bear Valley Visitor's Center: Mon–Fri: 9am–5pm, Sat/Sun and

holidays: 8am–5pm. Closed Christmas Day. Guided tours every Sunday from Memorial Day to Labor Day. Meet at the Bear Valley Visitors Center at Point Reyes National Seashore. Roundhouse tours on select Saturdays at 12:30pm during the spring and fall. These tours meet at the Roundhouse.

Cost: Free.

Bathrooms: Yes.

Facilities: Stroller friendly.

Food: Not usually, but on special event days, yes. Restaurants close by in Point Reyes Station and Olema.

What to Bring: Sunscreen, sunglasses, cash for food or picnic lunch, and camera.

Follow-Up Activities: 1) Strawberry Festival in late April celebrates the arrival of spring with blessing of the first fruit. Native American Dancers and demonstrators will be there along with food available for purchase. Don't forget to bring some cash! 2) Big Time is held in late July on a Saturday, 11am–5pm. Big Time is the traditional California Indian get together for dancing, trading, and socializing. Demonstrations, activities for kids, and Indian foods and crafts are for sale. For additional information, call (415) 464-5100. 3) For an on-line summary of the Miwok Indians, visit this Web site: <www.nps.gov/pore/history_miwok.htm> or <www.coastmiwok.com> then click on the "History" icon. 4) For additional information, contact the Miwok Archeological Preserve of Marin (MAPOM) at (415) 479-3281, 2255 Las Gallinas Avenue, San Rafael, CA 94903 or through the Web site: <www.mapom.com>.

Directions: <www.nps.gov/pore/visit_direct.htm>.

San Juan Bautista State Historic Park (Ages 5+)

(831) 623-4526; Hwy 156, San Juan Bautista, CA 95045
Plaza History Association: San Juan Bautista State Historic Park
(831) 623-4881; P.O. Box 787, San Juan Bautista, CA 95045
<www.parks.ca.gov/default.asp?page_id=563>

Description: This historic park, located in down town San Juan Bautista, includes the Plaza Hotel and stable, blacksmith shop, granary, jail, and several houses. The exhibits display what life was like in the California Mission during the Mexican era and during the precolonial days of the Native American.

Hours: 10am–4:30pm.

Cost: Free.
Bathrooms: Yes.
Facilities: Stroller friendly.
Food: No. Restaurants are nearby.
What to Bring: Sunscreen, sunglasses, camera, cash for food, and lots of gas in the tank.
Follow-Up Activities: 1) *Early Days in San Juan* is held annually on Father's Day weekend. The living history event features examples of life in the 1800s with an 1830 Mountain Men encampment, 1860–1870 buildings and clothing, and an 1890 bar room. 2) School trips require reservations with Reserve America at (831) 623-4528. Visit the Web site and look under the "School Groups" section for details.

Santa Cruz Mission (Ages 5+)

(831) 425-5849; 144 School Street, Santa Cruz, CA 95060
<www.santacruzstateparks.org/parks/mission/>

Description: This mission features exhibits about the Ohlone Indians who lived in the Santa Cruz region for thousands of years prior to the arrival of the Spanish missionaries.
Hours: Thur–Sun: 10am–4pm.
Cost: Free.
Bathrooms: Yes.
Facilities: Stroller friendly.
Food: No. Nearby restaurants.
What to Bring: Picnic lunch, sunscreen, and sunglasses.
Follow-Up Activities: *Tule Harvesting* in late August; *Storytelling* night on a Friday in late August; *Costuming Workshops* on Saturdays in August, September, and November; *Fiesta* in early October; *Living History Demonstrations* on Sundays in November; and a *First Night Living History Activity & Demonstration* on December 31. Visit the Web site: <www.sa ntacruzstateparks.org/education/events_list.php> for current information on dates and times.

Santa Cruz Museum of Art & History (Ages 3+)

has exhibit on the Ohlone Indians who lived in the Santa Cruz area. See the full entry in Chapter 8: Art & Performing Arts—Art Museums.

Missions

To learn more about California's missions, visit this Web site: <www.ca-missions.org>.

Sonoma Mission

(707) 938-1519; 114 East Spain Street, Sonoma, CA 95476
<www.iktome.com/svvb/mission.html>
Open 10am–5pm. $2/adult, $2/child.

Mission Dolores

(415) 621-8203   3321 16th Street, San Francisco, CA 94114
<www.missiondolores.org>

Open 8am–noon and 1–4pm. This serves as church, school, and museum.

Mission San Jose

(510) 657-1797; 43300 Mission Boulevard, Fremont, CA 94539
(P.O. Box 3314)
<www.ci.fremont.ca.us/Visiting/Attractions/HistoricAttractions.htm#Mission XE "Mission" >

Open 10am–5pm. The museum has a collection of artifacts, vestments, and memorabilia from the days when this served as a mission.

Mission Santa Clara, Santa Clara University

(408) 554-4023; 500 East Camino Real, Santa Clara, CA 95053
<www.scu.edu/visitors/mission>

For an on-line tour of the mission gardens: <www.scu.edu/map/tour/missiongardens>.

Santa Cruz Mission

(831) 425-5849; 144 School Street, Santa Cruz, CA 95060
<www.santacruzstateparks.org/parks/mission/>

See full entry in Chapter 9: Historical Outings—California History: Native American Indians section.

Mission San Juan Bautista

(831) 623-2127; Plaza, 2nd & Mariposa Street, San Juan Bautista
PO Box 400, San Juan Bautista, CA 95045
<www.parks.ca.gov/default.asp?page_id=563>
<www.oldmission-sjb.org/sightssounds.html>

Carmel Mission

(831) 624-3600; 3080 Rio Road, Carmel, CA 93923
<www.carmelmission.org>

Store open 9:30am – 4:30pm. Special Web site for fourth graders:
<www.carmelmission.org/4th_grade.htm>. This is still working as a church
as well as a museum. Annual *Fiesta* on the last Sunday of September.

Gold Rush

California's history is intricately linked to the Gold Rush. Use your
children's fascination with finding treasure to help them learn about
California's Gold Rush history.

Gold Rush Trail, San Francisco (Ages 8+)

(415) 981-4849; 57 Post Street, San Francisco, CA 94104
Email: contact@goldrushtrail.org.
<www.goldrushtrail.org>

Description: This is a walking trail that traces historic monuments and
buildings of the Gold Rush era. The trail runs from the south of Market
area to the Embarcadero, then back through downtown and the Financial
District to Chinatown and North Beach. The trail is broken into six dis-
tricts with museums and monuments to visit all along the way. Take a
district at a time and take the time to visit and enjoy. Visit the Web site for
maps, lists of museums, and places to see. This trail includes:
* the California Historical Society;
* the Pac Bell Museum;
* the Federal Reserve building;
* the Wells Fargo History Museum;
* the museum in the basement of the Union Bank of California,

which has an exhibit on the "Money of the American West"; and
• the Pacific Heritage Museum.

The Gold Rush Trail Foundation has established state certified history programs for 4th and 7th graders and has hosted many school groups.

Money of the American West, Union Bank of California
Old Bank of California Building
No Phone; California & Sansome Street, San Francisco, CA
Hours: Mon–Fri.
Cost: Free.
Bathrooms: Yes.
Facilities: Stroller friendly.
Food: No. There are restaurants in the Leides Dorff Alley between Montgomery and Sansome Streets.

Pac Bell Museum
Ground floor of the Pacific Bell Building
(415) 542-0182; 140 New Montgomery, San Francisco, CA
Hours: Tues, Wed, Thur: 10am–2pm.
Cost: Free.
Bathrooms: Yes.
Facilities: Stroller friendly.
Food: No. Restaurants are nearby.

Museum of the City of San Francisco (Ages 5+)
(415) 928-0289
Administrative Office: 945 Taraval Street, San Francisco, CA 94116
Exhibition space is at San Francisco's City Hall at the Civic Center (City Hall South Light Court, Grove and Van Ness).
<www.sfmuseum.org>

Description: This museum chronicles the history of San Francisco from its start as a Spanish garrison to the Gold Rush era, the historic 1906 Earthquake, the sinking of the Titanic, the end of World War II celebrations, and the more recent 1989 earthquake. For a virtual exhibit of the Gold Rush including its discovery at Sutter's Mill and chronology of the Gold Rush, visit: <www.sfmuseum.org/hist2/gold.html>.
Hours: At City Hall South Light Court: *Mon–Fri:* 8 am–8pm, *Sat:* noon–4pm. Closed Sundays.

Cost: Free.
Bathrooms: Yes.
Facilities: Stroller friendly.
Food: No, restaurants close by.
Follow-Up Activities: Don't miss the on-line exhibits of San Francisco and California history.

Oakland Museum of California (Ages 3+)

Virtual Exhibit of *California's Untold Stories: Gold Rush!* at: <www.museumca.org/goldrush>. In mid-May, free Gold Rush Family Day for kids over 3 years old from noon to 4pm.

Old Sacramento (All Ages)

(916) 558-3912 Events; (916) 442-7644 Visitor Center, Old Sacramento, CA
<www.oldsacramento.com>

Preserving historic Sacramento, Old Sacramento is an historic town within Sacramento with operating businesses and many museums. It is the site of many special events throughout the year. 1) Events in Old Sacramento include the Old-Fashioned Easter and Parade, Steam Train excursions in April, Thomas the Train Day in June, Gold Rush Days over Labor Day weekend, Octoberfest and Halloween Festival in October, and Heritage Holidays and Lamplight Tours in December. Look on the Web site under "Calendar." 2) Sacramento Museum Day means free admission to museums in Sacramento. Event occurs annually in February. Call (916) 264-7777 for more information.

Below are the museums and river cruise operators located in Old Sacramento.

Sutter's Fort
(916) 445-4422; 2710 L Street
Description: The original settlement is still available for self-guided tours.
Hours: Daily:10am–5pm.

Wells Fargo Museum
(916) 440-4263; Corner of Second and J Streets
Description: Stagecoaches, gold, mining, business, and commerce are all colorfully interpreted for visitors. Tours are avail-

able.

Hours: Daily: 10am–5pm.

Schoolhouse Museum

(916) 483-8818; Front and L Street

Description: This authentic one-room schoolhouse is available for school group tours.

Hours: Call for hours or to reserve tours.

Crocker Art Museum

(916) 264-5423; Third and O Street

<www.crockerartmuseum.org>

Description: This collection includes early Californian paintings, drawings by Old Masters, and contemporary Californian art. Family Sundays special events.

Hours: Tues–Sun: 10am–5pm.

Towe Auto Museum

(916) 442-6802; 2200 Front Street

Description: American cars are on exhibit.

Hours: Daily: 10am–6pm.

California Military Museum

(916) 442-2883; 1115 Second Street

Description: An interpretive museum with authentic clothing, equipment, and stories from our nation's rich military past.

Hours: Tues–Sun: 10am– 4:30pm.

Riverboat Cruises

(916) 552-2933; 110 L Street, Old Sacramento

River Otter Water Taxi

(916) 446-7704; L Street Landing - On the Waterfront

<www.riverotter.com>

Discovery Museum (All Ages)
"The Sacramento Museum of History, Science, Space & Technology"

<www.thediscovery.org>

Description: This museum is housed in two separate buildings. The Discovery Museum History Center is located in Old Sacramento, and appropriately focuses on historical exhibits. The Discovery Museum Science and Space Center is housed in another location.

Discovery Museum History Center (All Ages)
(916) 264-7057; 101 I Street, Old Sacramento CA 95814

Description: Located in Old Sacramento, next door to the California State Railroad Museum, the History Center has a Gold Rush exhibit, an authentic working print shop in the McClatchy Gallery, and imagination play stations with interactive exhibits to immerse children in history. The Community Gallery documents Sacramento's evolution from frontier town to a state capitol. The Agricultural Technology Gallery shows a historical survey of the technology used in agriculture.

Hours: Tues–Sun: 10am–5pm. Closed Mondays except for holidays and school tours. Closed Thanksgiving Day, Christmas Day, and New Year's Day. *Summer Hours (June, July and August):* Daily: 10am-5pm. Call to confirm hours.

Cost: $5/adult, $4/senior 60+, $4/youth 13–17, $3/child 6–12, free/child 5 & under.

Bathrooms: Yes.

Facilities: Stroller friendly.

Food: Snacks only. Restaurants are nearby.

Follow-Up Activities: 1) Many family events on weekends. Visit the Web site "Activities." 2) School group tours available. 3) Gold Rush Days and Ethnic Village is an Living History event with period costumes. All of Old Sacramento participates. The event takes place over Labor Day weekend. Check the Web site under "Activities" then "Special Events."

Discovery Museum Science & Space Center (All Ages)
(916) 575-3941; 3615 Auburn Boulevard, Sacramento, CA 95821

Description: The Science & Space Center has a planetarium and Nature Discovery room with insects and wildlife and is home to the Challenger Learning Center. The nature trail outside the museum provides an opportunity to be among the oaks and redwoods, have a picnic, and birdwatch.

Hours: Tues–Fri: noon–5pm, Sat & Sun: 10am–5pm. *Summer Hours (July and August):* Daily: 10am–5pm. Closed Memorial Day and the 4th of July. Every Tues–Fri at 2pm, there's a live animal presentation by the animal educator staff. Planetarium shows on weekends at 1pm & 3pm are free with admission.

Cost: $5/adult, $4/senior 60+, $4/youth 13–17, $3/child 6–12, free/child 5 & under.
Bathrooms: Yes.
Facilities: Stroller friendly.
Food: Snacks only. Restaurants are nearby.
Follow-Up Activities: 1) Many family events on weekends. Visit the Web site for "Activities" information. 2) School group tours available.

Challenger Learning Center

Located in the Discovery Museum Science & Space Center.
Description: Simulated Space Missions held on Friday evenings. *2003 Schedule:* February 7, May 2, June 20, July 18, October 10 from 6pm to 8:30pm. Visit Web site for the most current information.
Cost: $20/person; $15/person for 2 or more; $5 off/person for members. Reservations required: (916) 485-8836.

Seymour Pioneer Museum (Ages 5+)
Society of California Pioneers
(415) 957-1849; 300 Fourth Street, San Francisco, CA 94107
<www.californiapioneers.org>

Description: The museum is home to paintings depicting California landscapes and residents, a collection of costumes and accessories, historical artifacts such as gold pans and other equipment used during the Gold Rush era, and a photo gallery of the evolving California landscape and environment.
Hours: Wed–Fri: 10am–4pm. 1st and 3rd Saturday of every month: 10am–4pm.
Cost: $3/adult, $1/student or senior
Bathrooms: Yes.
Facilities: Stroller friendly.
Food: No, restaurants nearby.
What to Bring: Cash for parking.
Follow-Up Activities: Located across from Yerba Buena Gardens, this is close to Zeum, Metreon, ice skating, bowling, and the carousel. Park at the 5th & Mission Street Garage.

Wells Fargo History Museum (Ages 4+)

(415) 396-2619; 420 Montgomery Street, San Francisco, CA 94163
<www.wellsfargohistory.com/museums/sfmuseum.html>

Description: The museum displays artifacts important to the development of the Wells Fargo Corporation, California, and the American West. Exhibits include treasure boxes, the Wells Fargo stagecoach, gold, and original papers from the Wells Fargo office founded 100 years ago.
Hours: Mon–Fri: 9 am–5pm.
Cost: Free.
Bathrooms: Yes.
Facilities: Stroller friendly.
Food: No. Restaurants closeby.
What to Bring: Cash for parking and food.
Directions: Park at St. Mary's Square at 433 Kearny Street. The phone number is (415) 956-8106. Another option is the Portsmouth Square Garage at 733 Kearny, (415) 982-6353.

Out of Area...

The following parks, although out of our immediate area, are included because if you have a child like mine, it's nice to know where to go for gold panning.

Columbia State Historic Park (All Ages)

(209) 532-0150; (209) 532-4301
22708 Broadway, Columbia, CA 95310 (3 miles north of Sonora, off Hwy 49)
<www.parks.ca.gov/default.asp?page_id=552>

Description: This real town's Gold Rush era business district has been preserved from the 1850s with shop owners dressed in period costumes conducting business in the old-style. You can pan for gold by renting a gold pan for $5/person at the Matelot Gulch Mine Supply Store, (209) 532-9693, or take a tour of an active hardrock gold mine, at Hidden Treasure Gold Mine. For tours, sign up upon arrival at the Matelot Gulch Mine Supply Store for the Hidden Treasure Mine tour, located within the park at the corner of Washington and Main streets. Don't miss the stagecoach ride in town where you may get "held up" by the highway robber during your tour. There's a one-room schoolhouse, a general store, a jailhouse, a saloon, a hotel, a wonderful old-fashioned candy store, a firehouse, and a blacksmith making metal puzzles at the blacksmith shop.

Hours: Park facilities open at 8am. Most businesses open 10am–5pm. Call for winter hours for the gold mine tour and gold panning.

Cost: Free, but tours, rides, etc. cost extra. $5/person to rent the gold pan. Stagecoach ride: $6/adult, $3/child. Gold mine tour: $12/adult, $6/child.

Bathrooms: Yes, at the parking lot.

Facilities: Stroller friendly.

Food: Restaurants located within the park.

What to Bring: Cash for stagecoach ride, food, and souvenirs.

Follow-Up Activities: Jamestown and the Railtown 1897 Historic Park are just 6 miles away.

Hangtown's Gold Bug Park (Ages 4+)
City of Placerville – Parks & Recreation Department
(530) 642-5207; 2635 Gold Bug Lane, Placerville CA 95667
<www.goldbugpark.org>

Description: Gold Bug Mine, museum, and gold panning available. You can also take a tour of the Gold Mine Stamp Mill to learn how it crushes the gold ore to get the gold out of the rock.

Hours: Mid-April to October: daily 10am–4pm. November to mid-April: Weekends only: noon–4pm.

Cost: $3/adult, $1/child 5 to 16 years old, free/child under 5 years old. $2 gold pan rental for gold panning.

Bathrooms: Yes.

Facilities: Stroller friendly.

Food: Snacks only.

What to Bring: Picnic lunch.

Marshall Gold Discovery State Historic Park (Ages 5+)
(530) 622-3470; 310 Back Street, Coloma, CA 95613
<www.parks.ca.gov/default.asp?page_id=484>

Description: Try gold panning in the American River. "Live History

Days" every Thur–Sat in the spring and fall. For a detailed description of Coloma and the tours available, visit this Web site: <www.parks.ca.gov/default.asp?page_id=1142>.

Hours: *Park Hours:* 8am–5pm. *Museum and Building Hours:* 10am–4: 30pm. Closed Thanksgiving, Christmas, and New Year's Day.

Cost: Free.

Bathrooms: Yes.

Facilities: Stroller friendly.

Food: Yes.

Follow-Up Activities: Gold Discovery Day in late January 10am-4pm. This living history event features interactive period trade demonstrations like yarn spinning, blacksmithing, cornhusk doll making, and rope making. There is gold panning at Bekeart's Gun Shop; at the museum trough; and at the south fork of the American River, where gold was first discovered. There's also music and a Gold Rush history lecture series.

The California State Railroad Museum Web site has more Gold Rush history: <www.csrmf.org/doc.asp?id=15>. PBS has a Web site covering the Gold Rush: <www.pbs.org/goldrush> and Learning California's Web site <www.learncalifornia.org/doc.asp?id=491> also has information on the Gold Rush.

To learn about the process of government, YMCA (Young Men's Christian Association) has a wonderful *Youth and Government program* including the *Model United Nations* and the *California Youth and Government* programs. These are held on a yearly basis. To join, sign up with your local YMCA. These programs are geared for high school students. For additional information about these programs, you can go onto the Web site: <www.calymca.org>.

Chapter 10
Seasonal Events

The following events are only available seasonally. Some last only one day, while others last as long as one month. They are listed in chronological order.

Martin Luther King Day (Ages 5+)

Children's Discovery Museum, San Jose (Recommended for Ages 5+)

"Living the Dream" play during Martin Luther King Day. This play provides a very short and concise description of the beginning of the United States and the history of the constitutional amendments giving blacks their freedom and black men the right to vote. Then it describes the everyday realities of segregation during the 1940s–1960s, Martin Luther King Jr.'s experience with prejudice, his rallying cry for civil disobedience, and his dream to make the country a place where all are treated equally. The actors teach the audience *We Shall Overcome*, the rallying song sung by Martin Luther King Jr. The show is wonderfully performed, bringing to life the realities of life in the early half of the 20th century for Black Americans. It covers a lot of ground in 30 short minutes for only $1 per person!

Chinese New Year Festival & Parade

Chinese Chamber of Commerce (All Ages)
(415) 982-3000; 730 Sacramento Street, San Francisco, CA 94108
<www.chineseparade.com>
<www.chineseparade.com/route.htm>

Description: The parade lasts about two hours and features dancing lions and dragons as the main attraction.

Schedule: Usually takes place in February. Times vary every year as the Lunar New Year changes with the lunar calendar. Check the Web site for specific information on exact dates/times and routes on an annual basis. The parade begins at 5:30pm, starting at Market and Second streets. See the Web site for current route.

Cost: Free along the street. You can also purchase bleacher seats for $30/person, plus $4.50/order for shipping and handling by calling (415) 391-9680 or via the Web site. Children under 2 are free. The bleacher seats are located on Kearny Street, between Bush and Sutter streets.

Follow-Up Activities: For the legend of the New Year Chinese Dragon: <www.moonfestival.org/legends/dragon.htm>.

April/Easter (All Ages)
Many events such as Easter egg hunts are produced through the local community. Check with the Local Parks and Recreation departments for details. Old-fashioned Easter Parades or Egg Hunts are held at Old Sacramento and Columbia. See respective entries under California History: Gold Rush and Animal Kingdom: Farms.

Cal Day at the University of California, Berkeley (Ages 4+)
Visitor Services
(510) 642-5215;
101 University Hall, 2200 University Avenue, Berkeley, CA 94720
<www.berkeley.edu/calday>

Description: A don't-miss event where research museums and university departments, which are rarely open to the general public, share their collections and new research with the community. Many children oriented activities. Visit the Web site above for the schedule of events, map, and parking information. Here's a sample of the huge selection of events:

> Hands-on Archaeology for Kids, Play with Clay, Make Your Own Prehistoric Art, Demonstrating the Magic of Chemistry, Discovering Families of Planets, Robotic Racing Cars, Maps for Kids, Young People's Music Fair, Essig Museum of Entomology open, Museum of Paleontology open with tours, The Physics of Music, Hands on Physics Lab for all ages, and much more.

Hours: Takes place throughout the UC Berkeley campus on a weekend day in mid-April from 9am–4pm.
Cost: Free.
Bathrooms: Yes.
Facilities: Stroller friendly.
Food: Both on campus and off campus. There are plenty of restaurants and lawns.
What to Bring: Picnic lunch. It's a good idea to wear comfortable walking shoes and to dress in layers.

Community Day at Stanford (All Ages)
Stanford University
(650) 724-2933; Stanford, CA (along Serra Street facing the main quad)
<www.stanford.edu/dept/news/neighbors/communityday/index.html>

Description: Just beginning its third year in early April 2004, this event is simialr in concept to Cal Day at Berkeley. It features a children's carnival with pony rides, petting zoo, and face painting; demonstrations and lectures from the science departments; music and art tours at the Cantor Arts Center; and much more.
Hours: Early April 10am-4pm.
Cost: Free.
Bathrooms: Yes.
Facilities: Stroller friendly.
Food: Yes.
What to Bring: Wear comfortable walking shoes, bring sunscreen, sunglasses, and cash for food.

Cinco de Mayo (All Ages)

Cinco de Mayo Festival and Parade, San Jose
(408) 923-1646; 288-9470
Market and Santa Clara Streets, San Jose, CA 95113
<www.sjgif.org>

Description: The parade and festival celebrate freedom for the Mexican people. It ends at Almaden Boulevard and Park Avenue, the site of the festival.
Schedule: It is held on the first Sunday in May closest to Cinco de Mayo (May 5th). The parade is from 9am–noon. The festival is from 10am–6pm at Guadalupe River Park.
Cost: $1/person, free/child under 12.
What to Bring: Cash for vendors (food, crafts, etc.).
Follow-Up Activities: For a history of Cinco de Mayo:
<www.carnaval.com/cinco/cinco_history.htm>.

Cinco de Mayo, San Francisco
(415) 256-3005; Civic Center Plaza, San Francisco
<www.carnaval.com/sf/cinco_links.htm>
<www.latinbayarea.com/events/thisyear>

Schedule: First Sunday in May at the Civic Center Plaza, San Francisco, 11am–6pm. Parade starts at Mission Street.
Cost: Admission: $5. Free for children under 5.
What to Bring: Cash for vendors (food, crafts, etc.).

Memorial Day: Civil War Reenactments (Ages 5+)

Ardenwood Historical Farm has battle reenactments on Memorial Day weekend. Battle reenactments all three days, with two battles on both Saturday and Sunday at noon and at 3pm. On Memorial Day, there's only one battle at noon. The entry line can be time consuming. Plan on at least 30-minute wait at the entry. See entry under Chapter 1: Animal Kingdom—Farms section.

Casa de Fruta in June

Office: 831-637-0051; Mail Order: 800-543-1702
6680 Pacheco Pass Highway, Hollister, CA 95023
<www.casadefruta.com>

See entry under Chapter 1: Animal Kingdom—Farms section.

Roaring Camp Railroads

See full entry in Chapter 6: Transportation Favorites—Trains section.

Old Fashioned Independence Day Celebration (All Ages)

Ardenwood Historic Farm

See entry under Chapter 1: Animal Kingdom—Farms section.

Wilder Ranch State Park (All Ages)

(831) 426-0505/831-423-9703
1401 Coast Road, Santa Cruz, CA 95060
<www.scparkfriends.org/wilder/index.html>

Description: Enjoy an old-fashioned celebration with live music, children's parade, hayrides, games, and crafts. Period costumes and docent-led tours show what a dairy ranch was like 100 years ago.

Hours: 10am–4pm, July 4th.

Cost: $5 park entrance fee.

Bathrooms: Yes, at the parking lot.

Facilities: Stroller friendly.

Food: Concessions only during the July 4th celebration. Ice cream, etc.

What to Bring: Cash for parking and concessions, sunscreen, sunglasses, picnic lunch, picnic blanket, and plenty to drink.

Moon Festival (All Ages)

(415) 982-6306; California & Grant Avenue, San Francisco, CA
<www.moonfestival.org>

Description: The Moon Festival is a Chinese celebration of the harvest.

Entertainment includes live performances by acrobats, dancers, and singers; martial arts demonstrations; arts and crafts; food; parade with costumed children and artisans holding giant puppets; lion dancers; and marching bands. Visit the Web site for maps and directions, as well as the entertainment schedule.

Schedule: Varies yearly based on the Lunar Calendar of the 15th of the 8th month, which falls usually from late August to September. Check the Web site for specific dates annually. Takes place 11am–6pm over a weekend, usually in September.

Cost: Free.

Follow-Up Activities: For the legend of the Moon Festival, visit this Web site: <www.moonfestival.org/legends/chango.htm>.

Kids' Faire California (All Ages)

866-444-EXPO; Alameda County Fairground, Pleasanton, CA; San Mateo Expo Center, San Mateo, CA

<www.thekidsfaire.com>

Description: This fair is dedicated to family entertainment. Funds raised contribute to literacy programs for Head Start and other community programs. There are drop-in arts and crafts, a circus, "Safariland" with camel and pony rides, an area where kids can plant a vegetable garden, "Clown Town" where kids can learn to juggle, watch clown antics and magic shows, NBC-TV where kids can read a news story and be an anchor on TV, and a "Meet the Characters" pavilion where kids can meet famous TV characters (Dora the Explorer, Madeline, Scooby Doo, Spiderman, Bob the Builder, Arthur, Winnie the Pooh, and more). Like all fairs, there are rides, jump houses and slides, and musical entertainment on multiple stages.

Schedule: Mid-September, 10am–5pm on consecutive weekends at the Alameda County Fairgrounds and at the San Mateo Expo Center in San Mateo.

Cost: $6/adult, $2/child ages 2–12. $1 off Internet ticket purchase.

Bathrooms: Yes.

Food: Yes.

What to Bring: Sunscreen; sunglasses; and extra cash for parking, food, products, and entertainment.

Renaissance Pleasure Faire (Ages 3+)
Casa de Fruta
(800) 52-FAIRE (523-2473); (707) 552-5271
For directions: 10021 Pacheco Pass (Hwy 152 East), Hollister, CA 95023
<www.renaissancepleasurefaire.com>

Description: Do knights, jousts, castles, and armor interest your child? Visit the Renaissance Pleasure Faire to see what life was like in England during the Renaissance. Costumed actors dressed as well-known historical figures play the roles of their famous characters. Converse with Shakespeare, Queen Elizabeth, Robin Hood, and others. See artisans at work using techniques of the Renaissance. Watch jousts, archery contests, and other games of yesteryear.

Schedule: Annually in the fall from mid-September to mid-October on Sat & Sun: 10am–6pm.

Cost: Free Parking. *Advance Tickets*: $14.50/adult, $6/child 5–11. *Tickets at the Gate*: $18.50/adult, $7.50/child 5–11. *Discount Coupons*: on-line.

Bathrooms: Yes.

Facilities: Stroller friendly, but dusty trails.

Food: Yes—Outside food and drinks are not allowed.

What to Bring: Can be very hot. Bring camera; sunglasses; hats; sunscreen; and extra cash for food, drinks, souvenirs, etc.

Halloween

Roaring Camp Railroads has a special event on the *Legend of Sleepy Hollow*. See the full entry in Chapter 6: Transportation Favorites—Trains section.

Holiday Season

Many communities have visits with Santa, breakfast with Santa, Children's Holiday Parades, etc. Check with your local Parks and Recreation Department and its catalog, or your city's civic center, to find details on your community's events.

Allied Arts Guild's Children's Holiday Party (Ages 2+)

(650) 322-2405; 75 Arbor Road, Menlo Park, CA 94025
<www.alliedartsguild.org>

Description: The Allied Arts Guild has beautiful Spanish architecture and gardens and an annual holiday party that in the past, included a lunchtime magician; Truly Scrumptious, the music box dancer from *Chitty Chitty Bang Bang*; and pictures with Santa. This is very appropriate for the toddler crowd. Call in advance to make reservations.

Hours: Mon–Sat: 10am–5pm. Reopens in the fall of 2003. Party in early/mid December. Make your reservations early to avoid disappointment.

Cost: Reservations required. $16 per person.

Bathrooms: Yes.

Food: Included as part of the event.

What to Bring: Dress warm. Bring camera and cash.

Dickens' Christmas Fair (Ages 4+)

The San Francisco Cow Palace, Lower Exhibition

(415) 897-4555 (Mon–Fri: 9am–5pm); (415) 469-6065 Cow Palace
2600 Geneva Aveue, San Francisco, CA 94134
<www.dickensfair.com>
<www.renaissance-faire.com/Renfaires/Dickens-Faire.htm>

Description: The Dickens Christmas Fair is a living history event with many forms of entertainment. In the past, it has had Irish and Scottish dance performances, shows such as the *Pirates of Penzance* and *Alice in Wonderland*, a Christmas parade, musicians including a bagpipe performer and an harpist, and carolers. We saw chimney sweeps, a falcon, and an artisan weaving on a homemade loom. Many attendees come in period costume and it's great to see the beautiful clothes and decorations of a Victorian Christmas. The food is great, albeit pricey. There isn't much offered in the way of arts and crafts activities, and they cost extra. However, the shows, music, and dancing are wonderfully done and well worth the time and cost.

Schedule: Weekends after Thanksgiving to just before Christmas from 11am to 8pm.

Cost: $6 parking at the Cow Palace. *Advance tickets* by phone or online:

$16/adult; $6/child (5–11yrs); $13/student, senior, or military person-nel. $2 processing charge per order. *At the gate*: $20/adult; $8/child; $16/student, senior, or military.

Bathrooms: Yes, but no baby changing stations. Stroller friendly.

Food: Yes, including fish and chips, hot chocolate, afternoon tea (scones, tea sandwiches, pastries, etc), roasted chestnuts, English beer, and more.

What to Bring: Dress warmly. Bring your camera and extra cash for park-ing, food, and shopping.

Dunsmuir Historic Estate Holiday Events (3+)

(510) 615-5555; 2960 Peralta Oaks Court, Oakland, CA 94615
<http://dunsmuir.org>

Description: Experience an old-fashioned 19th century Christmas at Dunsmuir Historic Estate. The beautifully decorated Mansion is open for tours. When you purchase the tickets, you must select a time to tour the mansion. There are carolers, holiday crafts boutique, teas, carriage rides, children's arts and crafts, and visits with Father Christmas. Holiday Teas are separate and require advanced reservations. Dress in layers and plan on getting a bit messy if your children want to participate in arts and crafts activities. The children's arts and crafts have been hosted by the Museum of Children's Art in Oakland in the past and are included with admission.

Schedule: Late November—mid-December Fri–Sun: 11am–5pm. Gates close at 4pm for entry. Check event schedule on the Web site or call for specific dates.

Cost: *Advance Tickets:* $11/adult, $10/senior (62+), $7/child 6–13, free/ child under 6. *At the Gate*, prices increase by $4 per person. Tickets can be ordered in early October. *Holiday Teas*: $18 per person, advanced res-ervations required. Reserve early to avoid disappointment. These are very popular! There are also Children's Teas with Father Christmas. Menu for Holiday Teas (Served by volunteers in period costumes): holiday blend tea, scones, tea sandwiches, breads, and sweets

Bathrooms: Yes.

Facilities: Stroller friendly.

Food: Holiday café offers sandwiches, soups, salads, etc. in the Garden Pavilion; no reservation required. Holiday Teas and Children's Teas re-quire reservations in advance.

What to Bring: Camera, warm coats, and cash for snacks and hot cocoa.

Filoli Gardens Children's Luncheon Party (Ages 5+)
(650) 364-8300; 86 Cañada Road, Woodside, CA 94062
<www.filoli.org>

Description: The holiday parties have entertainers such as magicians, ventriloquists, and dancers. There are also visits with Santa and Mrs. Claus.
Schedule: Four parties held on a Saturday in early December, at 11am, noon, 1pm, and 2pm.
Cost: $30 per person.
Bathrooms: Yes.
Facilities: Stroller friendly.
Food: Yes.
What to Bring: Camera and warm jacket.

Prince & Princess Tea (Ages 12 & under)
Garden Court, The Palace Hotel
(415) 546-5010; 2 New Montgomery Street, San Francisco, CA 94105
<www.gardencourt-restaurant.com>

Description: The Princess Tea serves pastries and sandwiches. Keeping with the princess theme, a crown and scepter are included for the little princess. The belle époque Garden Court provides an opulent backdrop, with crystal chandeliers, mirrored doors, and harp music at teatime.
Hours: Year-round on Saturdays 1–3pm in the Garden Court. Call (415) 546-5089 for reservations. Special holiday events are also available during the holiday season; check the Web site for details in August.
Cost: $20/child.
Bathrooms: Yes.
Facilities: Stroller friendly.
What to Bring: Camera and warm jacket.

Teddy Bear Tea for Children (Ages 3+)
At The Ritz-Carlton, San Francisco
(415) 773-6198; 600 Stockton Street, San Francisco, CA 94108
<www.ritzcarlton.com/hotels/san_francisco/dining/venues/lobby_lounge>

Description: This event inclludes holiday storytelling, singing, and dancing with the elf and teddy bear. In the past, the menu included hot chocolate, teddy bear cutout cookies, peanut butter and jelly sandwiches, egg salad, and ham and cheese sandwiches.

Schedule: After Thanksgiving to December 24. There are 2 seatings daily: the first is 10–11:30am and the second is 1–2:30pm. Reservations are required. Call number above starting August 1, at 9am, to make reservations. Reservations are guaranteed with credit card; cancellations require 3 days prior to the event or a $25 cancellation fee applies.

Cost: *Tea Service*: $58/person. Teddy Bear Tea price includes tax, gratuity, and charity donation.

Bathrooms: Yes.

Facilities: Stroller friendly.

What to Bring: Camera and warm jacket; don't forget cash for parking.

For even more teatime suggestions, visit this Web site: <www.parentsnet.org/npn_teas.html>.

Nutcracker Ballet Performances

See Chapter 8: Art & Performing Arts—Ballet Performances section.

Section II
Classes to Take

Chapter 11
Local Resources

Many community groups offer afterschool classes and summer camps. The major players are the local Parks and Recreation Departments of the cities, the local YMCAs (Young Men's Christian Associations), and the JCCs (Jewish Community Centers). Although the YMCAs and the JCCs have religious affiliations, they do not require anyone to be any particular religion; access is open to all. The Parks and Recreation Departments of the cities do not require residency in the specific city but may charge a slightly higher fee for nonresidents.

These community centers have a huge assortment of classes, field trips, and community events such as free concerts and shows at the local parks, special holiday events including Christmas Tree lighting, children's holiday parades, breakfasts with Santa, and more. Look first at these resources because they tend to be cost-effective and are convenient to your locale. Don't forget to check with the neighboring community centers, since each center has a unique offering. A large range of classes is offered by these centers including art, drama, theater, music, science and nature, computers, sewing, cooking, and sports.

I've included additional resources for classes on science and nature, art, music, drama, swimming, dance, ice skating, and bowling. Remember that these are also wonderful for birthday parties. Most facilities will offer birthday parties. Just ask!

Jewish Community Centers (JCC's)

Addison–Penzak Jewish Community Center (Silicon Valley)

(408) 358-3636; 14855 Oka Road, Los Gatos, CA 95032
<www.sanjosejcc.org/html/our_programs.html>

Albert L. Schultz Jewish Community Center (Palo Alto)

(650) 493-9400; 4000 Middlefield Road, T-2, Palo Alto, CA 94303
<www.paloaltojcc.org>

Berkeley Richmond JCC

(510) 848-0237; 1414 Walnut Street, Berkeley, CA 94709
<www.brjcc.org>

Contra Costa JCC

(925) 938-7800; 2071 Tice Valley Boulevard, Walnut Creek, CA 94595
<www.ccjcc.org>
<www.ccjcc.org/departments.htm>

Jewish Community Center of San Francisco

(415) 346-6040; 1808 Wedemeyer Street, San Francisco, CA 94129
<www.jccsf.org>

The North Peninsula Jewish Community Center

(650) 591-4438; 2440 Carlmont Drive, Belmont, CA 94002
<www.pjcc.org>
New facility at end of 2003: 800 Foster City Boulevard, Foster City, CA 94002.

Osher Marin Jewish Community Center

(415) 444-8000; 200 North San Pedro Road, San Rafael, CA 94903

Local Parks & Recreation Departments

Local city Parks and Recreation Departments are wonderful resources. They offer a myriad of classes and activities, including art, music, theater, gymnastics, dance, ice skating, T-ball, soccer, little league, basketball, martial arts, science, and manners classes. They also offer special field trips and outings, and have special holiday events like visits with Santa and gingerbread house decorating. Don't forget to check with your local Parks and Recreation Departments, as they have different offerings. Ask to be put on your favorites' mailing lists so you won't miss the quarterly catalogs, especially the summer ones, which are a wonderful resource for summer camps.

You do not need to be a resident of the offering city to take advantage of these classes. There is usually a slightly higher fee for non-residents, but the activities are open to everyone. Listed below are online activity guides or catalogs with class descriptions and schedules.

Alameda Recreation and Parks
(510) 748-4565; 1327 Oak Street, Alameda, CA 94501
<www.ci.alameda.ca.us/arpd/index.html>

Albany
(510) 524-9283; 1249 Marin Avenue, Albany, CA 94706
<www.albanyca.org/recreation.html>

Belmont Parks and Recreation Department
(650) 595-7441; 1255 Ralston Avenue, Belmont, CA 94002
<www.belmont.gov/localgov/prec/index.html>

Belvedere–Tiburon Recreation Department
(415) 435-4355; 1505 Tiburon Blvd. Ste A, Tiburon, CA 94920
<www.btrecreation.org>
Summer camps on Angel Island for ages 6–13 from mid-June to August.
Other day camps available for ages 3½—5. Registration starts in early
March.

Berkeley
(510) 981-5150; 2016 Center Street, Berkeley, CA 94704
<www.ci.berkeley.ca.us/parks>
<www.ci.berkeley.ca.us/onlineservice/parks/RecreationCatalog.pdf>

Brisbane Recreation Department
(415) 467-6330; 50 Park Place, Brisbane CA 94005
<www.ci.brisbane.ca.us/Recreation/recreati.htm>

Burlingame Parks and Recreation Department
(650) 558-7300; 850 Burlingame Avenue, Burlingame, CA 94010
<www.burlingame.org/p_r/classes/classes.htm>

Campbell Recreation and Community Services Department
(408) 866-2105; 1 West Campbell Avenue #C-31, Campbell, CA 95008
<www.ci.campbell.ca.us/communityandarts/recreation.htm>

Concord Parks and Recreation
(925) 671-3329
In Person: 2974 Salvio Street, Concord, CA
By Mail: 1950 Parkside Drive, MS/10, Concord, CA 94519-2578
<www.ci.concord.ca.us/recreation/activityguideinfo.htm>

Cupertino Parks and Recreation Department
Quinlan Community Center
(408) 777-3102; 10185 N. Stelling Road, Cupertino, CA 95014
<www.cupertino.org/update/rec/rec.htm>

Daly City Parks and Recreation Department
(650) 991-8001 Administration
(650) 991-8015 Parks
(650) 991-8001 Recreation
111 Lake Merced Boulevard, Daly City, CA 94015
<www.lonicera.com/dcprkrec>

Danville Community Center
(925) 314-3400; 420 Front Street, Danville, CA 94526
<www.ci.danville.ca.us>
Click on "Departments," then "Community Services," then "Activity Guide" for the recreation catalog.

Dublin
Shannon Park and Community Center
(925) 556-4500; 11600 Shannon Avenue, Dublin, CA 94568
<www.ci.dublin.ca.us/html/recreation.html>

El Cerrito Recreation Department
(510) 215-4370; 7007 Moeser Lane, El Cerrito, CA 94530
<www.el-cerrito.com/recreation/>

Emeryville Recreation Department
(510) 596-3782; 4300 San Pablo Avenue, Emeryville, CA 94608
<www.ci.emeryville.ca.us/rec/recreation.html>

Foster City
(650) 286-3380; 650 Shell Boulevard, Foster City, CA 94404
<www.fostercity.org/Services/recreation/index.cfm>

Fremont Recreation Services Division
(510) 494-4600; 3350 Capital Avenue, Fremont, CA 94538
<www.ci.fremont.ca.us/Recreation/ClassRegistrationAndInformation>
<http://regerec.ci.fremont.ca.us/Start/>

Gilroy Community Services Department
(408) 846-0460; 7351 Rosanna Street, Gilroy, CA 95020
<www.ci.gilroy.ca.us/comserv/recguide.html>

Greater Hayward Area Recreation and Park Foundation (H.A.R.D.)
(510) 881-6700; 1099 E Street, Hayward, CA 94541
<http://hard.dst.ca.us/index.html>

Lafayette Parks and Recreation
(925) 284-2232; 500 St. Mary's Road, Lafayette, CA 94549
<www.ci.lafayette.ca.us>

Livermore Park and Recreation District
(925) 373-5700; 71 Trevarno Road, Livermore, CA 94551
<www.larpd.dst.ca.us>

Los Altos Recreation Department
(650) 947-2790; 97 Hillview Avenue, Los Altos, CA 94022
<www.ci.los-altos.ca.us/recreation>

Los Gatos–Saratoga Community Education and Recreation
(408) 354-8700, ext 221, or ext 225
123 East Main Street, Los Gatos, CA 95030
<www.lgsararec.org>

Menlo Park Community Services Department
(650) 330-2200; 701 Laurel Street, Menlo Park, CA 94025
<www.menlopark.org/departments/dep_comservices.html>

Mill Valley Recreation
Mill Valley Community Center
(415) 383-1370; 180 Camino Alto, Mill Valley, CA 94941

Millbrae
(650) 259-2360; 477 Lincoln Circle Millbrae, CA 94030
<www.ci.millbrae.ca.us/parksandrec.html>

Milpitas
408) 586-3210; 457 E. Calaveras Boulevard, Milpitas, CA 95035
<http://ci.milpitas.ca.gov/citydept/planning/recreation/default.htm>

Monterey
(831) 646-3866; 546 Dutra Street, Monterey, CA 93940
<www.monterey.org/rec>

Moraga Parks and Recreation Department
(925) 376-2520; 2100 Donald Drive, Moraga, CA 94556
<www.ci.moraga.ca.us/park.htm>

Morgan Hill
(408) 782-0008; 17555 Peak Avenue, Morgan Hill, CA 95037
<www.morgan-hill.ca.gov/html/gov/dept/recreation.asp>

Mountain View Recreation Department
(650) 903-6331; 201 South Rengstorff Avenue, Mountain View, CA 94040
<www.ci.mtnview.ca.us/citydepts/cs/recreation.htm>

Mountain View Recreation Activity Guide:
<www.ci.mtnview.ca.us/citynews/pdf/Activity_Guide.pdf>

Newark Recreation and Community Services Department
Silliman Activity Center
(510) 742-4400; 6800 Mowry Avenue, Newark, CA 94560

Community Center
(510) 742-4437; 35501 Cedar Boulevard, Newark, CA 94560
<www.ci.newark.ca.us/rc/rcrec.html>

Novato Parks, Recreation & Community Services

(415) 897-4323; 917 Sherman Avenue, Novato, CA 94945
<www.ci.novato.ca.us/parks/index.cfm>

Oakland Parks and Recreation

(510) 637-0274; 1520 Lakeside Drive, Oakland, CA 94612
<www.oaklandnet.com/parks/programs>

Orinda Parks and Recreation

(925) 254-2445; 26 Orinda Way, Orinda 94563
<www.ci.orinda.ca.us/parksandrec>

Pacific Grove Recreation Department

(831) 648-5730; 515 Junipero Avenue, Pacific Grove, CA 93950
<www.pacificgroverecreation.org>

Pacifica

(650) 738-7381; 170 Santa Maria Avenue, Pacifica, CA 94044
<www.ci.pacifica.ca.us/RECREATION/rec.html>

Palo Alto Arts & Culture Department

<www.city.palo-alto.ca.us/artsculture>
(650) 463-4952; 1305 Middlefield Road, Palo Alto, CA 94301
Palo Alto Arts & Culture Catalog: <www.paenjoy.org>

Piedmont Recreation Department

(510) 420-3070; 358 Hillside Avenue, Piedmont, CA 94611
<www.ci.piedmont.ca.us/welcome.htm>
On-Line Registration: www.ci.piedmont.ca.us/welcome.htm

Pinole Recreation Department

(510) 724-9002; 2131 Pear Street, Pinole, CA 94564
<www.ci.pinole.ca.us/recreation>

Pittsburg Parks and Recreation

(925) 252-4842; 65 Civic Avenue, Pittsburg, CA 94565
<www.ci.pittsburg.ca.us>

Pleasant Hill Recreation and Parks District

(925) 676-5200
Community Center
320 Civic Drive, Pleasant Hill, CA 94523

Aquatics, Adult/Youth Sports Leagues
147 Gregory Lane, Pleasant Hill, CA 94523
<www.pleasanthillrec.com>

Pleasanton Parks and Community Services

(925) 931-5340; 200 Old Bernal Avenue, Pleasanton, CA 94566
<www.ci.pleasanton.ca.us/parks.html>

Portola Valley, Town Center Resources

(650) 851-1701; 765 Portola Road, Portola Valley, CA 94028
<www.portolavalley.net/community/cr_classes.shtml>

Redwood City Parks, Recreation & Community Services

(650) 780-7250; 1400 Roosevelt Avenue, Redwood City, CA 94061
<www.redwoodcity.org/safari>

Richmond Recreation & Parks

(510) 620-6793; 3230 MacDonald Avenue, Richmond, CA 94804
<www.ci.richmond.ca.us/~recweb>

San Anselmo Parks and Recreation

(415) 258-4640; 525 San Anselmo Avenue, San Anselmo, CA 94960
<www.townofsananselmo.org/recreation>

San Bruno Recreation Services Department

(650) 616-7189; 567 El Camino Real, San Bruno, CA 94066
<www.ci.sanbruno.ca.us/Parks/rsw/Recreation.html>

San Carlos
(650) 802-4382; 600 Elm Street, San Carlos, CA 94070
<www.cityofsancarlos.org/deptindex/1,1009,deptid-43,00.html>

San Francisco
<www.parks.sfgov.org>
http://civiccenter.ci.sf.ca.us/recpark/activity.nsf/Activities?OpenView

San Jose Department of Parks, Recreation & Neighborhood Services
(408) 277- 4661; 4 N. Second Street, Ste 600, San Jose, CA 95113
For Recreation Activity Guides for San Jose Community Centers: <www.ci.san-jose.ca.us/prns/centers.htm>
<www.ci.san-jose.ca.us/prns/rcssa.htm>

For San Jose Special Events calendar, visit this Web site: <www.ci.san-jose.ca.us/prns/prnsevents.htm>

Almaden Community Center
(408) 268-1133; 6445 Camden Avenue, San Jose, CA 95120
Alviso Community Center
(408) 251-6392; 5050 North 1st Street, San Jose, CA 95002
Berryessa Community Center
(408) 251-6392; 3050 Berryessa Avenue, San Jose, CA 95132
Camden Community Center
(408) 559-8553; 3369 Union Avenue, San Jose, CA 95124
Evergreen CC
(408) 270-2220; 4860 San Felipe Road, San Jose, CA 95135
Gardner Community Center
(408) 279-1498; 520 W. Virginia Street, San Jose, CA 95125
George Shirakawa Community Center
(408) 277-3317; 2072 Lucretia Avenue, San Jose, CA 95122
Hank Lopez Community Center
(408) 251-2850; 1694 Adrian Way, San Jose, CA 95122
Kirk Community Center
(408) 723-1571; 1601 Foxworthy Avenue, San Jose, CA 95118
Mayfair Community Center
(408) 729-3475; 2039 Kammerer Avenue, San Jose, CA 95116
Millbrook/Mt. Pleasant Community Center
(408) 274-1343; 3200 Millbrook Drive, San Jose, CA 95148

Moreland West Community Center
(408) 871-3820; 1850 Fallbrook Avenue, San Jose, CA 95130
Olinder Community Center
(408) 279-1138; 848 E. William Street, San Jose, CA 95116
Roosevelt Community Center
(408) 998-2223; 901 East Santa Clara Street, San Jose, CA 95116
Sherman Oaks Community Center
(408) 292-2935; 1800A Fruitdale Avenue, San Jose, CA 95116
Solari Community Center
(408) 224-0415; 3590 Cas Drive, San Jose, CA 95111
Southside Community Center
(408) 629-3336; 5585 Cottle Road, San Jose, CA 95123
Starbird Community Center
(408) 984-1954; 1050 Boynton Avenue, San Jose, CA 95117
Watson Community Center
(408) 280-7355; 550 N 22nd Street, San Jose, CA 95112
Theater Programs
(408) 984-1954
Youth Arts Demonstration Project (YADP)
(408) 277-5144

San Leandro
(510) 577-3462; 835 E.14th Street, San Leandro, CA 94577
<www.ci.san-leandro.ca.us/slrechumansvcs.html>

San Mateo
(650) 522-7400; 330 West 20th Avenue, San Mateo, CA 94403
<www.ci.sanmateo.ca.us/dept/parks/index.html>

San Rafael
(415) 485-3333; 618 B Street, San Rafael, CA 94901
<www.cityofsanrafael.org/cs/recreation.htm>
<http://cityofsanrafael.org/cs/>

San Ramon Parks and Community Services
(925) 973-3200; 12501 Alcosta Boulevard, San Ramon, CA 94583
<www.ci.san-ramon.ca.us/parks>

Santa Clara Parks & Recreation Department
(408) 615-2260; 1500 Warburton Avenue, Santa Clara, CA 95050
<http://cho.ci.santa-clara.ca.us/205.html>

Santa Cruz Parks and Recreation Department
(831) 420-5270; (831) 420-5250 Registration Office
323 Church Street, Santa Cruz, CA 95060
<www.santacruzparksandrec.com>

Saratoga
(408) 868-1248; (408) 868-1249
19655 Allendale Avenue, Saratoga, CA 95070
<www.saratoga.ca.us/recreation.htm>

Sausalito Parks and Recreation Department
(415) 289-4152; 420 Litho Street, Sausalito, CA 94965
<www.ci.sausalito.ca.us/business/park-rec>

South San Francisco
(650) 829-3800; 33 Arroyo Drive, S. San Francisco, CA 94080
<www.ci.ssf.ca.us/depts/rcs/default.asp>

Sunnyvale Parks and Recreation
Sunnyvale Community Center
(408) 730-7350; 550 E. Remington Drive, Sunnyvale, CA 94087
<www.ci.sunnyvale.ca.us/leisure-services/>

Town of Los Gatos
(408) 354-8700 ext. 221 or 225
123 E. Main Street, Los Gatos, CA 95030
<www.lgsararec.org>

Town of Moraga
Parks and Recreation Activities
(925) 376-2520; 2100 Donald Drive, Moraga, CA 94556

Walnut Creek
Recreation Classes, Heather Farm Community Center
(925) 943-5858; 301 N. San Carlos Drive, Walnut Creek, CA 94596
<www.ci.walnut-creek.ca.us/leisure>

Walnut Creek Civic Arts Education Program
(925) 943-5846
<http://arts-ed.org>
Civic Park Campus
N. Broadway and Civic Drive, Walnut Creek, CA 94596

Shadelands Campus
111 N. Wiget Lane & Ygnacio Valley Road, Walnut Creek, CA 94598

Young Men's Christian Associations (YMCAs)

The Web site for U.S. YMCAs is <www.ymca.net/>.

Here are the Web sites of YMCAs in the Bay Area.

Mt. Diablo Region YMCA
<www.mtdiabloregionymca.org>

Peninsula Family YMCA
<www.peninsulafamilyymca.org>

Presidio Community YMCA
<www.presidioymca.org>

San Ramon Valley YMCA
<www.srvymca.org>

Sonoma County Family YMCA
<www.scfymca.org>

YMCA of San Francisco
<www.ymcasf.org>

Covers San Francisco, San Mateo, Marin, La Honda, Suisun City,

Sausalito YMCAs Branch Locations:
<www.ymcasf.org/peninsula/location.html>

YMCA of Santa Clara Valley
<www.scvymca.org>

YMCA of the East Bay
<www.ymcaeastbay.org>

Peninsula Family YMCA
(650) 286-9622; 1877 South Grant Street, San Mateo, CA 94402
<www.ymcasf.org/peninsula>

The YMCA of the Mid-Peninsula (Multiple branches)
<www.ymcamidpen.org>

Sequoia YMCA
(650) 368-4168; 1445 Hudson Street, Redwood City, CA 94061
<www.ymcamidpen.org/sequoiay.php>

Palo Alto Family YMCA
(650) 856-9622; 3412 Ross Road, Palo Alto, CA 94303
<www.ymcamidpen.org/pafy.php>

Indoor pool, swim lessons, youth and teen programs, sports programs, camps, child care.

Page Mill YMCA
(650) 858-0661; 755 Page Mill Road, Building B, Palo Alto, CA 94304
<www.ymcamidpen.org/pagemilly.php>

El Camino YMCA
(650) 969-9622; 2400 Grant Road, Mountain View, CA 94040
<www.ymcamidpen.org/elcaminoy.php>
Swim lessons for 6-month-olds to adults. Outdoor pool.

YMCA of Santa Clara Valley
<www.scvymca.org/metro/html/locations.html>

Southwest YMCA
(408) 370-1877; 13500 Quito Road, Saratoga, CA 95070
<www.scvymca.org/southwest>

Northwest YMCA
(408) 257-7160; 20803 Alves Drive, Cupertino, CA 95014
<www.scvymca.org/northwest>

Central YMCA
(408) 298-1717; 1717 The Alameda, San Jose, CA 95126
<www.scvymca.org/central>

East Valley Family YMCA (Milpitas & Berryessa)
(408) 715-6500; 1975 S. White Road, San Jose, CA 95148
<www.scvymca.org/eastvalley>

South Valley Family YMCA
(408) 226-9622; 5632 Santa Teresa Boulevard, San Jose, CA 95123
<www.scvymca.org/southvalley>

Chapter 12
Science & Arts Education

Science Education

Don't let the terms "science" and "education" fool you. These classes and programs are lots of fun and probably should be categorized as "edu-tainment." Review the list of possible programs below and you'll see what I mean.

California Academy of Sciences Golden Gate Park
Encompasses: Steinhart Aquarium, Natural History Museum, and Morrison Planetarium
(415) 750-7145; 55 Concourse Drive, San Francisco, CA 94118 (reopens 2008)
Temporary Location: 875 Howard Street, San Francisco, CA 94103
<www.calacademy.org>

Description: Family activities include guided field trips. The Junior Academy offers classes for older children ages 8–14. These classes include topics such as marine mammals, birds, insects, the savanna habitat, manatees, old ways living skills (methods used by early humans to make fire, beads, and string), astronomy, etc. On the Web site, look under "Education," then "Course Catalogs" icons. For the calendar of events: <www.calacademy.org/events/calendar>.

Hours: *Winter:* 10am–5pm, *Summer:* 9am–6pm (Memorial Day to Labor Day). First Wednesday of the month: open until 8:45pm. On Saturday mornings, there's *Children's Story Time* geared for children 3–7 years old. These are held at 10:30 am at the Skulls Exhibit Hall. Books chosen are from the Bio-Diversity Center Library based on monthly topics.

Cost: First Wednesday of each month is free to the public. $8.50/adult;

$5.50/youth (12–17), student w/ ID, & senior 65+; $2/child (4–11); free/child 3 & under. There are a few days each year where San Francisco residents of certain zip codes may visit for free. *Planetarium tickets*: $2.50/adult, $1.25/youth (6–17) & senior 65+. (Planetarium closed until 2008)

Camp Galileo (Ages 6–13)
Galileo Educational Services, LLC
(800) 854-3684; 5332 College Avenue, Suite 203, Oakland, CA 94618
<www.galileoed.com>

Arts, sciences, and the outdoors camp. This camp is sponsored by Galileo Educational Services; Klutz, Inc.; and the Tech Museum.

Chabot Space & Science Center (Ages 4+)
(510) 336-7300; (510) 336-7373 Box Office
10000 Skyline Boulevard, Oakland, CA 94619
<www.chabotspace.org>

Description: 1) For kids 4–8 years old, there is a free afterschool program on weekday afternoons called the "Discovery Club." Registration is required. Call the Discovery Lab instructor/coordinator at (510) 336-7362 or e-mail dlaffoon@chabotspace.org. For children ages 4–7, the Discovery Lab is open on weekday afternoons. 2) Summer camps are weeklong, half-day. Past camp topics have included robotics, principles of flight (what does it take to get to outer space?), ecology, the moon, Mars, etc. These camps are appropriate for children in first through eighth grades. 3) A wonderful "Visit the Future" program "is a career simulation in which families work with a practicing scientist and take on the role of scientists to tackle a problem in that field as a team. Two-hour programs, offered at the Challenger Learning Center." For more information about future programs, call the Challenger Learning Center at (510) 336-7355.
Hours: Closed Mondays. Open: Tues–Sun: 10am–5pm. *Spring Break Extended Hours:* Sat., March 30–Sat., April 6: Full facility open 10am–9pm daily. *Discovery Lab Hours:* Closed Mondays. Tues–Thur: 1–3pm; Fri: 1–4pm, Sat: 10:30am–12:15pm, 1–4pm; Sun: noon–4pm.

Children's Discovery Museum (Ages 4–10)
(408) 298-5437; 180 Woz Way, San Jose, CA 95110
<www.cdm.org>

Description: Provides programs including "My First Circle Time" for toddlers and "We're 5 and 4, We Explore" workshops with topics on bubbles, water, spiders, circles, kitchen chemistry, and more. Workshops for children ages 6 to 10 cover gears, solar power, and the properties of water such as water tension and water pressure. Check the Web site calendar (under the "Information" icon). If you're a member, CDM sends a monthly calendar with detailed descriptions of classes and events.

Hours: Closed Mondays. Tues–Sat: 10am–5pm. Sun: noon–5pm.

Cost: $7/adult or child, $6/senior. Infants under 1: free. Parking rates vary from $3 to $7 at the city lot across the street on Woz Way.

Bathrooms: Yes.

Facilities: Stroller friendly.

Food: Café.

Crab Cove Visitor Center (Ages 3+)
(510) 521-6887; 1252 McKay Avenue, Alameda, CA 94501
<www.ebparks.org/parks/crab.htm>

Description: Besides a small exhibition area, there are wonderful family oriented naturalist programs on the weekends. It's a good idea to visit during a naturalist program since this will enrich your experience here. Visit the Web page for specific programs, dates, and times. Programs include the mud flats habitat, microscopes to view the microbes found nearby, birding hikes, reptiles, and predator vs. prey. Some programs require advanced reservations (510) 521-6887. The center hosts birthday parties.

Hours: Open March through November, Wed–Sun: 10am–4pm. For naturalist program schedule, visit the events web page: <www.ebparks.org/events.htm>.

Cost: Free to the Visitor Center, but there may be a parking fee, depending on the season. Some naturalist programs require a very small fee, but most programs are free.

Bathrooms: Yes.

Facilities: Stroller friendly.

Food: No.

What to Bring: Binoculars and magnifying glasses. Picnic lunch, sunscreen, and sunglasses.

Cybercamp (Ages 7–16)

(Nationwide)

1-888-904-CAMP

1-888-904-2267

<www.cybercamps.com> or <www.giantcampus.com/cybercamps>

These weeklong summer camps can be half-day, full day, or residential, depending on the child's age. They provide instruction in Web design, 3-D animation, digital media (graphics, sound, etc), game design, programming, and robotics. In Northern California, these camps are located at West Valley (Saratoga), De Anza College (Cupertino), UC Berkeley, and Menlo College (Atherton). Check the Web site for pricing, locations, and camp courses.

Computer & Lego Camp (Ages 6–16)

TechKnowHow

(650) 325-5554

<www.techknowhowkids.com>

Locations on the peninsula and in the South Bay.

Destination Science (Ages 5–11)

(888) 909-2822

<www.destinationscience.org>

Destination Science services Marin, San Francisco, San Mateo, Contra Costa, and Santa Clara counties.

Environmental Volunteers

(650) 961-0545; 3921 E. Bayshore Road, Palo Alto, CA 94303-4326

The Environmental Volunteers who staff the Baylands in Palo Alto with docents offer S.N.A.K.E. Summer Camp. These camps are limited to 32 students in grades 2–6. They are held at the Keys School: 2890 Middlefield Road, Palo Alto, CA 94306, (650) 328-1711. Contact Environmental Volunteers for more information.

Exploratorium
(415) 563-7337; Palace of Fine Arts, 3601 Lyon Street, San Francisco, CA 94123
<www.exploratorium.edu>

Sunday afternoon science classes are for members only. Past class topics included weather, building bridges, sounds and music, and mirrors. For the fastest and easiest listing of the classes being offered, go to the Web site, click on the "Visit," then the "Events Calendar" icon, then do a search for "Science Classes." The Web site also has many "Web casts" and Web projects that showcase topics such as the bio-diversity of life, the science of cooking, and global climate change. It is, in essence, an online classroom. There is a summer day camp for members' children or grandchildren ages 7–10. These are full days (9am–4pm) for two weeks per session. Call for information (415) 561-0302.

Hayward Shoreline Interpretive Center
(510) 670-7270; (510) 881-6700 Reservations
4901 Breakwater Avenue, Hayward, CA 94545
<http://hard.dst.ca.us/index.html>

Description: Hayward Shoreline Interpretive Center provides an intro-duction to the San Francisco Estuary's ecology. The Interpretive Center has exhibits as well as weekend programs conducted by naturalists. These programs cover a wide range of topics that have included San Francisco Bay pirate history, the solar system and the universe from the Hubble Space Telescope, how boats float, and builders of the natural world: sea-shells, snails, and spiders, etc. For the most current list of programs, dates, and times, visit the Web site. Once you're at the home page, click on the "Signature Facilities" on the left column of the window, then click on "Hayward Shoreline Interpretive Center." School programs are available during the weekdays by reservation only.

Hours: Sat & Sun: 10 am–5pm. Administrative office is closed Mondays and Tuesdays.

Cost: Free, some programs require a small fee.

ID Tech Camps (Ages 8–17)
(888) 709-TECH
<www.internaldrive.com>

These camps focus on digital technology, including computer programming, Web design, computer graphics, digital music, and digital videos. These camps are held at UC Berkeley, Stanford, Santa Clara Universities, St. Mary's in Moraga, Dominican University, and Notre Dame de Namur.

Lawrence Hall of Science (Ages 4–18)
(510) 642-5132
Centennial Dr. near Grizzly Peak Boulevard, Berkeley, CA 94720
<www.lhs.berkeley.edu>

Description: Family workshops for children ages 3 to 7 are on Saturday mornings. During the week, there is a wonderful selection of classes, even for preschoolers, as well as science classes for home-schoolers ages 3 to 14. You may want to consider the affordable workshops/birthday parties. Summer camps (half-day, full-day, or residential) for ages ranging from 4–5 to high school teenagers. Supervised lunch hour and extended day care for summer camps are also available. Check the Web site and calendar for a full listing of the classes, programs, and summer camps offered.
Hours: Daily: 10am–5pm.

Mad Science of the Bay Area (Ages 5–12)
(877) 390-5437; 5409 Central Avenue, Suite 6, Newark, CA 94560
(650) 342-8342 San Mateo County
(510) 792-2795 Alameda County
(408) 262-5437 Santa Clara County
<www.madscience.org/southbay>

Description: Fun science classes in San Mateo, Santa Clara, and the western portion of Alameda counties. Programs include afterschool classes and summer camps. Check with your local Parks and Recreation Activity Guide to see if it is offered through your Parks and Recreation Department. Birthday parties for kids ages 5–12.

Ranger Explorers Summer Day Camp
(831) 335-3174
<www.mountainparks.org>

Description: The Mountain Parks Foundation runs a summer day camp called the Ranger Explorers. It is held June–August at various Santa Cruz County State Parks including Natural Bridges, Henry Cowell Redwoods

State Park, and Wilder Ranch State Park. For more information, contact Mountain Parks Foundation and visit the Web site in April for summer camp information.

Redwood Grove Nature Preserve (Ages 5+)

Through the Los Altos Parks and Recreation Department:
(650) 941-0950; (650) 917-0342; 482 University Avenue, Los Altos, CA 94022
<www.ci.los-altos.ca.us/recreation/fall/nature-preserve.pdf>

Description: In the spring and fall, a *Nature Fun* program is offered afterschool for ages 5 to 7. The program includes nature exploration, games, music, and arts and crafts. There are programs for school groups on nature, the Gold Rush, Ohlone Native Americans, archery, and bird watching. Summer programs are extremely popular and are on a first-come first-served basis. Register as early as possible to ensure placement. Hosts wonderful birthday parties.

Rotary Nature Center (Ages 6–15)

(510) 238-3739; 600 Bellevue Avenue, Oakland, CA 94610
<www.oaklandnet.com/parks/programs/rnc.asp>

Description: Weeklong summer day camps for children 6–15 years old. These science camps focus on different themes each week and include various topics such as bugs, birds, botany, and earth science. They also have extended care during the day.

Sally Ride Science Camps for Girls (Ages 11–14)

1-888-472-4386; Stanford University, Stanford, CA
<www.sallyridecamps.com/ScienceCamp/stanford/index.html>;
<www.sallyrideclub.com>

Description: Astronomer Sally Ride started this camp, which covers topics in astronomy, bioengineering, and structural engineering. These summer camps are held at Stanford University. She also started a company, Imaginary Lines, based in San Diego to help empower and encourage girls to explore and continue their interest in science and technology.

Science Adventures (Ages 6–12)
Science Enrichment Services, Inc.
1-800-4-SCIENCE (1-800-472-4362)

15412 Electronic Lane, Suite 201, Huntington Beach, CA 92649

<www.scienceadventures.com>

Description: Summer camps located in Alameda, Contra Costa, Santa Clara, Marin, San Francisco, San Mateo, and Sonoma counties. Camps cover a variety of science topics.

The Tech Museum of Innovation (Ages 9+)
(408) 294-TECH; 201 South Market Street, San Jose, CA 95113

<www.thetech.org>

Description: For older children, ages 9+, the Tech runs summer camps (members only). These are weekly half-day camps. The programs are:

- *Junior MD* and *Advanced MD* (be a doctor for a week),
- *Music Maestro* (learn sound engineering and MIDI techniques),
- *Hollywood Mogul* (write and direct a short movie using cutting edge software to record and edit the movie),
- *Lego Robo Techs* (build your own robots using LEGO® MINDSTORMS,
- *Mad Scientist* (learn about the scientists and the experiments that made them famous),
- *Web Guru* (design and build your own Web site).

Youth Science Institute (Ages 3+)
<www.ysi-ca.org>

Description: The Youth Science Institute has great hands-on science classes for kids from preschool on up. Summer camps and afterschool science classes are popular. These classes range from worms to temperature (such as the science of making ice cream), the planets, animal tracks, gravity, and rockets. There's an annual Wildlife Festival in mid-October 11am–4pm at Alum Rock Park, San Jose. This festival is free, but parking is $6/car. Class schedules and family science events are printed in the "Newsletter" on the Web site. You can also request to be placed on their mailing list for the newsletter. There three sites in Santa Clara County.

Vasona Lake County Park
(408) 356-4945; 296 Garden Hill Drive, Los Gatos, CA 95032
Mon–Fri: 9am–4:30pm, Sat–Sun by appointment.

Sanborn Center in Sanborn Park
(408) 867-6940; 16055 Sanborn Road, Saratoga, CA 95070
Tues–Fri: 9:30am–4:30pm, Sat–Sun: 12:30–4:30pm.

Alum Rock Park
(408) 258-4322; 16260 Alum Rock Avenue, San Jose, CA 95127
Tues–Sat: noon–4:30pm.

U.S. Space Camp (Ages 7–18)
Huntsville, Alabama
1-800-533-7281
<www.spacecamp.com>

Description: The NASA-affiliated Space Camp program requires children to be at least 9 years old and be in 4th grade. This is a residential camp that includes all room and board. There is a *Parent/Child Space Camp* for children ages 7–11; a *Space Academy Camp* for ages 12–14; and an *Advanced Space Academy* for teenagers 15–18. Unfortunately, the Moffett Field Space Camp closed due to financial difficulties.

Cool Science Web sites

There are wonderful Web sites that provide great science information. Listed below are some favorites.

Answers at Allstar Network
<www.allstar.fiu.edu>

Enchanted Learning
<www.EnchantedLearning.com>

Zoom Dinosaurs
<www.EnchantedLearning.com/subjects/dinosaurs>

How Do You Build Skyscrapers, Domes, Tunnels, Bridges, Dams, etc?
<www.pbs.org/wgbh/buildingbig/sitemap.html>

Hubble Site
(Cool Gallery of Photos from the Hubble Space Telescope)
<http://hubble.stsci.edu>

Kids Astronomy.Com
<www.KidsAstronomy.com>

Space Photos
<www.space.com>

Sites that Give Answers to "Why?" Questions –

World Kids Network
<www.worldkids.net>
Has answers to "Can fish hear?" "What's different between Whales and Fish?" etc.

What Is the Air Pressure Inside a Soap Bubble?
<www.sciencenet.org.uk/database/Physics/Original/p00324d.html>

The Why Files—Science Behind the News
<http://whyfiles.org>

Art Education

Creating art has great benefits. It helps nurture imagination, problem-solving skills, discipline, and patience. Children learn how to problem solve by correcting "mistakes" in the project. They develop their concentration, attention span, and patience since it takes time to complete a project.

When my daughter was three years old, she developed an attitude that things were "too hard" for her. What little concentration she had was tossed out the window when the painting she was working on didn't meet her expectations. She was frustrated and gave up on her self-initiated projects quickly. I had enrolled her in an art class but had some concerns that she wouldn't be able to sit through such a long class. I thought it was going to be very challenging because the class was over an hour long. To my surprise, she loved the class. She developed concentration, and her impatience quickly changed to patience. She brought home wonderful projects that required time and effort to complete. Within a month of starting the art class, she aspired to become an artist when she grew up. The patience and attention span she developed were unintended consequences of these art classes. But in retrospect, it makes a lot of sense that those skills were developed in the course of creating art.

There seem to be two camps in early childhood art education: "Open Art" and "Closed Art." The "Open Art" camp believes that art education for early childhood should be about pure exploration and creativity, that children should explore a variety of materials, textures, two- and three-dimensional projects, etc. Coloring books restrict children's creativity. Projects should not be done with a "cookie cutter" approach where the goal is in the end result looking exactly like the sample. "Open Art is an art process that allows the child to explore an art project on his own, uninhibited by outside expectations. It is a process that tends to lead to multiple interpretations, various end results, and even unpredictable directions. It is a process that thrives in a noncritical environment, in which the child's exploration is allowed to proceed without adult interference or correction. It is a process in which the *process itself* is more important than any adult-judged results."[2]

"The similarity of the work is a result of a ['Closed Art'] process in which the children are shown what they are going to do, shown how to do it, and often assisted in the process." "Closed Art" results in identical pieces of art work because "the *measure* of success is its close resemblance to the sample shown at the beginning of the process." [3]

"Open Art" believes in an open process while "Closed Art" believes in the end results.

As a parent who is neither an artist nor an educated art historian, I have wrestled with these philosophies and approaches. Perhaps my thoughts will help you arrive at your own insights. Here's the conclusion I've come to. I think that the "Open Art" process is very valuable in encouraging creativity and providing a positive and encouraging environment. I also agree with the prescription to withhold judgment, either positive or negative, on the child's work. Instead, factual observations can be made about the child's artwork that help the child see the effects of having mixed certain colors together, or how different use of line created the effects observed in the artwork. However, I saw how frustrated my daughter was in producing or even envisioning the art she wanted to create because she did not have the appropriate techniques and skills. Ideally, "Open Art" provides the techniques, then steps back to allow the child's originality to come through. But in some of the "Open Art" sessions I've seen, there has been very little guidance and basically just the materials are provided.

On the other hand, I was not impressed with the "Closed Art" approach that I saw in many preschools and day care centers, and even some art studios and art books, for the very reasons that Carolyn Holm, author of *Everyday Art for Kids*, cited. "Closed Art" sabotages the creativity that I was trying to nurture in my child.

Because of what I've read about coloring books restricting creativity, I've not asked nor required my daughter during her preschool years to do any coloring within the lines. The result was that my daughter's fine motor control skills were not honed. While coloring books do not encourage

[2] *Everyday Art for Kids* by Carolyn Holm pp8–9.
[3] *Everyday Art for Kids* by Carolyn Holm pp8–9.

creativity, I believe there is a place for them. Learning to color within the lines helps the child learn to develop fine motor control skills. However, I don't recommend coloring books exclusively and I don't believe that coloring is creative. I've found that providing my daughter with blank paper and quality coloring crayons with a clipboard in the car has been tremendously rewarding. She uses the time in the car as art sessions to experiment and be creative. It is open-ended and completely initiated by her. The artistic progress she has made from 4 years old to 5 years old, once I started the crayons and clipboard in the car, has been wonderful to see. I highly recommend it.

There is a compromise approach where the child is guided through a project framework with step-by-step techniques to help gain mastery of skills while providing freedom for individual creativity and variation. The results of this approach are works that look similar because they are the same projects, but with variations in each work.

I've spoken with artists to learn their views on these approaches and how they learned to become artists. They've told me that they were trained by learning the techniques. Creativity is something that comes forth later because they now have the skills to allow their creativity to produce what they envisioned.

One thing that seems to be a general consensus in the arts community is the setup of a workspace for doing art, and an environment where being messy is OK. The accessibility of the art materials helps children incorporate art into their everyday lives. See the recommended books for parents on how to set up the art area in your home.

Here's a guide to what to look for in an art class:
1. Art history introduction at each class, who the artist is, what his technique is, and what to notice about the art.
2. How the teacher talks to the students. Does the teacher encourage the child? There should not be judgmental comments from the teacher. How does the teacher talk about imitation? Imitation of other people's work helps us learn new techniques and can inspire us. The teacher should address the child's feelings of having made a "mistake." There are great children's books that are very appropriate

for working with these issues.

3. The techniques being taught in the class. Does the teacher teach about line, colors, composition, perspective, balance, etc?
4. Are there a variety of materials offered? Are they quality materials that are easy and fun to work with? Poor quality materials can be frustrating to use, both for children and adults, and may hinder the creative flow.

Recommended reading for parents:

Everyday Art for Kids by Carolyn Holm
"Projects to Unlock Creativity." "Over 250 fun & easy projects that get kids excited about art, Handy materials reference, Simple guidelines for providing a creative environment."
Doing Art Together by Muriel Silberstein-Storfer with Mablen Jones
"Discovering the joys of appreciating and creating art as taught at The Metropolitan Museum of Art's famous parent-child workshop."

Books about art for the preschooler:

I Am an Artist by Pat Lowery Collins, Robin Brickman (Illustrator).
Regina's Big Mistake by Marissa Moss.

Art Classes

Local community centers, such as the local Parks and Recreation Department, the YMCA, and the JCC, also sponsor art classes. See the listings at the beginning of the Classes section.

Below is a list of the art studios that provide art classes, including classes for young toddlers, in the Bay Area beyond your local community center. They are listed in alphabetical order.

A Painting Studio (Ages 5+)

(415) 333-9515; 300 Chenery Street, San Francisco, CA 94131

Almaden School of Music, Art, and Dance (Ages 5+)

(408) 267-3651; 5353 Almaden Expwy #12, San Jose, CA 95118

Artful I Studio (Ages 4 1/2+)

(408) 517-0377; 12201C Saratoga-Sunnyvale Road, Saratoga, CA 95070
<http://home.attbi.com/~artfuli>

The Art Room (Ages 4+)

(925) 299-1515; 50 Lafayette Circle, Lafayette, CA 94549
<www.theart-room.com>

California College of Arts and Crafts (Ages 12+)

(800) 447-1ART; (510) 594-3600
(510) 594-3710: Young Artist Studio (grades 6–8)
5212 Broadway, Oakland, CA 94618
<www.ccac-art.edu>

Summer courses for 6th–8th graders in the Young Artist Studio program and for high schoolers completing sophomore to senior years in the pre-college program with three college credits.

California Palace of the Legion of Honor (Ages 3+)

(415) 682-2483 Education Department
Lincoln Park, 100 34th Avenue, San Francisco, CA 94122
<www.thinker.org/legion>

Description: On Saturdays (10:30am –noon), there are special tours and art classes for children 3½ to 6 years old. These are free with museum admission. No preregistration required. Also at the same time, tours and classes are offered to children 7 to 12 years old, on the same basis. These class sizes are limited. Additional programs are offered, but require advanced registration.
Hours: Tues–Sun: 9:30am–5pm.
Cost: $8/adult, $6/senior 65 and over, $5/youth 12–17, free/child under 12.

Cantor Arts Center at Stanford University (Ages 3+)
(650) 723-4177; 328 Lomita Drive and Museum Way, Stanford, CA 94305-5060
<www.stanford.edu/dept/ccva>

Description: The art classes are held in Moorman Studio Classroom and galleries. Class information line: (650) 725-3155. The class schedule is also available online at: <www.stanford.edu/dept/ccva>.
Hours: Wed–Sun: 11am–5pm; Thur: 11am–8pm. Closed Mon, Tues, and holidays.

Community School of Music & Arts (5+)
(650) 961-0342; 253 Martens Avenue, Mountain View, CA 94040
<http://csmaca.org>

Clay Studio (Ages 5–17)
(415) 777-9080; 743 Harrison Street, San Francisco, CA 94107
www.theclaystudio.com

Offers clay instruction and hand building for children. Afterschool and Saturday morning classes are available.

Civic Arts Education (Ages 2+)
(925) 943-5846; Studio E, 1313 Civic Drive, Walnut Creek, CA 94596
<http://arts-ed.org>

Available for birthday parties.

De Colores (Ages 2+)
(650) 347-1089; 49 N. San Mateo Drive, San Mateo, CA 94401
<www.decolores-art.org>

Available for birthday parties.

Gymboree Play & Music Programs (Ages 1½–5)

(408) 378-5318; 1600 Saratoga Avenue, #517, San Jose, CA 95129
(408) 629-5813; 222 Oakridge Mall, San Jose, CA 95123
(408) 777-8470; 10123 N. Wolfe Road, #1017, Cupertino, CA 95014
(510) 739-6150; 39138 Fremont Hub #221, Fremont, CA 94538
(650) 949-5798; 664 Los Altos Rancho, Los Altos, CA 94024
(650) 494-8400; 3908 Middlefield Road, Palo Alto, CA 94303-4733
(650) 364-3420; 2531 El Camino Real, Redwood City, CA 94061
<www.playandmusic.com/b2c/customer/programIndex.jsp>

Now has art classes for 18 month olds to 5 year olds. Classes include music and creative movement. Available for birthday parties, too.

Habitot Children's Museum (Ages 2+)

(510) 647-1111; 2065 Kittredge Street, Berkeley, CA 94704
<www.habitot.org>

Art area for self-directed art projects. Geared toward toddlers and preschoolers. Wonderful selection of art, music, and drama classes, as well as camps. Available for birthday parties.

Jewish Community Center of San Francisco (Ages 3–14)

(415) 346-6040; 1808 Wedemeyer Street, San Francisco, CA 94129
<www.jccsf.org>

Art and ceramic classes for children.

Junior Center of Art and Science (Ages 2–17)

Lakeside Park (by Lake Merritt/Oakland's Fairyland)

(510) 839-5777; 558 Bellevue Avenue, Oakland, CA 94610
<www.juniorcenter.org>
<www.oaklandnet.com/parks/facilities/points_junior_center.asp>

Description: Drop-in art activities and pottery studio for all ages, including preschoolers. Afterschool art and science classes 4–6pm for children ages 5+. Registration is required. Summer art camps for children 5–16. During the summer, drop-in activities are also available.
Hours: *September–May:* Tues–Fri: 10am–6pm; Sat: 10am–3pm.
June–August: Mon–Thur: 8:30am–5:30pm.
Cost: Varies, depending on the class/program. Call for details.

Kids N' Clay (Ages 5+)
(510) 845-0982; 1824 5ᵗʰ Street, Berkeley, CA 94710
<www.kidsnclay.com>

Ceramics studio offers classes to children 5 and older (up to teens) after school and on Saturdays. Summer camps available. Ask to be on the mailing list. The mailing goes out in January. Summer camps sign up in February.

Kollage Community School for the Arts
(650) 592-8842
Physical address: 801 Granda Street, Belmont, CA 94002
Mailing address: P.O. Box 532, Belmont, CA 94002
<www.kollage.org>

Museum of Children's Art (MOCHA) (Ages 18 months+)
(510) 465-8770; 538 Ninth Street, Oakland, CA 94607
<www.mocha.org>

Art studios designed for pre-schoolers as well as big kids.

Pacific Art League (Ages 5+)
(650) 321-3891; 668 Ramona Street, Palo Alto, CA 94301
<www.pacificartleague.org>

Palo Alto Art Center (Ages 18 months+)
(650) 329-2366; 1313 Newell Road, Palo Alto, CA 94303
<www.city.palo-alto.ca.us/artcenter/generalinfo.html>

Look at the Palo Alto *Enjoy* catalog for the schedule of classes. Great family workshops on weekends, too.

the Painting Shop (Ages 5+)
(408) 448-4833; 1080-G Blossom Hill Road, San Jose, CA 95124

Purple Crayon (Ages 2+)
(415) 831-0693; 301 Cornwall, San Francisco, CA 94118
<www.purplecrayon.com>

The Randall Museum (Ages 2+)
(415) 554-9600; 199 Museum Way, San Francisco, CA 94114
<www.randallmuseum.org/events.cfm>

Richards Arts Crafts & Framing (Ages 5+)
(925) 447-0471; 4502 Las Positas, Livermore, CA 94550

Art project birthday parties, including ceramic painting, tie dye T-shirts, etc. Afterschool and Saturday classes.

Richmond Art Center (Ages 3½+)
(510) 620-6772; Civic Center Plaza, Richmond, CA 94804
<www.therichmondartcenter.org>

San Francisco Children's Art Center (Ages 3+)
Fort Mason Center
(415) 775-0991 x107; Fort Mason Center, Bldg. A, San Francisco, CA 94123
<www.mocfa.org>

San Jose Museum of Art
(408) 271-6840; 110 South Market Street, San Jose, CA 95113
<www.sjmusart.org>

Hours: Tues–Sun: 11am–5pm, Fri: 11am–10pm. Closed Mondays, Thanksgiving, Christmas, and New Year's Day. Kids Art Sunday is on the last Sunday of each month. These art classes/workshops are free.

The Santa Cruz Mountains Art Center
(831) 336-3513; 9341 Mill Street, Ben Lomond, CA 95005
<www.mountainartcenter.org>

Children's ceramic and art classes offered. Call (831) 336-4ART for more details.

Sharon Art Studio (Ages 5-15)

Golden Gate Park Arts & Crafts Division at McLaren Lodge
(415) 753-7004; 501 Stanyan Street, San Francisco, CA 94117
<www.sharonartstudio.org>

Ceramics, glass, jewelry making, drawing, painting, and mix media classes offered.

Silicon Valley Art Museum

1870 Ralston Avenue, Belmont, CA 94002
<www.svam.org/Art_Tech>

Online art lesson plans.

Studio One Art Center

(510) 597-5027; 365 45th Street, Oakland, CA 94609
<www.oaklandnet.com/parks/facilities/points_studio_one.asp>

The Marvegos Fine Art School

Saratoga Studio: (408) 866-0671
18776 Cox Avenue, Saratoga, CA (at Quito Village)

Fremont Studio: (510) 445-1507
<www.marvegos.com>

Triton Museum of Art (Ages 5+)

(408) 247-3754; 247-9340
1505 Warburton Avenue, Santa Clara, CA 95050
<www.tritonmuseum.org>

Summer camp available.

University Art (supply store w/ classes)

(408) 297-4707; 456 Meridian Avenue, San Jose, CA 95126
<www.universityart.com/class.htm>

Young at Art Studio (Ages 4+)

(408) 255-1414; 19701 Stevens Creek Boulevard, Cupertino, CA 95014

Art Supplies Stores

Besides taking art classes, it's good to encourage your child to do art at home. *Doing Art Together* author Muriel Silberstein-Storfer suggests setting up a workspace in the home and providing good quality paints, brushes, pastels, paper, etc. Here's a list of art supplies stores in the Bay Area to help with your search.

Aaron Brothers
<www.aaronbrothers.com>

Stores in Daly City, San Francisco, Berkeley, Concord, Dublin, Fremont, Pinole, San Ramon, Walnut Creek, Redwood City, San Mateo, Campbell, Cupertino, Sunnyvale, and San Jose.

Amsterdam Art Supplies
(510) 649-4800; 1-800-994-2787
1013 University Avenue, Berkeley, CA 94710
<www.amsterdamart.com>

Lakeshore Learning Store
<www.lakeshorelearning.com>

Stores in Walnut Creek, San Jose, and San Leandro. The San Leandro store is the clearance warehouse.

Michaels
<www.michaels.com>

Stores in Redwood City, San Mateo, Dublin, Emeryville, Union City, Fremont, Milpitas, Cupertino, Sunnyvale, and San Jose.

Morrison School Supply
(650) 592-3000; 400 Industrial Road, San Carlos, CA 94070
(408) 749-1114; 560 E El Camino, Sunnyvale, CA 94087

Great source of 11x14 and 8x11 white construction paper!

Richard's Arts Crafts & Framing
(925) 820-4731; 225A Alamo Plaza, Alamo, CA 94507
(925) 447-0471; 4502 Las Positas, Livermore, CA 94550

University Art
<www.universityart.com>

Stores in San Francisco, Palo Alto, San Jose, and Sacramento.

Music Education

Learning to play a musical instrument has many benefits. Besides developing music appreciation, the discipline of learning an instrument gives you opportunities to learn life lessons. There are times when learning new skills is hard, and the student has great difficulty accomplishing new tasks. Oftentimes, this is when the student wants to quit. It's important to learn that skills and tasks that are hard require practice, but with practice comes mastery. It's important to learn not to give up for trivial reasons, to learn the discipline of having to practice daily, even when it's hard and not so fun.

In the course of dealing with difficulty, the student should also learn to be patient and kind to himself; he must give himself the time to learn. The goal is daily incremental improvement. Sometimes, it's two steps forward and one step backward. It's important not to expect perfection, but rather expect to do one's best. Mistakes are not failures, but the means to learn and improve. These are important life lessons that can be learned through the discipline of playing an instrument. Of course, these life lessons can be learned through many different pursuits, including sports and hobbies, as long as you have commitment and dedication.

Playing an instrument demands great physical coordination. It requires the eyes and brain to read the notes and translate them to the hands/ breath, etc. It requires listening to the music and cooperating with other instruments in the orchestra, ensemble, or symphony. These tasks require a great deal from children's brains, resulting in general development of the brain and, therefore, intelligence. In recent years, there has been a product trend of cassettes and videos to increase an infant's intelligence. The most recent study shows that there is an effect while listening to the music, but it is very short-lived. These products try to cash in on the public's misunderstanding that these passive activities increase the baby's or child's intelligence.

From my experience, there are several distinct stages in musical development in early childhood. The first stage is just music appreciation, which can be developed by the parent or caregiver. Start by singing and allowing yourself to be silly to foster creativity. Singing lullabies and children's songs helps develop the child's sense of pitch, rhythm, and—most importantly—love of music. Once the child starts singing along with you, it's time for introductory music classes such as Music Together, Kindermusic, and Gymboree Music. These programs develop music appreciation and basic musicianship in a fun, stimulating, and nonthreatening environment. They all believe that your child is inherently musical and help develop musical skills through play.

Making music at home with your child, and using the skills you've learned in these programs, is a great way to encourage daily music play. It's a great idea to start a "music kit" that contains rhythm instruments (maracas, egg shakers, train whistle, drum set, tambourine, sticks, spoons, etc.) Music Together also sells its collections via cassette or CD, with a songbook with lyrics for each collection. This is a great way to bring the Music Together experience home. Gymboree Music and Play Programs also sell CD and rhythm instruments. I highly recommend the *Gymboree Singing Together* cassette and songbook for the toddler or preschool-age child. It has finger plays, counting and chants for rhythm development, as well as old-time favorite tunes.

Once your child is comfortable with music—singing in pitch and with basic rhythm— it's probably time for a group music class that will prepare your child to take private music lessons. This stage should be in the 4- to 5-year-old range. The goals of the group lessons should be learning the following concepts and putting these new skills into practice.
1)   Rhythm, keeping a steady beat.

2) Keeping count (your child need only be able to count to six, as almost all music measures are 2 beats up to a maximum of 6 beats per measure).

3) Distinguishing whether a musical piece or phrase is fast or slow.

4) Distinguishing whether the note is a high note or low note.

5) Differentiating between right and left hand.

6) Being able to distinguish whether it's a major key (sounds happy) or a minor key (sounds sad).

7) Learning the types of notes (whole notes get 4 beats, half notes get 2 beats, quarter notes get 1 beat, eighth notes get ½ beat, etc.).

8) Learning to read the music: understanding the clefs (treble clef and bass clef), the number of beats per measure, and reading the notes on the musical staff.

9) Being able to identify the piano key to the note on the musical staff.

This lays the foundation for private music lessons. However, consider the emotional maturity and the readiness of the child before starting private lessons, as this step requires the discipline and commitment to practice the instrument on a daily basis.

Music Classes

Local Parks and Recreation Departments also sponsor group music classes for beginners. See Chapter 11: Local Resources—Parks and Recreation Departments section.

Do Re Mi Music Studio
(888) 458-2208

Gymboree Play & Music Programs (Infants–5)

(408) 378-5318; 1600 Saratoga Avenue, #517, San Jose, CA 95129
(408) 629-5813; 222 Oakridge Mall, San Jose, CA 95123
(408) 777-8470; 10123 N. Wolfe Road, #1017, Cupertino, CA 95014
(510) 739-6150; 39138 Fremont Hub #221, Fremont, CA 94538
(650) 949-5798; 664 Los Altos Rancho, Los Altos, CA 94024
(650) 494-8400; 3908 Middlefield Road, Palo Alto, CA 94303-4733
(650) 364-3420; 2531 El Camino Real, Redwood City, CA 94061
<www.playandmusic.com/b2c/customer/programIndex.jsp>

Keynote Music

(925)855-8863; 480L San Ramon Valley Road, Danville, CA 94526

Kids in Tune (Ages 18 Months–7 years)

(800) 720-0887; (510) 887-1304; P.O. Box 336, Mt. Eden, CA 94557

> **Danville:** The Grange Hall, 743 Diablo Road, Danville, CA 94526
> **Oakland/Montclair:** St. John's Episcopal Church, 1707 Gouldin Road, Oakland, CA 94611
> **Los Altos:** Foothill Congregational Church, 461 Orange Avenue, Los Altos, CA 94022

Teaching based on the Kodaly method. Offers classes through preschools and local Parks and Recreation Departments. Call to request brochure for details. The following cities have Parks and Recreation Departments that feature Kids in Tune: Alameda, Concord, Fremont, Los Altos, Milpitas, Newark, Pleasant Hill, Redwood City, San Leandro, and San Mateo.

Kindermusik (Infants & Up)

<www.kindermusik.com>

Provides early childhood instruction in music for newborns to children age 7. Visit the Web site for curricula information and educator location.

Music Together (Age 1—5)

<www.musictogether.com>

Nationwide music and movement program for babies and preschoolers. Go to the Web site for city locator and program closest to you. The classes can also be found through various city Parks and Recreation Departments. Certain locations have International Music Together featuring music and songs from various countries and languages. You can also purchase the music collections and rhythm instruments online.

Music Together of the Mid-Peninsula
<www.musictogether.info>
Serves Mountain View, Sunnyvale, Palo Alto, and Menlo Park.

Music Together of Santa Cruz/Santa Clara County
<www.cruzers.com/~musictogether/hp/hp.html>
Serves Cupertino, Los Gatos, Saratoga, Campbell, Capitola, and Santa Cruz.

Music Together of Marin
(415) 388-2464
<www.music4families.com>
Serves Mill Valley/Fairfax and San Rafael.

Music Together of San Francisco
(415) 596-0299; 575 Kelmore Street, Moss Beach, CA 94038
<www.musictogethersf.com>

San Francisco Music Together
(415) 431-9793; 88 Haight Street, San Francisco, CA 94117
<www.sfmusictogether.com>

Music Together in the Tri-Valley
(925) 551-7722
www.musictogether.net/newinfo.htm
Serves Walnut Creek, Danville, Pleasanton, and Livermore.

Do Music
(650) 366-4463
<www.domusictogether.com>
Serves Foster City, Redwood City, and San Carlos.

East Bay Music Together
(510) 843-8641; 2316 Webster Street, Berkeley, CA 94705
http://eastbaymusictogether.com/cgi-bin/page.cgi?name=home
Serves Berkeley, Moraga, and Walnut Creek.

Half Moon Music
<www.halfmoonmusic.com>
Serves San Mateo, Burlingame, Belmont, Half Moon Bay, Bonny Doon, San Mateo, Belmont, and Burlingame. Classes offered through Parks and Recreation Departments.

Almaden School of Music, Art, & Dance
Almaden Plaza
(408) 267-3651; 5353 Almaden Expressway, Ste 12, San Jose, CA 95118
<www.almadenschool.com>

Canon Music (Ages 3+)
(408) 996-8033; 10885 South Blaney Avenue, Cupertino, CA 95014
Also rents pianos on a monthly basis.

Community Music Center, San Francisco
(415) 647-6015; 544 Capp Street, San Francisco, CA 94110
(415) 221-4515; 741 30th Avenue, San Francisco, CA 94121
<www.sfmusic.org>

Community School of Music & Arts (Ages 4+)
(650) 961-0342; 137 E El Camino Real, Mountain View, CA 94040
<www.arts4all.org>

Peninsula Piano School
(650) 851-1999; 405 El Camino Real #232, Menlo Park, CA 94025
(650) 854-7006; Classes held at Cubberley Community Center:
(888) 742-6680; 4000 Middlefield Road, Room M7
<www.penpiano.com>

Polonsky Piano School (Ages 4+)
(408) 257-6181; 18572 Prospect Road #B, Saratoga, CA 95070
<www.polonskypianoschool.com>
Offers piano and violin classes. Summer arts camp.

San Francisco Conservatory of Music, Preparatory Division (Ages 4+)
(415) 564-8086; 1201 Ortega Street, San Francisco, CA 94122-4498
<www.sfcm.edu>

Provides early childhood music education for children ages 4–9. Private lessons are also available.

Sweetmusik Studios (Ages 3+)
(408) 973-1240; 20009 Stevens Creek Boulevard, Cupertino, CA 95014

World of Music
(408) 252-8264; 20015 Stevens Creek Boulevard, Cupertino, CA 95014

Drama Education

Children love to pretend and dress up. It's a wonderful way to develop their imagination and creativity, in addition to developing their public speaking skills and self-confidence. Many of the companies listed below provide drama classes, as well as performances, for children.

Bay Area Children's Theatre Company (Ages 4–16)
(510) 444-4942; 2501 Harrison Street, Oakland, CA 94612
<www.bayareachildrenstheatre.com>

Children's Fairyland Children's Theater (All Ages)
(510) 452-2259; 699 Bellevue Avenue, Oakland, CA 94610
<www.fairyland.org/schedule.html#daily>

Conservatory of Performing Arts (Ages 4+)
Children's Musical Theater, San Jose
(408) 288-5437 x22
1401 Parkmoor Avenue, Ste. 100, San Jose, CA 95126
<www.cmtsj.org>

Offers classes for children starting at age four. Tiny Tots Song & Dance (ages 4–5), Junior Talents Revue (ages 6–8), Rising Stars Revue (ages 9–12), and Master Acting Class (ages 12–20). Summer camps are available.

Children's Play House of San Jose (Ages 6+)
(Grades 1 – 9; Musicals)
(408) 578-PLAY (call between 3pm and 6 pm)

Offered at the Blossom Hill School in Los Gatos. Register through Los Gatos–Saratoga Department of Community Education and Recreation, at (408)354-8700 or via the Web site <www.lgsararec.org>.

Dublin Theatre Company Performing Arts Academy
(925) 551-5382; (925) 551-5382 x44 for birthday parties
6620 Dublin Boulevard, Dublin, CA 94568
<www.dublintheatre.com>

Classes offered through the Performing Arts Academy. On the Web site, select "Education" then "Performing Arts Academy." Offers classes in acting, singing, and dance. Birthday parties offered. A few courses are through the Parks and Recreation Departments of Livermore, Pleasanton, and San Ramon. These courses include "City Theatre Arts," "Creative Dramatics," and "Acting Is for Me." See the Parks and Recreation section under these cities for the Web sites.

Kaleidoscope Camp & Classes for Kids (Ages 4+)
Julia Morgan Center for the Arts
(510) 845-8542 ext.301; 2640 College Avenue, Berkeley, CA 94704
www.juliamorgan.org/kal.shtml

Spring and summer camps in the theater arts.

Kids on Broadway (Ages 6+)
(831) 425-3455; P.O. Box 3461 Santa Cruz, CA 95063
<www.kidsonbroadway.org>

Afterschool classes, workshops, and summer camps in theater arts for kids 6 and older. Classes include acting, voice, dance, improvisation, lighting, set construction, and costume design.

Palo Alto Children's Theater (Ages 5+)
(650) 329-2216; 1305 Middlefield Road, Palo Alto, CA 94301
<www.city.palo-alto.ca.us/support/links/pages/Arts/Childrens_Theatre>

Wonderful summertime theater for kids, including preschoolers, in an outdoor environment. You can bring a picnic and blanket. You can purchase cookies and hot dogs, too.

Peninsula Youth Theatre (Ages 3½+)
(650) 988-8798; 2500 Old Middlefield Way, Mountain View, CA 94043
<www.pytnet.org>

Santa Clara Junior Theatre (Ages 4+)
Santa Clara Community Recreation Center
(408) 244-SCJT; (408) 615-3161
969 Kiely Boulevard, Santa Clara, CA 95051
Email: scjt@vval.com

Register through the Santa Clara Parks and Recreation Department. For more information, see the Santa Clara Parks and Recreation Department in Chapter 11: Local Resources—Local Parks and Recreation Departments section.

Saratoga Children's Festival Theater (Ages 5+)
Tickets: (408) 868-1248; 19655 Allendale, Saratoga, CA 95070
<www.childrens-festival-theatre.com>

(Through the Saratoga Parks and Recreation Department) Performances held at the Saratoga Community Center.

Willows Theatre Conservatory (Ages 5+)
(925) 798-1300; 1975 Diamond Boulevard, Concord, CA 94520
<www.willowstheatre.org>

Young Performers Theatre (Ages 3+)
(415) 346-5550
Fort Mason Center, Building C, Room 300, San Francisco, CA 94123
<www.ypt.org>

Besides wonderful children's theater at very affordable prices, there are classes for even the youngest pretenders. Available for birthday parties.

Chapter 13
Physical Activities

Physical activity is not only fun, it is absolutely necessary for children's well being. Motor skill development is as important as academic development. A great time to visit toddler playgrounds is in the first two years, after babies learn to walk and are fairly confident on their feet. Many gymnastics programs have classes for infants to 4 year olds. Some swimming classes accommodate children as young as six months. Dance classes usually require the child to be at least 2 years old, generally 3 years old. Ice skating usually accommodates children three and older. Bowling seems to work well for kids over 3 years old.

Parks

National & State Parks

National Parks
1-888-GO-PARKS
<www.nps.gov>
<www.nationalparks.org>

California State Parks
(916) 653-6995
<http://parks.ca.gov>

County Parks

East Bay Regional Park District
<www.ebparks.org>

Includes Alameda and Contra Costa counties

Marin County Parks
<http://maps.openspacecouncil.org/Orgs/County_of_Marin.html>

Monterey County Parks
<www.co.monterey.ca.us/parks>

San Francisco Parks
<www.parks.sfgov.org/site/recpark_index.asp>

San Mateo County Parks
<www.co.sanmateo.ca.us/smc/department/esa/home/0,2242,5556687_
10575168,00.html>

Santa Clara County Parks
<http://claraweb.co.santa-clara.ca.us/parks/index.html>
<www.parkhere.org/site/0,4760,sid=12761,00.html>

Santa Cruz County Parks
<www.scparks.com>

Sonoma County Parks
<www.parks.sonoma.net>

Neighborhood Parks

The following Web sites provide information for each city's neighborhood parks. Some parks have water play areas. For those, it's a good idea to bring flip-flops, bathing suits, sunscreen, towels, a picnic lunch, and drinks. Don't forget your sunscreen and sunglasses, and some change for metered parking, too.

Alameda: <www.ci.alameda.ca.us/arpd/pdf/parks-activity-guide.pdf> or <www.ci.alameda.ca.us/arpd/parkfacil.html>
Belmont: <www.belmont.gov/localgov/prec/parks.jpg>
Berkeley: <www.ci.berkeley.ca.us/parks/parks.html>
Brentwood: <www.ci.brentwood.ca.us/department/parks/parksdiv.cfm>
Burlingame: <www.burlingame.org/p_r/parks/parks.htm>
Campbell: <www.ci.campbell.ca.us/communityandarts/parks.htm>
Concord: <www.ci.concord.ca.us/recreation/playgrnd.htm>
Cupertino: <www.cupertino.org/just_visiting/what_to_do/index.asp>
Danville: <www.ci.danville.ca.us/parks/parkdes.htm>
Dublin: <www.ci.dublin.ca.us/DepartmentSub.cfm?PL=Rec&SL=prkfac>
El Cerrito: <www.el-cerrito.org/recreation/parks.html>
Emeryville: <www.ci.emeryville.ca.us/rec/recreation.html>
Foster City: <www.fostercity.org/Services/recreation/ParkGrid.cfm>
Fremont: <www.fremont.gov/Recreation/Playgrounds/default.htm>
Gilroy: <www.ci.gilroy.ca.us/comserv/parks.html>
Hayward: <www.ci.hayward.ca.us/community/recreation.html>
Livermore: <www.larpd.dst.ca.us/facilities_fs.html>
Los Altos: <www.losaltosonline.com/articles/2003/06/03/government/parks/news01.txt>
Los Altos Hills: <www.losaltoshills.ca.gov/recreation.html>
Los Gatos: <www.town.los-gatos.ca.us/services/6b.html>
Menlo Park: <www.menlopark.org/departments/com/parks.html>
Mill Valley: <www.cityofmillvalley.org/parks-facilities-main.html>
Millbrae:< www.ci.millbrae.ca.us/parksandrec/parklocations.html>
Milpitas: <www.ci.milpitas.ca.gov/citydept/planning/recreation/parkfacilityreservation.htm>
Monterey Area: <www.monterey.com/mc3/mc3a2.html>
Moraga: <www.ci.moraga.ca.us/reservtn.htm>

Morgan Hill: <http://mhwww.e21corp.com/html/citysvc/comm/facility.asp>

Mountain View: <www.ci.mtnview.ca.us/citydepts/cs/parks.htm>

Newark: <www.newark.org/pw/pwmapar.html>

Oakland: <www.oaklandnet.com/parks/facilities/parks.asp>

Orinda: <www.ci.orinda.ca.us/parksandrec/parksandtrails/parksandtrails.html>

Pacific Grove: <www.pacificgroverecreation.org>

Palo Alto: <www.paloaltoonline.com/paw/paonline/com_info/parks.shtml>

Piedmont: <www.ci.piedmont.ca.us/html/visitor/parks.htm>

Pleasant Hill: <www.pleasanthillrec.com/facilities.html>

Pleasanton: <www.ci.pleasanton.ca.us/pdf/sumag03pgs6465.pdf>

Portola Valley: <www.portolavalley.net/community/cr_parks_recreation.shtml>

Redwood City: <www.ci.redwood-city.ca.us/parks/parks_all.html>

Richmond: <www.ci.richmond.ca.us/~recweb/public.html#parks>

San Anselmo: <www.townofsananselmo.org/parks>

San Carlos: <www.cityofsancarlos.org/is/display/0,1124,deptid-19_isid-432,00.html>

San Francisco: <www.sfgov.org/site/recpark_index.asp?id=1503>

San Jose: <www.sjparks.org/Parks/list.htm> or <www.ci.san-jose.ca.us/prns/parksppf.htm>

> **Lincoln Glen Park** (has water play and restrooms)
> Corner of Lincoln and Curtner Avenues, San Jose, CA
> Bring flip-flops for kids – the ground gets very hot.

For the list of parks within San Jose that have water play:
<www.sjparks.org/Features/chikdrenswaterfeatures.htm>

San Leandro: <www.ci.san-leandro.ca.us/slparks.html>

San Mateo: <www.cityofsanmateo.org/dept/parks/directory.html>

San Rafael: <www.cityofsanrafael.org/cs/parkrentals.htm>

San Ramon: <www.ci.san-ramon.ca.us/parks/parks.htm>

Santa Clara: <http://cho.ci.santa-clara.ca.us/3041.html>

Santa Cruz: <www.santacruzparksandrec.com/parks/neighborhoodparks.html>

Saratoga: <www.saratoga.ca.us/parkrental.htm>

Sausalito: <www.ci.sausalito.ca.us/business/park-rec/parks.htm>

Sunnyvale: <www.ci.sunnyvale.ca.us/leisure-services/facilities/index.htm>

Union City: <www.ci.union-city.ca.us/leisure/sites/parks.htm>
Walnut Creek: <www.ci.walnut-creek.ca.us/parks/parksmain.htm>

Swimming

The American College of Pediatrics recommends waiting until a child is 4 years old to introduce swimming lessons. For its policy statement regarding swimming programs for infants and toddlers, refer to the Web site: <www.aap.org/policy/re9940.html>. It concludes that children under 4 years of age do not have sufficient motor skills and that swim classes can lead parents to the false belief that their child is water safe.

I believe another reason infants should not take swim classes is because their little bodies lose body temperature too quickly, even in a 30-minute class and in an enclosed, heated pool. I've been in classes with 6 month-old infants who were so cold they were shivering in the middle of summer.

I started my child around her 2nd birthday. I found that to be the optimal age because she had not developed a major fear and aversion to the water yet. Children starting at an older age may have a tougher introduction to the water. Additionally, parent/child introductory swimming classes, offered to children under three years old, are wonderful transition classes prior to the child-only classes at the age of 3. The parent/child classes use songs and games to promote a secure and fun environment. It's absolutely critical that we, as parents, do not delude ourselves into believing that our children are water safe just because they have had swim classes. Parents should always supervise their children, especially when their children are in the pool, even if they have had swim classes.

You must decide for yourself when to introduce your children to swim classes, if ever. You should also consider your children's temperament to gauge when they are ready.

I think it's sufficient to take swim classes only during the warm weather, from late spring to early fall. During the winter, it gets very cold, even in an indoor heated pool. There can be quite a change in temperature from being in the pool to getting out of the pool, into the dressing area, and getting dressed. Also, during the cold weather season, so many kids have colds or the flu and yet continue to go to swim classes that I think it's better to avoid this environment entirely. After I stopped my daughter's winter swimming lessons, I noticed that she got sick less often. Lastly, I have not seen any significant regression when I've taken my daughter out of swim classes during the winter. I believe that classes during warm weather provide sufficient progress.

Many people find that the frequency of swimming classes plays an important role in how fast the child's swimming progresses. During the summer, it's ideal to provide multiple swimming sessions each week to help reinforce skills learned. Some swim schools provide summer intensive sessions that run daily for two weeks. Others provide 2 or three classes per week during the summer. I find that a class once a week is sufficient if you have access to a pool during the summer to allow your child the chance to practice what she has learned and just to play.

Be aware that pool facilities vary from site to site. Some facilities are indoor; some outdoor with a dome; while others are outdoor, exposed to the sun and weather. Some pools are very shallow teaching pools, while some are much deeper. Some pools are heated to 90°F, appropriate for young children who lose body temperature very quickly in the water, while other pools are cooler, appropriate for older kids and adults. It is important that the facility you choose be a good fit with your needs. If you have very young children, choose a pool that is well heated (to 90°F), indoor, or domed, to prevent sun damage to tender baby skin. Shallow pools are wonderful for the very first classes because they help children feel more comfortable and secure. However, shallow pools can also become crutches that impede progress because children depend on their ability to stand up and fail to gain confidence in their ability to swim in deeper water.

When my daughter was three, she learned to do the dog paddle at a deeper pool. A beautiful new indoor teaching pool opened and I switched her to this school, since it was winter and I wanted her to stay warmer. Unfortunately, my daughter's skills and confidence regressed because this pool was shallow and it became a crutch. During the two sessions that she took classes at this pool, she became afraid to go into deeper pools and was afraid to swim on her own. When I switched her back to the previous swim school, her confidence returned very quickly and she was again swimming on her own.

Teaching methods also vary from school to school. Some methods are very gentle and are suitable for sensitive children. However, the gentler methods may take more time to produce results. Other methods are more no-nonsense, with faster progress, but not appropriate for all personalities. As a parent, you know your child and what style works best. So, in your search for swimming classes, consider both the facility and the school's teaching methods. To get a better feel for the teaching methods and approaches, it's a great idea to visit the schools, see the facilities firsthand, and talk to other parents there.

Even within a school, different teachers have different styles. You may not be able to choose teachers at a particular school. Each swimming school has its pros and cons. You have to be the judge of what works best for your child.

Local Parks and Recreation Departments, JCCs, and the YMCAs offer swimming classes in the summer. Your local high school or community colleges may also have swimming instruction, especially during the summer.

Swim Schools

Adventure Sports Unlimited
(831) 458-3648; 303 Potrero Street #15, Santa Cruz, CA 95060
<www.asudoit.com>

Aitken's Peninsula Swim School
(650) 366-9211; 1602 Stafford Street, Redwood City, CA 94063
<www.peninsulaswim.com>
Indoor/outdoor pool heated to 90°F.

Almaden Valley Athletic Club (AVAC)
(408) 267-4032; 5400 Camden Avenue, San Jose, CA 95124
<www.avac.us/swim.htm>
Indoor pool heated to 90°F, shallow teaching pool (2 feet deep).

Ann Curtis School Of Swimming
(415) 479-9131; 25 Golden Hinde Boulevard, San Rafael, CA 94903

Bay–O–Vista Swim School
(510) 357-8366; 1881 Astor Drive, San Leandro, CA, 94577
<www.bovswim.com>

Betty Wright Swim Center
(415) 494-1480; 3864 Middlefield Road, Palo Alto, CA 94303
<www.c-a-r.org/swim.html>
Specializes in swimming lessons for kids with developmental or physical disabilities.

California Sports Center
(408) 246-7795; 3800 Blackbird Avenue, San Jose, CA 95117
<www.calsportscenter.com/swimless.htm>
Lessons at the Fremont High School site in Sunnyvale.

Club Sport of San Ramon (Ages 6–18)
(925) 735-8500; 350 Bollinger Canyon Lane, San Ramon, CA 94583
<www.clubsportsanramon.com>
Swim team and tennis camps.

Club Sport (Ages 5–12)
(510) 226-8500; 46650 Landing Pkwy, Fremont, CA 94538
(925) 463-2822; 7090 Johnson Drive, Pleasanton, CA 94588
(925) 942-6382; 2805 Jones Road, Walnut Creek, CA 94596
or (925) 938-8700

Contra Costa Jewish Community Center
Offered through Mt. Diablo YMCA
(925) 979-9622; (925) 938-7800
2071 Tice Valley Boulevard, Walnut Creek, CA 94596
<www.mdrymca.org>
Outdoor 74°F pool. Open May–September.

DACA Swim School
(408) 446-5600; 21111 Stevens Creek Boulevard, Cupertino, CA 95014
<www.daca.org>
Indoor pool heated to 90°F.

Doug Senz Swim Lessons
(925) 356-2226; Pleasant Hill, CA
Starts in February.

Fremont Hills Country Club Swim School
(650) 941-9667; (650) 948-8261
12889 Viscaino Place, Los Altos Hills, CA 94022
<www.fremonthills.com>
Summer program.

Fremont Swim School
<www.fremontswimschool.com>
Fremont: (510) 657-7946; 42400 Blacow Road, Fremont, CA 94539
Livermore: (925) 373-7946; 2821 Old First Street, Livermore, CA 94550
Newark: (510) 794-7946; 37400 Cedar Boulevard, Newark, CA 94560

Harriet Plummer Aquatic School
(925) 943-7331; 1150 Nogales Street, Lafayette, CA 94549

Harvey West Swimming Pool
(831) 420-6140; 275 Harvey West Boulevard, Santa Cruz, CA 95060
<www.santacruzparksandrec.com/guide/aqua.html>
Classes offered through the Santa Cruz Parks and Recreation
Department.

Highlands Swim School
Dolphins Swim Team
(650) 341-4251; 1851 Lexington Avenue, San Mateo, CA 94402
<www.highlandsrec.com/home.htm>

Jewish Community Center Fitness Center
(650) 493-6702; 655 Arastradero Road, Palo Alto, CA 94306
<www.paloaltojcc.org/html/aquatics.html>

Jim Booth Swim School
(831) 722-3500; 25 Penny Lane, Watsonville, CA 95076

Jim Gorman's Swimming & Diving Instruction
Madera Oaks
(650) 854-6699; 3249 Alpine Road, Portola Valley, CA 94028
Pool heated to mid-80°F.

Johnson Aquatics
(415) 479-3813; 424 El Faisan Drive, San Rafael, CA 94903

Joinville Swim Center
(650) 522-7460; 2111 Kehoe Avenue, San Mateo, CA 94403
<www.ci.sanmateo.ca.us/dept/parks/locations/bayside.html>
Select the Activity Guide on the left column of the Web site. Birthday
parties, too.

Kona Kai Swim & Racquet Club
(408) 249-5699; 680 Hubbard Avenue, Santa Clara, CA 95051
<www.konakaiclub.com/swimming.html>

Le Petit Baleen
(650) 588-7665; 434 San Mateo Avenue, San Bruno, CA 94066
(650) 726-3676; 775 Main Street, Half Moon Bay, CA 94019

Livermore Valley Tennis Club (6 months+)

(925) 443-7700; 2000 Arroyo Road, Livermore, CA 94550
www.lvtc.com
Swim classes for children over 6 months old. Tennis classes to children from 3 to 18 years old.

Los Gatos Swim & Racquet Club

(408) 356-2136; 14700 Oka Road, Los Gatos, CA 95032
<www.lgsrc.com>
Outdoor pool heated to 84°F.

Mission San Jose Aquatics

(510) 226-6752; Fremont, CA
<www.swimmsja.org>
Summer program. Uses the Ohlone College Pool at 43600 Mission Blvd. in Fremont and the American High School Pool at 36300 Fremont Blvd. in Fremont

Nancy's Mommy & Me Swim School

(415) 383-3801; Mill Valley, CA

San Jose Swim & Racquet Club

(408) 297-0067; 1170 Pedro Street, San Jose, CA 95126
Outdoor pool heated to ~84°F. Open April–August.

San Ramon Olympic Pool and Aquatic Park

(925) 973-3240; 9900 Broadmoor Drive, San Ramon, CA 94583
<www.sanramon.ca.gov> or <www.ci.san-ramon.ca.us/parks/index.htm>
Once on the Web site, choose the Parks and Recreation Activities Guide and select the appropriate brochure for the season. Outdoor pool heated to 80°F, open spring–fall. Birthday parties, too.

Santa Clara Swim Club

Santa Clara International Swim Center
(408) 246-5050; 2625 Patricia Drive, Santa Clara, CA 95051

Santa Cruz Swim School
(831) 426-7946; P.O. Box 455, Santa Cruz, CA
Summer program held at the Elks Lodge. Fall/winter programs at the teacher's house has a covered indoor 90°F pool. Web site is under construction; call for Web site address.

Junipero Serra High School: Swim School
(650) 345-7331; 451 W 20th Avenue, San Mateo, CA
<www.serrahs.com/Activities/Brochure99Html/brochure99html.htm>
Summer program.

Sherman Swim School
(925) 283-2100; 1075 Carol Lane, Lafayette, CA
Summer session begins in mid-June, Mon–Fri 3–7pm.

Sue's Swim School
(925) 837-2428; 2701 Store Valley Road, Alamo, CA

Strawberry Canyon Recreation Area Aquatics
UC Berkeley
(510) 643-2267; (510) 643-4397
Strawberry Canyon Center, Berkeley, CA 94720-4430
<www.oski.org/html/scra_aquatics2.htm>

Taft Swim School
(650) 349-7946; 57 E 40th Avenue, San Mateo, CA

Terra Linda Recreation Center
Through the City of San Rafael Parks and Recreation Department
(415) 485-3344; 670 Del Ganado Road, San Rafael, CA

Water Babies Swim School
(408) 377-4626; 973 Apricot Avenue, Campbell, CA 95008
Outdoor pool: March–September season.

West Coast Aquatics

(408) 259-4522; 1776 Educational Park Drive, San Jose, CA
<www.westcoastaquatics.org>

San Francisco Parks and Recreation Swimming Program:

<www.parks.sfgov.org/site/recpark_page.asp?id=1867>

Call the senior swimming instructor of each pool for specific dates and times.

Cost: $3/adult (18 and older)/swim, $28/12-swim scrip ticket, $12.25/5-swim scrip ticket. $5/family rate (2 adults and 2 children), 50 cents/child (17 and younger). Swim Lessons: $1 plus regular admission fee, $15/child's 10-lesson scrip ticket.

Balboa Park & Pool

(415) 337-4701; San Jose Ave and Havelock, San Francisco, CA 94112
Hours: Mon–Fri: 8am–8pm; Sat: 9am–6pm; closed Sun. Swim lessons on Tues & Thur: 5–5:30pm, and Sat: 10:20–11:05am. Indoor pool at 80°F.

Coffman Pool

(415) 337-4702; Visitacion and Hahn Streets, San Francisco, CA
Indoor pool at 80°F.

Garfield Pool

(415) 695-5001; 26th and Harrison Streets, San Francisco, CA
Indoor pool at 80°F.

Hamilton Pool

(415) 292-2001; Geary Blvd. and Steiner Street, San Francisco, CA
Indoor pool at 80°F.

Martin Luther King Jr. Pool

(415) 822-2807; 3rd Avenue and Carroll Street, San Francisco, CA
Two indoor pools at 80°F.

Mission Pool

(415) 695-5002; 19th St. and Linda, San Francisco, CA
Open in the summer only.

North Beach Pool

(415) 274-0200; Lombard and Mason Street, San Francisco, CA
Preschool swim lessons for kids 18 months–5 years are on Sat: 10:30–11am. Preschool swim: Wed. 3:15–3:45pm. Currently

being renovated.

Rossi Pool

(415) 666-7014; Arguello and Anza Streets, San Francisco, CA
Pre-school swim lessons for children under 4-foot tall are on
Saturday 10:30–11:15am. Indoor pool at 80°F.

Sava Pool

(415) 753-7000; 19th Avenue and Wawona Street, San Francisco, CA
Preschool swim lessons for children under 4-foot tall are held
on Sat: 10:15am– 11am. Indoor pool at 80°F.

Swim Clubs & Teams

While some swim clubs and swim teams focus on competitions, many
have noncompetitive programs as well. Many swim clubs/teams also provide swimming lessons for young infants and preschoolers. Don't overlook
these for your young child just because they sound competitive. Each club
or team has its own philosophy, so check out the Web sites, call, and visit
to get a feel for the team and to see if it's a good fit for your needs.

The United States Swimming Teams are associated with the U.S. National
Swim Team. To find more swim teams, visit the U.S. National Swim Team
Web site: <www.usswim.org>.

Alameda Island Aquatics (Ages 5+)

(510) 865-5484; 215 Beach Road, Alameda, CA 94502
<www.alamedaislanders.org>

Burlingame Aquatic Club

(650) 558-1298; 400 Carolan Avenue, Burlingame, CA 94010
<www.burlingameaquatics.com>

Uses the Burlingame High School pool. Burlingame Aquatic Center:
(650) 558-7322 and the Web site:

<www.burlingame.org/p_r/facility/burlingame_aquatic_center_schedule.htm>

Cabrillo Threshers Swim Team
P.O. Box 1686, Soquel, CA 95073
<www.cab-threshers.org> or E-mail: postmaster@cab-threshers.org
Uses the Cabrillo College pool.

Covington Swim Team (Ages 4+)
(650) 941-2406; P.O. Box 809, Los Altos, CA 94023
<www.losaltosmasters.org/youth/index.htm>
Summer swim team program.

DACA (De Anza Cupertino Aquatics)
(408) 253-SWIM (7946); P.O. Box 436 , Cupertino, CA 95015
<www.daca.org>
Uses the De Anza College pool.

Foothill Tennis and Swim Club
(650) 493-0920; 3351 Miranda Avenue, Palo Alto, CA 94304
<www.foothills-club.org>

Los Altos Mountain View Aquatics Club
(650) 599-2213
<www.lamvac.org>
Uses the Foothill College Pool: 12345 El Monte Road, Los Altos Hills;
Eagle Pool: off Church St. and S. Shoreline Blvd; and Rengstorff Pool at
Rengstorff Park: Crisanto Ave and S. Rengstorff Avenue

Morgan Hill Swim Club
(408) 782-0088
<www.makos.darkhorizons.org/Swim/index.html>
Practices at Live Oak High School or Britton Middle School, Morgan
Hill.

Osprey Aquatics (6+)
(408) 268-4379; 757 Harry Road, San Jose, CA 95120
<www.ospreyaquatics.com>
Uses Willow Glen Middle School pool for practices.

Pacific Coast Marlins Swim Club
At the Rafael Racquet Club
(415) 456-1153 ; 95 Racquet Club Drive, San Rafael, CA
<www.pacificcoastmarlins.com>

Peninsula Covenant Community Center
(650) 364-6272
<www.pcaswimteam.com>

San Ramon Valley Livermore Aquatics Swim Team
(925) 833-2407
<www.srvla.org>
Uses the San Ramon Olympic Pool and Aquatic Park site at 9900
Broadmoor, San Ramon, CA.

Santa Clara Swim Club
(408) 246-5050; P.O. Box 2672, Santa Clara, CA 95055
<www.santaclaraswimclub.org>
Uses Santa Clara International Swim Center: 2625 Patricia Drive, Santa
Clara, CA 95051.

Santa Cruz County Aquatics
(831) 246-2059; SCCA, P.O. Box 1616, Soquel, CA 95073
<www.santacruzcountyaquatics.com>

Silicon Valley Aquatics Association (SVAA) Club (Ages 5+)
(408) 227-5884; P O Box 36205, San Jose, CA 95159
Silver Creek Office: (408) 239-0504
<www.siliconvalleyaquaticassociation.org/introprogram.htm>

Sunnyvale Swim Club
(408) 235-9874; P.O. Box 2580, Sunnyvale, CA 94087
<www.sunn.org>
Uses the Fremont High School pool.

Stanford Campus Recreational Association (SCRA) (Ages 5+)

(650) 948-2483; 591 Middlebury Drive, Sunnyvale, CA 94087
<www.scra-swim.org>
Attn: Scott Shea.

Terrapin Swim Team (Ages 5+)

(925) 680-8372; 4180 Treat Blvd. Ste. K, Concord, CA 94518
<www.terrapinswim.com/index2.htm>
Uses Concord Community Pool 3501 Cowell Road, Concord, CA.
Coach Paul 680-8372 x206 and the Brentwood Swim Center 195
Griffith Road, Brentwood, CA. Coach Chris 680-8732 x205.

Tsunami Aquatics

(925) 443-1755 x.1003; P.O. Box 1217, Livermore, CA 94551
<http://tsunamiaquatics.org/classes.htm>

University Club Palo Alto
Palo Alto Swim Club

(650) 493-2375; 3277 Miranda Avenue, Palo Alto, CA 94304
<http://ucpaloalto.com/aquatic_home.htm>

Walnut Creek Aquabears

(925) 939-5990; PO Box 3462, Walnut Creek, CA 94598
<http://aquabears.org>
Uses Clarke Memorial Swim Center at Heather Farm Park.

West Coast Aquatics

(408) 259-4522; P.O. Box 32188, San Jose, CA 95152
<www.westcoastaquatics.org>
Uses the Independence High School and the Silver Creek High School
pools.

West Valley Swim Club

(408) 867-0161 (SHS pool); (408) 395-5341 (fax/office)
P.O. Box 1180, Los Gatos, CA 95031

Summer swimming classes in 2-week sessions from mid-June to August.
Uses the Saratoga High School Aquatic Center.

Dancing

Dance is a great way to help young children develop motor coordination. It also helps them develop an understanding of rhythm and exposes them to the idea that musical rhythm and motion can go together. Since performance is part of a dance curriculum, don't overlook these dance companies as a wonderful source of dance performances. For performance schedule and additional information, visit the Web sites or call.

Dance Schools

For more dance studios:<www.dancemastersofcalifornia.org/
studios.htm>.

Aspire! Dance
Part of Dublin Theatre Company
(925) 551-5382 x45; (925) 551-5382 x44 for birthday parties
6620 Dublin Boulevard, Dublin, CA 94568
<www.dublintheatre.com>

Ballet, jazz, hip-hop, and musical theater classes. Click on the Aspire! Dance button on the left column of the Web site. Performing arts classes under the Performing Arts Academy. On the Web site, select "Education" then "Performing Arts Academy." The Performing Arts Academy offers classes in acting, singing, and dance. Birthday parties offered.

Axis Dance Company (Ages 5+)
(510) 625-0110; 1428 Alice Street, Suite 201, Oakland, CA 94612
<www.axisdance.org>
Eighth Street Studio: 2525 8th Street, Berkeley, CA
Alice Arts Center: 1428 Alice Street, Oakland, CA
For information on performances: <www.axisdance.org/performances/calendar.html>.

Beaudoins School Of Dance
(650) 326-2184; 464 Colorado Avenue, Palo Alto, CA 94306
<www.beaudoins-studio.com>

Branham Dance Center
(408) 269-1363; 1088 W. Branham Lane, San Jose, CA 95112
Tap, jazz, ballet, and hip-hop.

California Academy of Performing Arts
(925) 376-2454; 370 Park Street, Ste E, Moraga, CA 94556
Ballet, jazz, tap, and character.

Center Stage Dance Co.
(408) 723-2623; 1095 Malone Road, San Jose, CA

Dance 10 Dancers
(510) 339-3345; 900 Santa Clara Avenue, Alameda, CA

Dance Academy USA (Ages 2+)
(408) 257-3211; 21269 Stevens Creek Blvd #600, Cupertino, CA 95014
<www.danceacademyusa.com>
Ballet, jazz, hip-hop, tap, street funk, lyrical, yoga, musical theater, and voice.

Dance Affair (Ages 3+)
(408) 243-4834; 2905 Park Avenue, Santa Clara, CA 95050
<www.thedanceaffair.com>
Hip-hop, jazz, tap, and musical theater.

Dance Art Studio
(408) 293-1930; 1094 S Second Street, San Jose, CA

Dance Attack!
(408) 356-6456; 14110 Blossom Hill Road, Los Gatos, CA 95032
<www.danceattackstudios.com>
<www.danceattackstudios.com/schoolsched.html> For class schedule
Ballet, jazz, hip-hop, tap, break dancing, modern, voice, and acting lessons offered.

Dance Attack!
(408) 245-5432; 120 Carroll Street, Sunnyvale, CA 94086
Ballet, tap, jazz, lyrical, and hip-hop. Has some of the same teachers as Dance Attack! Los Gatos, but different owners.

Dance Attack School Of Dance
(650) 965-3310; 1350 Grant Road, Mountain View CA 94040

Dance Connection (Ages 3+)
(650) 322-7032; 4000 Middlefield Road, Palo Alto CA 94303
<www.danceconnectionpaloalto.com>
Jazz, ballet, hip-hop, tap instruction. *Nutcracker* performance in early December. There's a tea party prior to the performance to help the little ones understand the story.

Dance Effects
(408) 374-6123; 58 E. Campbell Avenue Campbell, CA 95008

Dance with Sherry Studio
(415) 499-1986; 4140 Redwood Highway, Ste 4, San Rafael, CA

Dance Mission Theatre (Ages 2½+)
(415) 826-4441; 3316 24th Street, San Francisco, CA 94110

Happy Feet
(415) 381-0811; 15 Montford Avenue, Mill Valley, CA 94941
Ballet, tap, jazz.

Jazz N Taps
(925) 484-0678; 3015 Ste 1 Hopyard Road, Pleasanton, CA 94588
Ballet, tap, jazz, and hip-hop

Jensen Performing Arts (Ages 2+)
(408) 262-0770; 1491 N. Milpitas Boulevard, Milpitas, CA 95305
<www.jpadance.com>
Ballet, tap, jazz, lyrical, tumbling, voice/song/dance, TnT Dancers.

Lafayette Dance Center (Kids 'N Dance)
(925) 284-7388; 3369 Mt. Diablo Boulevard, Lafayette, CA 94549

Martis Dance School
(650) 949-3467; 201 Covington Road., Los Altos, CA 94024

Menlo Park Academy of Dance
(650) 323-5292; 1163 El Camino Real, Menlo Park, CA 94025
Ballet, tap, jazz, tumbling hip-hop, and voice.

Mission Dance & Performing Arts
(510) 651-2783; 42068 Osgood Road, Fremont, CA 94539
<http://missiondance.neatscape.com>
Ballet, break dance, hip-hop, jazz, tap, lyrical, and more.

San Juan School of Dance
(650) 948-6287; 140 3rd Street, Los Altos, CA 94022
(408) 267-5525; 1557 Meridian Avenue, San Jose, CA 95125
<www.sanjuandance.com>
Ballet, pointe, tap, jazz, lyrical, song and dance.

Saratoga School of Dance

(408) 866-4691; 18778 Cox Avenue, Saratoga, CA 95070

Ballet, tap, and jazz.

Shawl–Anderson Dance Center (Ages 3+)

(510) 654-5921; 2704 Alcatraz Avenue, Berkeley CA 94705

<www.shawl-anderson.org>

Ballet, jazz, and modern dance classes

Stapleton School of the Performing Arts

(415) 454-5759; P.O. Box 331, San Anselmo, CA 94979

Main Studio: 118 Greenfield Avenue, San Anselmo, CA 94960

Satellite Studio: 2240B Fourth Street, San Rafael, CA

<www.stapletonschool.org>

Ballet, hip-hop, boys' and teen classes offered.

Turning Pointe Dance Studio

(408) 946-0564; 2673 Cropley Avenue, San Jose, CA

<www.geocities.com/edanceclass/index.htm>

Ballet, jazz, hip-hop, modern dance classes.

Valley Dance Theatre

(925) 243-0925; 443-6953

20 South L Street, Livermore, CA 94550

<www.valleydancetheatre.com>

Ballet, tap, jazz, and swing dance classes.

Yoko's Dance & Performing Arts Company (Ages 3+)

(510) 651-STAR (7827); 42400 Blacow Road, Fremont, CA 94539

<www.yokosdance.com>

Tap, jazz, lyrical, hip-hop, and ballet.

Ballet Schools

Academy of American Ballet (Ages 5+)
(650) 366-1222; 275A Linden Street, Redwood City, CA 94061
<www.geocities.com/julia_ball_us/aab.html>

Academy of Classical Ballet (Ages 5+)
(510) 452-5140; 452 Santa Clara Avenue, Oakland, CA
<www.acb-oakland.com>

Alonzo King's LINES Ballet
(415) 863-3040 ext. 287 or 239
26 Seventh Street, 5th Floor, San Francisco, CA 94103
<www.linesballet.org>

Ballet San Jose Silicon Valley School (Ages 4+)
(408) 288-2820, ext. 223
40 North First Street, San Jose, CA
<www.balletsanjose.org/school.html>

The Open Division for children ages 4 to 14 has classes once a week and Saturday classes. The Adult/Teen Division is on a drop-in basis. The Professional Division is for students 7–18 years old who are interested in professional ballet. They must attend a minimum of two classes per week. Class fees: $15/class, $235: 1 class per week ($13.06/class), $451: 2 classes per week ($12.53/class), $540: 3 classes per week ($10/class).

Berkeley Ballet Theater
(510) 843-4687; Box Office: (510) 843-4689
2640 College Avenue, Berkeley, CA 94704
<www.berkeleyballet.org>

Berkeley City Ballet
(510) 841-8913; 1800 Dwight Way, Berkeley, CA 94703

Ballet and Theatre Arts of Danville
School of the Danville Ballet Company
(925) 831-9256; 190F Alamo Plaza, Alamo, CA 94507
<www.danvilleballet.org/Pages/school/index.html>

Conservatory of Classical Ballet (Ages 3½+)
(510) 568-7728; 1035 Mac Arthur Boulevard, San Leandro, CA. 94577
<www.conservatoryofballet.com>

Contra Costa Ballet Centre (Ages 3½+)
(925) 935-7984; 2040 North Broadway, Walnut Creek CA 94596
<www.contracostaballet.org>

Marin Ballet Center for Dance
(415) 453-6705; 100 Elm Street, San Rafael, CA
<www.marinballet.org>

Marin Dance Theatre (Ages 3+)
St. Vincent's School Campus
(415) 499-8891; One St. Vincent Drive, San Rafael, CA 94903
<www.mdt.org>
Preballet classes for 5– to 6-year-olds.

Mountain View Ballet Company and School
(650) 968-4455; 2028 Old Middlefield Way, Mountain View, CA 94043
<www.westernballet.org/school>

Pacific Ballet Academy (Ages 3½–15)
(650) 969-4614; Mailing: P.O. Box 765, Los Altos, CA 94023
Campus: 259B Polaris Avenue, Mountain View, CA
<www.pacificballet.org>

This school provides preballet through preprofessional levels of ballet
training. The curriculum is based on the Russian style of ballet. Preballet
classes for 3½- to 5-year-olds include stretching, skipping, hopping, and
galloping steps with creative and folk dances. Check the Web site for more
detailed information for older students ages 6–15. A few classes on week-

day and Saturday mornings for moms & tots and preballet. Most classes are after school. Summer classes and intensive summer camps.

Professional Ballet School
(650) 598-0796; 425 Harbor Blvd. #3, Belmont, CA 94002
<www.yabt.org>

Santa Clara Ballet School
(408) 247-9178; 3086 El Camino Real, Santa Clara, CA 95051
<www.geocities.com/vienna/strasse/7530/TheSchool.htm>

Western Ballet Company & School
(650) 968-4455; 2028 Old Middlefield Way, Mountain View, CA 94043
<www.westernballet.org>

Gymnastics

For toddlers and young preschoolers, playgrounds at the local parks are probably sufficient. During winter, when it's cold and rainy, you might want to consider the Gymboree Play, Junior Gym, Little Gym, or My Gym Programs.

Gymboree Play Programs (Ages Infants–4)
1-877-4-GYMWEB (1-877-449-6932)
<www.playandmusic.com/b2c/customer/programIndex.jsp >

Mon–Fri: 6am–9pm, Sat: 7am–3pm PST. Call or visit the Web site for a program location closest to you. Gymboree has classes for babies 0–6 months, 6–12 months, 10–18 months, 14–28 months, 2 year olds, 3- to 4-year-olds.

> (925) 866-8315; 2570 San Ramon Valley Boulevard, San Ramon, CA
> (925) 227-0725; 2457 Stoneridge Mall Road, Pleasanton, CA
> (415) 492-1418; 2180 Northgate Mall, San Rafael, CA
> (408) 629-5813; 925 Blossom Hill Road, San Jose, CA
> (925) 866-8315; 3191 Crow Canyon Place, San Ramon, CA

(650) 364-3420; 2531 El Camino Real, Redwood City, CA
(650) 875-3588; 731 Kains Avenue, San Bruno, CA
(415) 776-2111; 2675 Geary Boulevard, San Francisco, CA
(831) 642-9186; 650 Del Monte Ctr., Monterey, CA
(925) 685-7773; 1975 Diamond Boulevard, Concord, CA
(650) 494-8400; Charleston Shopping Ctr, Palo Alto, CA
(510) 739-6150; 39138 Fremont Hub, Fremont, CA
(650) 949-5798; 664 Rancho Shopping Center, Los Altos, CA
(415) 383-9771; 406 Strawberry Village, Mill Valley, CA
(408) 378-5318; 1600 Saratoga Avenue, San Jose, CA

Junior Gym (Ages 6 months+)
(650) 548-9901; 101 South B Street, San Mateo, CA
<www.juniorgym.com>

Parent/toddler classes for babies 6 months–3 years old, gymnastics classes for kids 3–10 years old, sports skills class for kids 4+, cheerleading skills for girls 5+, yoga for kids 6+, and self-defense for kids 5+.

The Little Gym (Ages 4 months–12 years)
(925) 736-3141; 3490 Blackhawk Plaza Circle, Danville, CA 94506
<www.tlgdanvilleca.com>

(510) 794-6660; 5700 Newpark Mall Road, Newark, CA 94560
<www.thelittlegym.com>

(408) 366-2222; 5357 Prospect Road, San Jose, CA 95129
<www.tlgsanjoseca.com>

MiniGym Explorations (Ages 8 months–8 years)
(408) 559-4616; 559-3631; 4115 Jacksol Drive, San Jose, CA 95154
<www.minigymexplorations.com>

Parent/me classes for babies 8 months–3 years old; "Exploragym Preschool" for children 3–4 years old; and summer camps for children 3½ –8 years old. Birthday parties available for kids up to 7 years old.

My Gym Children's Fitness Center (Ages 3 months–9 years)

(408) 279-9700; 1262 S. Bascom Avenue, San Jose, CA 95128
(925) 244-1171; 180 Market Place, San Ramon, CA 94583
<www.my-gym.com>

Gymnastics and exercise incorporating dance, music, and games. Birthday parties are offered also.

For the older kids, preschool age and up, who want to really do some cartwheels and learn more gymnastics skills, here are some schools specializing in gymnastics for the older child. Visit the USA Gymnastics Web site for additional gyms: <www.usa-gymnastics.org/search/club-locator-CA.html>.

Airborne Gymnastics

(408) 986-8226; 2250 Martin Avenue, Santa Clara, CA 95050
<www.airborne-gymnastics.com>

Almaden Valley Gymnastics Club

(408) 268-1272; 19600 Almaden Road, San Jose, CA 95120
<www.almadengymnastics.com>

California Sports Center

(408) 269-5437 (KIDS); 832 Malone Road, San Jose, Ca 95125
(408) 280-5437; 336 Race Street, San Jose, CA 95126
(408) 264-5439; 3001 Ross Avenue, San Jose, Ca 95124
<www.calsportscenter.com>

Cal West Gymnastics

(510) 651-5870; 4883 Davenport Place, Fremont, CA 94538
<www.calwestgym.com>

Demaray's Gymnastics Academy

(510) 661-0576; 40511 Albrae Street, Fremont, CA 94538

Diablo Gymnastics School
(925) 820-6885; 2411-J Old Crow Canyon Road, San Ramon , CA 94583
<www.diablogym.com>

Encore Gymnastics
(925) 932-1033 ; Mailing: P.O. Box 30113, Walnut Creek, CA 94598
999 Bancroft Road, Concord, CA 94518
<www.encoregym.com>

Gold Star Gymnastics Academy
(650) 694-7827; 92 W El Camino Real, Mountain View, CA 94040
<www.goldstargym.com>

Golden Bear Recreation Center, UC Berkeley
(510) 642-9821 or (510) 642-0792
25 Sports Lane #4428, Berkeley, CA 94720
<www.oski.org/html/gbgym2.htm>
<http://calbears.berkeley.edu/facilities/gbrc/default.asp>
Available for birthday parties.

GymWorld Academy of Gymnastics
(415) 482-8580; 555 E. Francisco Blvd. #19, San Rafael, CA
<http://members.aol.com/gymworldsr>

Gymtowne Gymnastics
(650) 589-3733; 300 Piedmont Avenue, Ste 604, San Bruno, CA 94066
<www.gymtowne.com>

Head Over Heels
(510) 655-1265; 1250 45th St Suite E, Emeryville, CA 94608
<www.hohgymnastics.org>

Livermore Gymnastics Center
(925) 371-1688; 703 Debra Street, Livermore, CA 94550

Marin Elite Gymnastics Academy (MEGA)
(415) 257-MEGA; 72 Woodland Avenue, San Rafael, Ca 94901
<www.megagymnastics.com>

Menlo Park Gymnastics
(650) 858-3480; 501 Laurel Street, Menlo Park, CA 94025
<www.menlopark.org>

Michael Anthony's School of Gymnastics
(925) 671-0262; 2330-A Bates Avenue, Concord, CA 94520
<www.magym.com>

Morgan Hill Gymnastics (Ages 3+)
(408) 778-2882; 140 Mast Street, Suite B, Morgan Hill, CA 95037

My Gym Children's Fitness Center
(Ages 3 months–9 years)
(408) 279-9700; 1262 S. Bascom Avenue, San Jose, CA 95128
(925) 244-1171; 180 Market Place, San Ramon, CA 94583
<www.my-gym.com>

Gymnastics and exercise incorporating dance, music, and games. Birthday
parties are offered also.

Pegasus Gymnastics Academy (Ages 1+)
(408) 946-6607; 1450 Great Mall Drive, Milpitas, CA 95035

S.A.S. Gymnastics
(925) 462-5877; 1056-B Serpentine Lane, Pleasanton, CA 94566
<www.sasgym.com/sys-tmpl/doo>

San Francisco Gymnastics (Ages 1+)
(415) 561-6260; P.O. Box 29427, San Francisco, CA 94129
Building 920 - The Presidio, San Francisco

San Rafael Gymnastics Club

(415) 456-1290; 267 Playa Del Rey, San Rafael, CA 94901

Available for birthday parties. Cheerleading program.

Santa Cruz Gymnastics Center

(831) 462.0655; 2750-B Soquel Avenue, Santa Cruz, CA 95060

<www.scgym.com>

Top Flight Gymnastics (Ages 1½+)

(510) 796-3547; 5127 Mowry Avenue, Fremont, CA 94538

<www.eteamz.com/topflight>

Available for birthday parties.

Tri Valley Gymnastics

(925) 606-0936; 180 Wright Brothers Avenue, Livermore, CA 94550

<http://tvgymnastics.com>

Twisters Gym

(650) 967-5581; 2639 Terminal Boulevard, Mountain View, CA 94043

<www.geocities.com/twistersgym>

West Valley Gymnastics School

(408) 374-8692; 1190 Dell Avenue #1, Campbell, CA

<www.wvgs.com>

Links to Web sites of Gymnastics Clubs in Northern California:
<www.norcal-gymnastics.org>.

Ice Skating

Ice skating has become an extremely popular sport in recent years. It is a wonderful summertime activity to escape from the heat. It is also a great birthday party destination. Be advised that public skating sessions vary from facility to facility, so plan ahead; get information on public sessions to avoid disappointment prior to your outing. For skating classes, don't forget to check your local Parks and Recreation Departments, as their programs may provide better times or values than participating directly with the facility. Ice skating classes typically provide instruction for kids 3 years and older.

Belmont Iceland
(650) 592-0532; 815 Old County Road, Belmont, CA 94002
<www.belmonticeland.com>
$7/adult, $6/youth 17 & under, $4/child 4 & under, $3/skate rental.

Berkeley Iceland
(510) 647-1615; 2727 Milvia Street, Berkeley, CA
<www.berkeleyiceland.com/eastbay/berkeley>
$7/adult, $6/youth 17 & under, $4/child 4 & under, $3/skate rental.

Dublin Iceland
(925) 829-4445; 7212 San Ramon Road, Dublin, CA 94568
<www.dubliniceland.com/eastbay/dublin>
$7/adult, $6/youth 17 & under, $4/child 4 & under, $3/skate rental.

Eastridge Ice Arena
(408) 238-0440; 2190A Tully Road, San Jose, CA 95122
<www.eastridgeicearena.com>

Fremont Iceplex
(510) 490-6621; 44388 Old Warm Springs Road, Fremont, CA 94538
<www.iceoplex.com/Locations/fremont.htm>
$6/admission including skate rental, $2.50/skate rental only.

Ice Chalet, Vallco Fashion Park

(408) 446-2906; 10123 Wolfe Road, Cupertino, CA 95008
<www.icecenter.net/cupertino>
$10 with skate rental. $7 admission, skate rental $4.

Ice Oasis

(650) 364-8090; 3140 Bay Road, Redwood City, CA 94063
<www.iceoasis.com>
$8/person 13 & older; $7/child 12 and under, $7/senior; $3/skate rental.

The Ice Center, San Mateo

(650) 574-1616; 2202 Bridgepointe Parkway, San Mateo, CA 94404
<www.icechalet.com>

$10/admission includes skate rental, $7/admission only, $5/senior admission and rental, $4/skate rental only.

Kristi Yamaguchi Embarcadero Center Ice Rink

Embarcadero Center in Justin Herman Plaza

(415) 956-2688; Foot of Market, San Francisco, CA 94111
<www.sfgate.com/listings/venue.php?events,v4297>

Hours: Open only November–January each year. Sun–Thu: 10am–10pm; Fri–Sat: 10am–11:30pm. 90-minute public skate sessions begin on every even hour starting at 10am. Parking is validated up to four hours after 5pm on weekdays, and after 10am on weekends.
Cost: $7/adult, $3.50/child 8 and under, $3.5/skate rental only.

Oakland Ice Center

(510) 268-9000; 519 18th Street, Oakland, CA 94612
<www.oaklandice.com>

$7.50/adult, $6.50/child 12 & under, $6.50/senior, $2.50/skate rental.

Redwood Empire Ice Arena

(707) 546-7147; 1667 W. Steele Lane, Santa Rosa, CA 95403
www.snoopyshomeice.com

$7/ person 12 & older, $5.50/child under 12, $2/skate rental only.

San Jose Ice Center
(408) 279-6000; 1500 S. 10th Street, San Jose, CA 95112
<www.icecentresj.com>

$7/person 13 & older, $6/child 12 & under, $4/senior, $3/skate rental only.

Winter Lodge
(650) 493-4566; 3009 Middlefield Road, Palo Alto, CA 94306
<www.winterlodge.com>

$7/admission, $3/skate rental only.

Yerba Buena Ice Skating & Bowling Center
(415) 777-3727; 750 Folsom Street, San Francisco, CA 94107
<www.skatebowl.com>

$6.50/adult, $5/child 12 & younger, $4.50/senior; $2.50/skate rental only, $10/freestyle sessions.

Bowling

AMF Cabrillo Lanes
(408) 724-1155; 580 Auto Center Drive, Watsonville, CA 95076
<www.amfcenters.com>

AMF Mel's South Shore Bowl
(510) 523-6767; 300 Park Street, Alameda, CA 94501
<www.amfcenters.com>

AMF Mission Lanes
(408) 262-6950; 1287 South Park Victoria, Milpitas, CA 95035

AMF Moonlite Lanes
(408) 296-7200; 2780 El Camino Real, Santa Clara, CA 95051
<www.amfcenters.com>

AMF Mowry Lanes
(510) 794-7777; 585 Mowry Avenue, Fremont, CA 94536
<www.amfcenters.com>

AMF Redwood Lanes
(650) 369-5584; 2580 El Camino Real, Redwood City, CA 94061
<www.amfcenters.com>

AMF Saratoga Lanes
(408) 252-2212; 1585 Saratoga Avenue, San Jose, CA 95129
<www.amfcenters.com>

ARC Nineteenth Avenue Bowl
(650) 341-5813; 830 S Delaware, San Mateo, CA 94402

Bel Mateo Bowl
(650) 341-2616; 4330 Olympic Avenue, San Mateo, CA 94403

Boardwalk Bowl
(831) 426-3324; 115 Cliff Street, Santa Cruz, CA 95060
<www.boardwalkbowl.com>

Brentwood Bowl
(650) 583-1056; 237 El Camino Real, South San Francisco, CA 94080-5920

Brunswick Delta Bowl
(925) 757-5424; 3300 Delta Fair Boulevard, Antioch, CA 94509

Cambrian Bowl
(408) 377-2354; 14900 Camden Avenue, San Jose, CA 95124
<http://cambrianbowl.com>

Castro Village Bowl

(510) 538-8100; 3501 Village Drive, Castro Valley, CA 94546
<www.diningtips.com/castrovillagedining/shops.html>

Classic Bowling Center

(650) 878-0300; 900 King Drive, Daly City, CA 94015
<www.classicbowling.com>

Clayton Valley Bowl

(925) 689-4631; 5300 Clayton Road, Concord, CA 94521
<http://claytonvalleybowl.com>

Cloverleaf Family Bowl

(510) 656-4414; 40645 Fremont Boulevard, Fremont, CA 94538
<www.cloverleafbowl.com>

Danville Bowl

(925) 837-7272; 200 Boone Court, Danville, CA 94526

Diablo Lanes

(510) 671-0913; 1500 Monument Boulevard, Concord, CA 94520
<www.diablolanes.com>

Fourth Street Bowl

(408) 453-5555; 1441 N Fourth Street, San Jose, CA 95112

Gilroy Bowl

(408) 842-5100; 7554 Monterey Street, Gilroy, CA 95020

Granada Bowl

(925) 447-5600; 1620 Railroad Avenue, Livermore, CA 94550
<www.gobowling.com/granada>

Harvest Park Bowl
(925) 516-1221; 5000 Valfour Road, Brentwood, CA 94513
<www.harvestparkbowl.com>

Holiday Bowl
(510) 538-0300; 29827 Mission Boulevard, Hayward, CA 94544
<www.holidaybowl.tv/flash.html>

Homestead Lanes
(408) 255-5700; 20990 Homestead Road, Cupertino, CA 95014
<www.homesteadlanes.com>

Moraga–Rheem Valley Bowl
(925) 376-4495; 489 Moraga Road, Moraga, CA 94556

Paddock Bowl
(925) 685-7812; 5915 Pacheco Boulevard, Pacheco, CA 94553
<http://paddockbowl.com/index.cfm>

Palo Alto Bowl
(650) 948-1031; 4329 El Camino Real, Palo Alto, CA 94306
<www.fun2spare.com>

Serra Bowl
(650) 992-3444; 3301 Junipero Serra Boulevard, Daly City 94014
<www.fun2spare.com>

Sea Bowl
(650) 738-8190; 4625 Coast Highway, Pacifica, CA 94044
<www.seabowl.com>

Yerba Buena Ice Skating & Bowling Center
Rooftop at Yerba Buena Gardens
(415) 777-3727; 130 Third Street, San Francisco, CA 94107

Appendices

Appendix A
Calendar Index

This calendar is provided to help you plan your outings. I have pulled out the follow-up activities' special events from the entries to help you search for outings based on the time of year. For more detailed information, use the alphabetical index to locate the entries.

For a general San Francisco Bay Area events Web site:
<www.sfgate.com/eguide/events>

First Saturday of Each Month
- Antique & Classic Aircraft Exhibit: Watsonville Airport
- Chantey Sings: Hyde Street Pier, San Francisco

Second Saturday of Each Month
- Costumed Living History event "A Day in the Life 1901": Hyde Street Pier

Third Saturday of Each Month:
- Living History Demonstration: Wilder Ranch State Park, Santa Cruz
- Sea Music Festival for kids: Hyde Street Pier
- Young Eagles Program children 8–17 fly over SF Bay for free: San Carlos Airport

January
- Auld Lang Syne Express (lighted train): Niles Canyon Railway & Museum, Sunol Depot
- Great blue heron & great egret nesting season (late January— early March): Elkhorn Slough Reserve
- Nighttime tidepooling trip: Fitzgerald Marine Reserve

- New Year's Cruise: Angel Island/Tiburon Ferry
- Whale-watching trip: Seymour Marine Discovery Center

February
- Chinese New Year Parade, San Francisco, CA

March
- Departure of Northern Elephant Seals: Natural Bridges State Beach, Point Reyes National Seashore
- Monarch butterflies leave on migration routes: Natural Bridges State Beach, Pacific Grove Monarch Preserve, Ardenwood Historic Farm

Early March
- Great American Train Show: Cow Palace, Daly City (see South Bay Historical Railroad Society entry)
- Johnny Appleseed Day: Ardenwood Farm
- Oakland Zoo summer camp registration begins

Late March/April
- Filoli Gardens: Annual Easter Egg Hunt

April
- Cal Day: U.C. Berkeley (see Chapter 10: Seasonal Events)
- Community Day at Stanford University (see Chapter 10: Seasonal Events)
- Historic Trolley Service: Light-rail San Jose: April–September and winter holiday season
- New baby animals (chicks, lambs, and kids): Slide Ranch *Spring Fling* event
- Spring activities on the farm: baby animals, gardening, bees, sheep and wool, etc.: Ardenwood Historic Farm
- Spring Open House & Model Railroad Show: South Bay Historical Museum, first weekend in April and November

Easter
- Easter Egg Hunt: Casa de Fruta, Filoli Gardens
- Wildflower walks: See Nature Preserves section
- Gardens
- Baby chicks and ducklings on farm tours April–July: Deer

Hollow Farm

Late April (Earth Day celebrations)

- Earth Day celebration with Maypole dancing, old ways of butter making, wool shearing, and spinning, etc.: Hidden Villa
- Berkeley Bay Festival: Berkeley Marina Shorebird Nature Center
- Pacific Coast Dream Machines: Half Moon Bay, last Sunday in April
- Strawberry Festival (Native American celebration): Kule Loklo, Point Reyes National Seashore
- Old Fashioned Easter and Parade: Old Sacramento
- Steam train excursion: Old Sacramento

May

- Spring Train Festival: Golden Gate Railroad Museum, Hunter's Point Naval Shipyard, San Francisco
- Great American Train Show: Marin Center, San Rafael (See South Bay Historical Railroad Society)
- MG Car Show: Jack London Square
- Wings of History Air Museum sponsors an air show; Young Eagles get to ride for free: South County Airport
- Cinco de Mayo weekend: San Jose and San Francisco
- Cinco de Mayo weekend: Portuguese Heritage Festival: History Park, San Jose

May Day

- Annual Garden Tour: Heather Farms, Walnut Creek
- Astronomy Day in early May: Morrison Planetarium, California Academy of Sciences, San Francisco (reopens 2008)
- May Day celebration of spring with Maypole dancing: Hayward Shoreline Interpretive Center
- Hillsborough Classic Car Show & Carnival, First Sunday in May
- Historic Trolley Service: Light-rail San Jose, April–September and Christmas season.
- May Fireworks: Angel Island/Tiburon Ferry
- Pow-wows: Casa de Fruta
- Strawberry picking: Chapter 2: Plant Kingdom—Coastal Berry Picking Farms section

- Woodside Days, first Sunday in May: Woodside Store

Late May

- Native American Pow-Wow: Casa de Fruta
- Annual Insect Fair: Youth Science Institute Sanborn Nature Center

Memorial Day Weekend

- Cherry picking season begins: Chapter 2: Plant Kingdom—Brentwood Fruit Farms & Orchards section
- Civil War Reenactment: Ardenwood Farm, Roaring Camp & Railroad
- Multicultural Festival: History Park, San Jose
- Memorial Day Cruise: S.S. Jeremiah O'Brien
- Watsonville Fly-In & Air Show: Watsonville Airport

June

- Historic Trolley Service: Light-rail San Jose: April–September and winter holiday season.
- Day Out with Thomas the Train: California State Railroad Museum, Old Sacramento

Early June

- Celtic Festival: Ardenwood Farm
- PortFest: Jack London Square, Oakland
- Annual Wildlife Fair: Sulphur Creek Nature Center

Mid-June

- Fruit picking—boysenberries, olallieberries, and strawberries at the coastal farms; nectarines, plums, and apricots at Brentwood farms
- Early Days in San Juan Living History Event: San Juan Bautista State
- Fire Truck Day & Antique Engine Show: Ardenwood Farm
- Father's Day weekend: Historic Park:
- Heritage Day is on 2nd Saturday in June: Old Borges Ranch
- Father's Day tide pooling trip: Seymour Marine Discovery Center

Late June

- Palo Alto Concours D'Elegance, Classic Car Show: Stanford University

- Vertical Challenge Helicopter Air Show: Hiller Aviation Museum, San Carlos Airport

July

- Berry picking—boysenberries, raspberries
- Big Time (Native American celebration): Kule Loklo, Point Reyes National Seashore (late July)
- Fruit picking: nectarines, peaches, plums, apricots, and raspberries
- July 4th celebration with fireworks: Jack London Square
- Summer program to watch the stars open to the public (July–September): Lick Observatory, San Jose
- Old Fashioned Independence Day Celebration: Ardenwood, Wilder Ranch State Park
- Ringling Brothers & Barnum & Bailey Circus, July – August time frame
- Independence Day Celebration: U.S.S. Hornet Museum
- Old Fashioned Independence Day Celebration: Wilder Ranch

August

- Dragon boat races: Jack London Square, Oakland
- Early August: Annual Steinbeck Festival: National Steinbeck Center
- Historic Trolley Service, Light-rail San Jose: April–September and winter holiday season
- Summer Gathering of Mountain Men: Roaring Camp Railroads

Late August/September

- Fruit picking—asian pears: Chapter 2: Plant Kingdom—Brentwood Fruit Farms & Orchards section
- Moon Festival: San Francisco
- Kenneth C. Patrick Visitor Center: Labor Day Sunday Sand Sculpture Contest: Point Reyes National Seashore
- History Cruise on the San Francisco Bay. August and September on Saturdays: Presidential Yacht Potomac
- Tule harvesting, storytelling: Santa Cruz Mission

September
- Annual Art Show of Bay Area Artists: Jack London Square
- Boat Show: Jack London Square
- Gold Rush Days over Labor Day weekend: California State Railroad Museum
- Great Train Robberies reenactment: Roaring Camp Railroads, Felton
- Historic Trolley Service, Light-rail San Jose: April–September and winter holiday season.
- History Cruise on the San Francisco Bay, August and September on Saturdays: Presidential Yacht Potomac
- Railfan Photographer's Day: Portola Railroad Museum, Portola
- Watsonville Airport Open House in the Fall

Mid-September to mid-October:
- Annual Sea Music Festival: Maritime Museum, San Francisco
- Annual Trade Feast Celebration: mid-September: Miwok Park/ Marin
- Air Expo: Moffett Field, Palo Alto
- Fruit Picking—apples: Gizdich Ranch
- Harvest Festival: Wilder Ranch State Park, Santa Cruz
- Museum of the American Indian
- Redwood Grove Nature Preserve: Open houses on the 3rd Sunday of the following months: September, January, and May
- Renaissance Pleasure Faire: Casa de Fruta
- Slide Ranch: Harvest Festival

October
- 1880s Harvest Fair: Roaring Camp & Railroads
- Cable Car Bell Ringing Competition: Union Square, San Francisco
- Fleet Week & Parade of Ships: San Francisco: Marina Green, Fisherman's Wharf, Ferry Building
- Ghost Train & Reenactment of the Legend of Sleepy Hollow: Roaring Camp Railroads
- Halloween Festival: Old Sacramento
- Monarch butterfly releases in Los Gatos, San Jose, and Walnut Creek: Magical Beginnings Butterfly Farms
- Octoberfest: Old Sacramento

- Pumpkin Patch: Uesugi Farms, Casa de Fruta, Grant & Covington, Mountain View
- Wildlife Education Day: McClellan Ranch Park, Cupertino

Early October
- Fiesta: Santa Cruz Mission

Mid-October
- Apple Butter Festival w/ apple butter making, canning, pumpkin patch, etc.: Gizdich Ranch
- California International Air Show: Salinas Municipal Airport
- Fleet Week Cruise: Angel Island/Tiburon Ferry, *SS Jeremiah O'Brien*
- Harvest Festival at the Farm: UC Santa Cruz Farm & Garden, 2nd Saturday in mid-October
- Wildlife Festival: Youth Science Institute, Alum Rock Park, San Jose

Weekend after Columbus Day
- Annual Half Moon Bay Art & Pumpkin Festival: Lemos Farm

Late October
- Haunted Train: Ardenwood
- Monarch butterflies return to Natural Bridges, Pacific Grove, Ardenwood Farms, and Point Lobos State Reserve, etc.
- Haunted Forest and the Phantom Express Train: Oak Meadow park, Los Gatos
- Spookomotive Halloween Train: California State Railroad Museum

November
- Annual Mountain Men Rendezvous: Roaring Camp Railroads
- Bird watching season for migratory birds: see Nature Preserves section
- Dickens Christmas Fair, Cow Palace, San Francisco: See Seasonal Events section
- Old Fashioned 19th Century Christmas: (mid-November—mid-December): Dunsmuir Historic Estate
- Victorian Christmas: Ardenwood

December

- Northern elephant seals breeding season (December—March): Año Nuevo State Reserve, Point Reyes National Seashore
- Holiday Train: Billy Jones Wildcat Railroad, Oak Meadow Park Los Gatos
- Santa's Yuletide Express: California State Railroad Museum
- Dickens Christmas Fair: Cow Palace, San Francisco: See Seasonal Events
- Holiday Teas: Dunsmuir Historic Estate, Oakland
- Great American Train Show: Marin Center, San Rafael (See South Bay Historical Railroad Society)
- Heritage Holidays: Old Sacramento
- Historic Trolley Service: Light-rail San Jose: April—September and winter holiday season
- Lamplight Tours: Old Sacramento
- Holiday Train of Lights: Niles Canyon Railway & Museum, Sunol Depot
- Nutcracker Ballet: See Chapter 8: Art & Performing Arts— Ballet Performance section
- Santa trains in early December: Portola Railroad Museum, Portola
- *Deck the Halls, Peter & the Wolf:* San Francisco Symphony
- *Fantasy of Lights* drive through: Vasona Lake Park, Los Gatos
- Victorian Holiday Celebration: Wilder Ranch State Park, Santa Cruz
- Santa Trains: Western Railway Museum, Suisun (December weekends before Christmas)

Early December

- Victorian Christmas: Ardenwood Historic Farm, Newark
- Parent/Child Luncheon Parties with Santa and Mrs. Claus: Filoli Gardens
- Children's Puppet Show and Holiday Teas: Gamble Garden
- Holiday Hoe Down: Old Borges Ranch

Mid-December

- Pioneer Christmas: Roaring Camp Railroads, Felton

Late December/early January

- South Bay Chapter: Annual bird count walk: Audubon Society

- Nighttime tide pooling trip: Fitzgerald Marine Reserve
- Annual Bird Count Walk: Rancho Del Oso Nature & History Center
- First Night Living History Activity & Demonstration: Santa Cruz Mission

Appendix B
Free Activities Index

Many activities are free, such as performing arts, parks, and special free days at museums and zoos. However, remember that the free days at the museums and zoos may also mean crowds. So, expect to be in a crowded space and prepare accordingly. It's also probably a good idea to visit early in the morning before the crowds get too big. Please refer to the Alphabetical Index to help you locate the entries.

First Tuesday of Every Month:
- Asian Art Museum
- California Historical Society
- Cartoon Art Museum "Pay What You Wish" Day
- San Francisco Museum of Modern Art
- Seymour Marine Discovery Center at Long Marine Labs at UC Santa Cruz, Santa Cruz: (831) 459-3800

First Wednesday of Every Month:
- Asian Art Museum, Civic Center
- California Academy of Sciences (comprised of Steinhart Aquarium, Natural History Museum, and Morrison Planetarium), Golden Gate Park
- Cartoon Art Museum
- Coyote Pointe Museum
- Exploratorium
- San Francisco Zoo

First Thursday of Every Month:
- Berkeley Art Museum
- Center for the Arts, Yerba Buena Gardens

First Friday of Every Month:
- Santa Cruz Museum of Art and History (MAH)

Second Sunday of Every month:
- Oakland Museum of California

Every Tuesday
- California Palace of the Legion of Honor, Lincoln Park

Every Thursday
- San Francisco Museum of Modern Art also has ½ price every Thursday night, 6pm–9pm.
- UC Berkeley Botanical Gardens

Free Everyday
- Agate Beach County Park, Bolinas: tide pooling: (415) 499-6387
- Arastradero Preserve, Palo Alto: (650) 329-2423
- Art galleries
- Asilomar State Beach: Tide pooling
- Basic Brown Bear Factory Tour, San Francisco: (800) 554-1910
- Bay Model Visitor Center, Sausalito: (415) 332-3870
- Baylands Nature Preserve, Palo Alto: (650) 329-2506
- Berkeley Marina Shorebird Nature Center, Berkeley: (510) 644-8623
- Bolinas Lagoon Preserve, Stinson Beach: (415) 868-9244
- Botanic Garden, Tilden Nature Preserve Regional Park, Berkeley: (510)841-8732
- Cal Day at U.C. Berkeley: (510) 642-5215
- Cantor Art Center, Stanford University, Stanford: (650) 723-4177
- Children's Events (at libraries and stores)
- Chinese New Year Parade, San Francisco: (415) 982-3000
- Community Concerts, East Bay <www.CommunityConcerts.com>
- Community School of Music & Arts: Free concert series, Mountain View: (650) 961-0342
- Computer History Museum History Center, Mountain View: (650) 810-1010

- Cupertino Memorial Park Amphitheater: Summer Concerts, Cupertino: (408) 777-3120
- Deer Hollow Farm: Rancho San Antonio Preserve, Los Altos: (650) 965-FARM for Farm Tour Reservations
- Don Edwards San Francisco Bay National Wildlife Refuge, Fremont and Alviso: (510) 792-0222 & (408) 262-5513, respectively
- Dreyer's Grand Ice Cream Tour, Union City: (510) 471-6622
- Emma Prusch Farm, San Jose: (408) 926-5555
- Fitzgerald Marine Reserve, Moss Beach: (650) 728-3584
- Foothill Observatory, Foothill College, Los Altos Hills: (650) 949-7334
- Gamble Garden, Palo Alto: (650) 329-1356
- Gardens at Heather Farms, Walnut Creek: (925) 947-6712
- Gold Rush Trail, San Francisco: (415) 981-4849
- Golden Gate Fortune Cookie Company, San Francisco: (415) 781-3956
- Golden Gate Live Steamers Club, Tilden Park, Berkeley: free train rides on Sundays noon–3pm. <www.ggls.org>
- Hakone Gardens, Saratoga: (408) 741-4994
- Half Moon Bay: Annual Half Moon Bay Art & Pumpkin Festival on weekend following Columbus Day (See Lemos Farms entry)
- Intel Museum, Santa Clara: (408) 765-0503
- Japanese Friendship Garden, San Jose: (408) 277-5254
- Japanese Tea Garden, San Mateo: (650) 522-7409
- Jelly Bean Factory Tour, Fairfield: (800) 522-3267
- Junior Center of Art and Science, Oakland: (510) 839-5777
- Kule Loklo, replica Coast Miwok Village: (415) 464-5100
- Levi-Strauss Visitor Center, San Francisco: (415) 501-6000
- Linden Tree: Wednesdays in the Courtyard Music Series, Los Altos: 1-800-949-3313
- Marin French Cheese Company Tour, Petaluma: (800) 292-6001
- Marine Mammal Center, Marin Headlands, Sausalito: (415) 289-7325
- Maritime Museum, San Francisco Maritime National Historic Park, San Francisco: (415) 561-7100

Francisco: (415) 564-8086
- San Francisco Fire Department Museum, San Francisco: (415) 563-4630
- San Francisco Youth Arts Festival, Yerba Buena Gardens: (415) 759-2916
- San Jose Museum of Art, San Jose: (408) 271-6840
- Santa Clara University, Music at Noon series, Santa Clara: (408) 554-4429
- Santa Cruz Mission: (831) 425-5849
- Santa Cruz Natural History Museum, Santa Cruz: (831) 420-6115
- Scharffen Berger Chocolate Maker Factory Tour, Berkeley: (510) 981-4050
- Shakespeare in the Park <www.sfshakes.org/park/index.html>
- Shoreline Park, Mountain View: (650) 965-7474
- Sigmund Stern Grove Festival, San Francisco: (415) 252-6252
- South Bay Historical Railroad Society, Santa Clara: (408) 243-3969
- Stanford Linear Accelerator, Menlo Park: (650) 926-2204
- Strybing Arboretum & Botanical Gardens, San Francisco: (415) 661-1316
- Sulphur Creek Nature Center, Hayward: (510) 881-6747
- Sunset Magazine's Demonstration Gardens, Menlo Park: (650) 321-3600
- Tassajara Symphony Orchestra: Free Kids' Concerts, Pleasanton: (925) 820-2494
- Tiburon Railroad–Ferry Depot Museum, Tiburon: (415) 435-1853
- Triton Museum of Art, Santa Clara: (408) 247-3754
- U.C. Santa Cruz Arboretum, Santa Cruz: (831) 427-2998
- U.S. Geological Survey, Menlo Park: (650) 329-4390 Recording, (650) 329-5392 Tour requests
- Watsonville Airport, Watsonville: (831) 728-6075
- Wells Fargo History Museum: (415) 396-2619
- Whole Foods Groceries Store Tours: See Chapter 7: How Things Work—Site Tours section.
- Wildlife Festival: Youth Science Institue, Alum Rock Park: (408) 258-4322

- Woodside Store: (650) 851-7615
- Yerba Buena Gardens Festival, Esplanade of Yerba Buena Gardens, San Francisco: (415) 543-1718

Appendix C
Alphabetical Index

C

Check List — Before You Go

1) Call to confirm dates, times, costs, and directions.

2) Print out maps/directions from the World Wide Web.

3) Bring some cash, in various denominations from quarters and dollar bills to larger bills.

4) Extra changes of clothing and shoes in the car (at least for the kids, but it's a good idea for the adults, too) for unexpected messes.

5) Bring lots of bottled water or drinks because fun can be a thirsty business. It's always a great idea to have some fruit, yogurt, cheese sticks, or other snacks handy for the trip home.

6) Sunscreen

7) Sunglasses

8) Jackets

9) Binoculars

10) Camera

11) Umbrella

About the Author

Elina Wong is a former product line manager in the health care industry and a former market researcher with Apple Computers, Inc. She has a bachelor's degree in biochemistry from U.C. Berkeley and a master's degree in health finance and management from the Johns Hopkins Bloomberg School of Public Health.

She lives in Los Gatos, California, with her husband and two young daughters. She has been an active full-time mom for the past six years, with many adventure miles logged on her car.

Both of her parents were music teachers. Her hobbies include piano and photography. She is passionate about her children's education.

Feedback Please!

We welcome your feedback!
Please send to: Kids EdVentures
P.O. Box 1090, Los Gatos, CA 95031-1090
or e-mail to: feedback@www.kidsedventures.com
*Please feel free to use a separate piece of paper for
additional comments or space.*

Have you found someplace or something special? (Please provide as much detail as possible: Web site, address, telephone number, organization name, event, and why you would recommend it.)

Please share your experiences on your outings and classes with us so we can make this an even better book! Submit your review on our Web site: www.KidsEducationalAdventures.com or mail it to us.

Which section(s) of *Kids' Adventures* is(are) the most useful? Why?

Which section(s) of *Kids' Adventures* did you like least? Why? How would you improve it?

Please circle:
Are you a parent, educator, homeschooler, scout leader, or other?
If other, please specify:_____

How old are the kids?_____

Where do you live?
City:_____**State:**_____
Zip Code: _____**Country:**_____

Would you like to receive a free copy of our electronic newsletter with updates and events? If yes, please provide your e-mail address:

_____

Updates & Notes

Please use the following pages to keep track of changes and updates.